IN THE ABSENCE OF PREDATORS

In the Absence of
PREDATORS

Conservation and Controversy
on the Kaibab Plateau

Christian C. Young

UNIVERSITY OF NEBRASKA PRESS
LINCOLN AND LONDON

"N"

Designed and composed by
Todd Duren of Firefly Design. Set in Filosophia,
Birch, and Blackoak fonts.

TO MOM AND DAD

Contents

List of Illustrations and Maps — ix

Acknowledgments — xi

Introduction — 1

1. Buckskin Mountain — 7

2. Beasts in the Garden — 22

3. A Deer Dilemma — 39

4. Getting to the Bottom of Things — 61

5. Taking Notice of the Kaibab Deer — 82

6. Scientific Expertise in the Midst of Controversy — 110

7. Big Game Management Plans on the Kaibab — 135

8. The Exception That Proved the Rule — 173

Epilogue — 206

Notes — 217

Bibliography — 249

Index — 263

Illustrations and Maps

ILLUSTRATIONS

Kaibab deer on exhibit at the Milwaukee Public Museum	2
High desert north of the Kaibab Plateau	9
Corral at the Ryan site	30
Typical intermediate range vegetation	49
Zane Grey's *The Deer Stalker*	72
R. H. Rutledge inspecting heavily browsed forage	108
Investigating committee members look out over the canyon	141
Inspecting the vegetation of the forest	142
D. I. Rasmussen's 1932 population graph	155
Rasmussen's food web of the Kaibab biotic communities	156
Deer population data	192
Rasmussen's famous deer graph	199
Aldo Leopold's version of Rasmussen's graph	202
Browse line on vegetation in 1930	203
Browse line in 1942	204
Vegetation largely recovered by 1948	208
"Nature Fights Back" on the Kaibab	210
Kaibab doe on Walhalla Plateau	213

MAPS

The Kaibab Plateau and surroundings	8
Locations on the Kaibab Plateau	120

Acknowledgments

What a pleasure it is, at last, to look back on this project and recall all of the people who have helped with the logistics of writing this book and contributed to my thinking along the way. And what a daunting task, when I consider how likely it is that I will forget someone whose name surely belongs here.

I am especially fortunate to count so many very good friends among my colleagues, who have commented insightfully on my work and made it tremendous fun at the same time. These include: Jay Taylor and Matt Klingle; Juan Ilerbaig, Mary Thomas, Rob Ferguson, Kai Barth, Michael Reidy, and John Jackson; Kevin Francis and Karin Matchett; Joe Julik and Rett Young. I have also had the help of my oldest and best friends, Scott Koehler, John Flaa, and George Vacek.

A few friends have gone above and beyond the standard expectations of both friendship and collegiality. Steve Fifield (the Duke) read and commented on earlier versions in addition to accompanying me on a grand tour of the West. Mark Largent (the King) provided invaluable advice and insightful comments on a very late version of the entire manuscript.

Others have provided encouragement and advice based on their extensive experience, and I have benefited greatly. They are Gar Allen, Mark Barrow, Gregg Mitman, Paul Farber, Jane Maienschein, Jim Collins, Bill Robbins, Tom Dunlap, Bruce Fall, Joe Cain, Douglas Allchin, Ken Waters, and particularly Sally Gregory Kohlstedt.

A few uniquely positioned people have given their help generously. I owe debts to Dave Rasmussen, Dale McCullough, Barbara Stein, and especially to Teri Cleeland.

Of course, Michelle has made this work possible with support of every imaginable sort, and I love her for managing to keep my life simple.

Finally, it is a great privilege to thank John Beatty and Keith Benson, who have given what I could not have asked for, usually because I did not know what I needed. They have enriched my work and my life in many ways.

This book is dedicated to my parents, Joyce and Les Young.

In the Absence of Predators

Introduction

In the end the starved bones of the hoped-for deer herd,
dead of its own too-much, bleach with the bones of the
dead sage, or molder under the high-lined junipers.

ALDO LEOPOLD

Predators help to keep natural communities in balance, and in the absence of predators, prey populations can increase to the brink of starvation and beyond. Aldo Leopold, author of the first textbook on game management, called this an irruption. Although early in his career he believed that deer and other game could be maintained in abundance in the absence of predators, he realized later that deer needed predators to avoid irruptions and the disastrous population crashes that inevitably followed.[1]

The case of an apparent deer irruption and crash on the Kaibab Plateau in the 1920s became a textbook lesson of how human interference can threaten the long-term outcome of game managers' ambitious plans. In the early twentieth century, conservationists hoped to protect game by removing the enemies of the most desirable species. On the Kaibab, these removals reportedly allowed the deer population to increase beyond the local supply of vegetation. When later ecologists such as Leopold assessed the situation with hindsight, they concluded that when food ran short, starvation quickly took its toll on the deer with a vengeance that predators could not have matched.[2]

Based on the way the Kaibab lesson became known through popular essays and textbooks, scientists in the 1950s and 1960s believed prey populations benefited from predation. In the Kaibab case, overprotection ultimately led to starvation of the deer. The common-sense notion that predators limited prey populations became part of an argument that predatory animals should be included in management plans rather than exterminated, and by the 1990s the public had gotten the message. For many, the lesson has become so obvious that they can no longer comprehend the motivations that led conservationists in 1906 to protect—and thus doom—the Kaibab deer. Popular wildlife writer and photographer Erwin Bauer describes "the terrible lesson of the Kaibab," where game refuges become "death traps" when protectionists remove predators and hunters. He notes that "the predators' natural role is to keep plant eaters in balance with their food supply."[3] The Kaibab lesson also appears on display at the Field Museum of Natural History in Chicago. There, visitors read that human tinkering with animal communities leads to disaster, not wildlife protection. A stuffed cougar hangs suspended upside down by a rope accompanied by the question, "What happened when we tried to

The lesson of the Kaibab deer appears on exhibit in natural history museums. In this example, from the Milwaukee Public Museum in Milwaukee, Wisconsin, a buck and doe stand just below the rim of the Grand Canyon (in front of a painted backdrop) while a crouching mountain lion lies in wait. This exhibit was created around 1970. Photo by the author.

'protect' mule deer by killing wild predators on Arizona's Kaibab Plateau?" The answer: Many deer starved because humans interfered in "the intricate web of living things." A less elaborate diorama carrying the same message appears at the Milwaukee Public Museum and undoubtedly at countless other natural history museums.[4]

While wildlife managers seem to have succeeded in educating the public, the scientific basis of the classic Kaibab story lost credibility after an ecologist questioned the data on which Leopold built his lesson. Changes in livestock grazing and drought in northern Arizona may have caused the overpopulation and starvation of the deer, meaning that perhaps predator removal played at most a minor role.[5]

What really took place on the Kaibab Plateau in the 1920s? The disputed role of predators may be even less significant than the fact that no one ever got an accurate estimate of the deer population during that critical period. Given these disclaimers, there must be some reason that the case captured intermittent but worldwide attention. Part of the answer comes in acknowledging that the romanticized West fascinated Americans, especially in places like the Kaibab Plateau, which seemed to lie beyond the reach of the closed frontier. Nowhere is this better demonstrated than by the involvement of Western novelist Zane Grey.[6] The more significant answer requires a closer look at the activities and motivations of researchers and government officials on the Kaibab Plateau in the early twentieth century. Those researchers and officials faced new challenges about the workings of nature to which solutions were neither readily available nor easily implemented. A more complete history of the Kaibab case requires an examination of these challenges within the context of early-twentieth-century American biological science.

Historical examination of the Kaibab case has generally relied on secondary accounts of the case that too often simplify it into a few key events: establishment of the preserve, divided jurisdiction of the preserve between state and federal agencies, and unheeded warnings about overpopulation of the deer. Such accounts allow historians and scientists alike to blame the protracted controversy on a failure to apply ecological knowledge properly in a practical setting. With this explanation, problems do not yield to ecological solutions because ecologists cannot overcome the inertia of outdated assumptions about nature. In fact, the misguided notion that fundamental scientific principles in ecology would have solved a game-management controversy fits a general pattern of expectation that controversies are about deficiencies of facts and can be resolved by providing the requisite data. But controversies are sometimes about disagreements over theory, and these cannot be resolved by assembling more evidence. In reality, most controversies in science are about both facts and theories, whether or not scientists realize this added complexity in the midst of endless debates and fact gathering.[7] The assumption that controversies in game management resulted from a lack of facts can be traced to the widespread comments of the scientists themselves.[8]

Historians of this case also tend to focus on controversies of facts, examining the way scientists involved in the Kaibab investigations increased their expertise by gathering new data. Rarely equipped to assess the meaning of these newly found facts, however, historians then assume that the failure to resolve controversies based on the introduction of new evidence resulted from social or political pressures outside the scientific process. These scholars often begin with the assumption that scientific expertise solved problems when government bureaucracies attended to scientists' advice. When for various reasons policymakers and policy implementers ignored scientists, problems went unsolved and controversies continued. It is easy to focus on the reasons that led the makers and implementers of policy to ignore scientific expertise. In the process, however, historians themselves ignore the scientific side of the story. That is, they seek explanations for unresolved controversies, but they do not adequately examine the content of the science that they claim could have resolved those controversies.[9]

Throughout the events occurring on the Kaibab Plateau during the 1920s, science did not stand apart from controversy, like some kind of objective arbiter. While this point has been adopted within certain reaches of the environmental sciences in recent years, controversies like the Kaibab case might also be reexamined with the understanding that scientific knowledge and scientists themselves were implicated in the ongoing disagreements.[10] If scientists, government officials, and the public all expected scientific expertise to resolve management problems in the 1920s on the Kaibab Plateau, it will be important to begin by considering whether those expectations were unrealistic from the start. They hoped to base management plans on new facts about the deer, but what they found was that questions about the role of predators, the growth patterns of vegetation, and the behavior of deer involved theoretical questions that facts alone would not answer. The knowledge gained in the process was not worthless simply because it did not answer the immediate factual questions. In fact, scientists often sharpened disagreements among themselves and between other groups, recognizing the need to conduct further investigations into the problems that vexed them.[11]

Scientists, conservationists, environmentalists, bureaucrats, and the general public continue to accept the notion that the accumulation of facts within the science of ecology is essential to conservation. As such, ecology is seen as a "pure" science that can be "applied" to practical matters like wildlife management.[12] Historians of science and technology began viewing the pure versus applied science model as problematic in the early 1970s. They have argued that knowledge developed to solve practical problems must also be understood on its own terms. Technology, for example, represents a broad set of practices and knowledge production that is often quite separate from the traditionally narrow model of applied science. A revised model of technology focuses on the activities and traditions of researchers, artisans, and inventors, all of whom figure significantly in the history of technology.[13] This approach leaves something of a void in understanding what continues to be called applied science in fields like conservation, where connections to the conventionally pure science of ecology involve a simultaneous emergence of new practical concepts and methods.

One way to reconsider the relationship between ecology and wildlife management is to acknowledge that the distinction between pure and applied science rests on the motivations behind scientific activities. Scientists are motivated by the goal of solving both theoretical and practical problems, and most ecological and wildlife management studies have both pure and applied motivations. Beyond these goals, the activities of both pure and applied scientists often appear to be indistinguishable.[14] When scientists fail to solve practical problems, however, their authority is diminished in the eyes of many audiences, regardless of gains in knowledge or the development of new techniques. In order to recognize scientific contributions for more than their success in solving practical problems, scholars examine how communities of scientists succeed in meeting other criteria, such as the establishment of experimental investigations under controlled conditions. Those criteria might be irrelevant, however, for practically oriented audiences who want results that translate into economic gain without regard for the complexity of balancing experimental and natural conditions.[15] Deer management controversies, for example, continue to vex scientists, bureaucrats, and communities.[16] In such cases, scientists attempt to acquire the elusive ability to satisfy different audiences, thus linking pure and applied science in a complex web of activities, motivations, and audiences.

In the Kaibab story, no single or simplified connection is adequate to explain the relationship between ecology and wildlife management. Instead, examination of the complex web of interrelations between the two illuminates the emergence of scientific conceptions of predator-prey relationships and carrying capacity, as well as the failure of scientific expertise. In the account that follows, the web of activities includes the research of both scientists and game officials. Their motivations focus on ambitions for improved management of the game preserve. The audiences include the diverse community of scientists, preservation-minded nature lovers, utilitarian conservationists, hunters, ranchers, entrepreneurs in the tourism industry, and the government officials who cared about the fate of the deer.

The activities, motivations, and audiences of the scientists who studied the deer, predators, and broader natural communities on Kaibab Plateau combine to offer a kind of parable about science and wildlife conservation.[17] Here science and human society interacted with nature, and those interactions contributed to the production of scientific knowledge. Even when research was conducted cautiously with the best conceptual and methodological tools available, uncertainty was often very much a part of the scientific enterprise. Scientists responded to social and political concerns with new and often contentious questions that could be examined and challenged, accepted or dismissed, rather than with claims to objective truth about the world. Along the way, predators and prey became defined scientifically and popularly in new ways. Ironically, it was the absence of predators on the Kaibab that created interest in their importance.

1
—

Buckskin Mountain

Natural History

From the northern border of Arizona, just outside the town of Fredonia, a low, gray-green line rises in the distance to mark the southern horizon. It is a long mountain ridge, rising almost a mile above the surrounding sagebrush. In the late nineteenth century, the ridge was known as Buckskin Mountain, an apt name for a place where Indians hunted deer for skins and meat. Buckskin Mountain became more widely known by another name, also appropriate for its topography and the history of its native cultures—Kaibab, a Paiute word meaning "mountain lying down." In the early 1870s, John Wesley Powell used this name in describing his expeditions through the Grand Canyon and explorations of the surrounding plateaus.[1] The Kaibab Plateau rises above the dry scrub grass and sage desert around Fredonia to an elevation of over nine thousand feet, before it drops precipitously into the Grand Canyon.

The splendor of the Kaibab Plateau is enhanced by its unique isolation. The various routes onto the plateau allow only limited human access and all but prohibit the migration of the deer. Each path onto the plateau presented a serious challenge to ranchers, hunters, and other travelers in the early twentieth century, and to this day none of these paths provides an easy migration route to or from the game preserve. Approaching from the north, the rugged, multicolored canyonlands of southern Utah suddenly give way to a broad sagebrush plain near the Arizona border, established along a precisely arbitrary straight line at thirty-seven degrees north latitude. Mule deer, known for their aversion to open places, seldom cross twenty miles of open ground and never in large numbers. Their movements tend to be limited to seasonal migrations.

Climbing several thousand feet in elevation onto the plateau, early visitors noted how the vegetation of the area quickly changed from dry

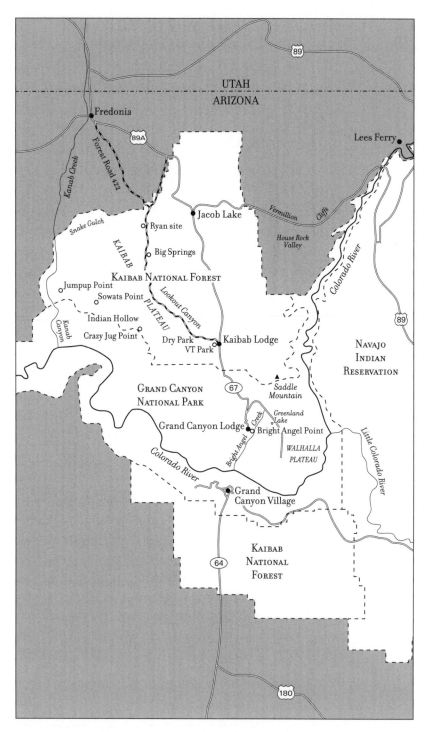

The Kaibab Plateau and surroundings

sage to scrubby pinyon pine and juniper, then to sparse groves of scrub oak. Above that, tall stands of ponderosa pine mix with a dense pine-spruce-fir forest. Hidden among the tall conifers, meadows and aspen groves provide ideal habitat for the deer. At eighty-two hundred feet above sea level, Jacob Lake is a crossroad between the northern and easterly approaches to the plateau. The road from the town of Marble Canyon, east of the Kaibab, follows a forty-mile route over sparsely vegetated desert through House Rock Valley before climbing into the forests around Jacob Lake. Travelers from Flagstaff could formerly cross the Colorado River only via Lees Ferry near Marble Canyon. It was the only vehicle crossing for several hundred miles. Navajo Bridge, built in 1928, replaced the Lees Ferry crossing and is still the only route across the Colorado between Glen Canyon Dam and Hoover Dam, a remote two-hundred-mile stretch of river.

The third route to and from the Kaibab Plateau is the most remote and treacherous of all. Following narrow trails from the South Rim of the

The high desert north of the Kaibab Plateau is sparsely vegetated, providing virtually no cover for mule deer. Very few big-game animals would cross twenty miles of open ground from the plateau to the canyonlands and forests in southern Utah. Photo by the author.

Grand Canyon, a traveler descends over five thousand vertical feet to the bottom of the canyon, only to face the Colorado River at one of its swiftest points. Today, one crosses the narrow Kaibab Suspension Bridge and follows Bright Angel Creek before climbing to the North Rim. The bridge over the raging Colorado was built in 1928. Before that, a swinging bridge built in 1921 barely survived high water and windstorms.[2] When President Theodore Roosevelt hiked through the canyon and crossed the Colorado in 1913, he crossed on a hand-cranked trolley suspended by a single cable.[3] The hike, about twenty miles from rim to rim, generally takes two or three days. Again, wildlife does not migrate to and from the Kaibab Plateau via the Grand Canyon. Kanab Canyon completes the isolation of the Kaibab Plateau to the west.

Partly because of its isolation and partly because of its accessibility to a famous natural feature, early conservationists agreed that the plateau would make an ideal game preserve. The limited access protected it from poachers. What made the Kaibab Plateau truly ideal for deer, however, was the forest that lay on its highest elevation along a ridge running nearly north to south. Similar stands of forestland were rare in the Desert Southwest. There, amid the pine forests, slight valleys opened into broad meadows like DeMotte Park (earlier known as VT Park) and Pleasant Valley, which became famous locations for viewing wildlife. Mule deer emerged each evening and browsed in the shadows as darkness approached. Visitors in the 1920s often counted over a thousand deer from the road during the summer months. At these higher elevations, wildlife found abundant vegetation for food and cover in the summer, but during the winter as much as ten feet of snow made the ridge uninhabitable for deer.[4]

Each year, the mule deer followed regular migration patterns from the higher elevations in the center of the plateau, to lower elevations to the east and west. The high summer ranges consisted of dense aspen groves along the edges of mountain meadows. In the fall, deer made their way through the thick cover of gullies and ravines to the winter range. There, they subsisted on cliff rose and juniper until spring, when they completed the cycle. The terrain, vegetation, and climate combined with deer behavior patterns to constrain their migration. They avoided the northern end of the plateau throughout the year, moving mainly east and west, from high to low, and back again. These behaviors seemed unalterable, regardless of the changing conditions of food and cover vegetation. Climatic fluctuations, including periods of drought, severely affected the abundance of forage at all elevations. The majority of the deer migrated to the west, where they wintered below seven thousand feet. The animals sometimes became trapped at higher elevations on narrow peninsulas like Sowats Point and Jumpup Point by heavy winter snows. Access to these areas was limited to relatively narrow routes. Vast wilderness areas such as Kanab Canyon and the Grand Canyon itself bordered these points.

Uneven distribution of the deer on these narrow stretches of land gave rise to widely divergent perceptions of the conditions of vegetation on the plateau in general. Confined on small sections of the range, groups of deer often consumed virtually all of the available forage, standing on their hind legs to reach upper branches and sometimes riding small trees to the ground by leaning against them. Such behavior gave the impression to many observers that the deer were desperate for food. Early wildlife biologists were mystified when deer ate every green twig in sight but would not move a few miles to another area where food was abundant.

On the east side of the plateau, a smaller portion of the deer population spent its winter. The deer foraged in places such as the lower meadows around Saddle Mountain and along the narrow plateau leading out to Greenland Point, now known as Cape Royal, at the end of the Walhalla Plateau. The Colorado River and the Grand Canyon restricted migration beyond these areas. During most years, deer migrated past the narrow "opening" to Greenland Point, leaving sections of the range completely untouched on that part of the plateau. Other years, however, some deer migrated onto Greenland Point, only to become trapped on the point by snow. They would then virtually destroy the vegetation at lower elevations near the end of the point. Depending on what part of the plateau visitors observed, and how the deer had survived the previous winter, human perceptions of the condition of vegetation varied enormously.

The most significant features of the plateau's natural history, according to most accounts, were the wolves, mountain lions, coyotes, and bears. Little is known about these "predators," as they came to be called, on the Kaibab before the twentieth century. Early reports from trappers and lion hunters contained exaggerations that served to enhance the reputation of such men as guides and frontier legends. These trappers and hunters served the interests of ranchers and a broader segment of society accustomed to fear wild, meat-eating beasts. Those beasts preyed upon livestock and peaceful forest creatures. In legend and in popular fact, they were feared and deservedly persecuted. For the protection of human communities and livestock, trappers and hunters exterminated carnivores. On the Kaibab Plateau, such an undertaking would not have been justified for the sake of a few deer. Common-sense assumptions that relatively abundant predators kept the deer population in check arose only after people began to perceive increasing deer numbers as a problem. The role of predators in the early natural history of the Kaibab, largely unknown and probably unknowable, can serve as a reminder that this story turns on human perceptions and interpretations of nature. Those interpretations—including the condition of vegetation, the number of deer, and the role of predators—depended on a wide variety of features in human history.[5]

HUMAN HISTORY

Native groups, now known to archeologists as Anasazi, occupied the land along the North Rim of the Grand Canyon. Those who lived on the North Rim left behind a record of their lifestyle in the form of pottery and woven baskets. Going back five thousand years, the ancestors of the Basketmakers left woven-twig figurines that resemble the wildlife of the Grand Canyon area. The majority of archaeological evidence for these civilizations comes from ruins and cavelike dwellings near or under the rim of the canyon, and those were not particularly close to the forested areas of the Kaibab. More recent residents of the area shared the plateau as a common hunting ground with nonresident bands. Some Anasazi campsites have been unearthed near the end of Walhalla Plateau, where—like the deer—human groups may have been trapped by winter storms.[6]

American Indians still living in the Grand Canyon area today include the Havasupai and Hualapai. Their ancestors were hunters, gatherers, and planters, known to have hunted animals large and small throughout the pine forests of the region. According to legends and archaeological evidence, the Havasupai and Hualapai both settled in the Grand Canyon in the twelfth century A.D. Their garments from this early era were of tanned buckskin, and deer played an important role in their subsistence culture. They did not necessarily hunt regularly on the North Rim, however, as deer were most likely plentiful on lands south of the canyon as well. Beginning around the same time, several Paiute bands moved into the area north of the Grand Canyon. They were hunters and gatherers, who depended upon the deer and pine nuts of the Kaibab forests. They moved with the seasons, occupying the Kaibab area most often in the fall, when nuts were plentiful and snows had not yet blanketed the higher elevations. In more recent times, Navajo groups also visited the Kaibab in search of deer for clothing, food, and other needs. Prior to settlement by

Mormon ranchers from Utah, the lands around the Kaibab supported an estimated population of 1,175 Paiute Indians. By the 1870s, that number had dwindled to about two hundred, and within the next decade the Paiute population dropped below one hundred. When the Kaibab Indian Reservation was established in 1907, fewer than eighty Paiute Indians remained. The decline resulted from starvation, as competition for scarce resources in the area increased and ranchers typically won in their efforts to divert water for cattle. Disease and outright warfare were rare in the remote Arizona Strip, that section of Arizona north of the Grand Canyon and south of the current border with Utah.[7]

Jacob Hamblin became an influential local leader among the early settlers, who knew the Kaibab as Buckskin Mountain. A Mormon missionary and explorer, Hamblin worked among the Indians and scouted the Grand Canyon. His trip around the canyon in 1862 was the first such recorded journey. He helped to arbitrate peace between Mormons and Indians during a period of strife. The village on the Kaibab Plateau, Jacob Lake, was named for Hamblin.[8]

The most famous explorer of the Grand Canyon region, John Wesley Powell, first came to Arizona in 1869 at the age of thirty-five. He was a veteran of the Civil War and had lost most of his right arm after being wounded at the Battle of Shiloh in 1862. As a professor of geology in Illinois after the war, he began studying the Rocky Mountain region, becoming simultaneously interested in Indian cultures. To extend his research, Powell proposed an expedition of the Colorado River that would begin on the Green River in Wyoming. He obtained support for the expedition from universities, railroad companies, the Smithsonian Institution, and Congress. His famous first running of the Colorado through the Grand Canyon has been repeatedly described, while his own account remains perhaps the most vivid.[9] The year after running the canyon, Powell returned to begin ethnological studies on the Kaibab and surrounding lands. He was also scouting for a second expedition through the canyon. That expedition began again in Wyoming, but delays forced the party to pull out upriver from the canyon and spend the winter of 1871–72 in Kanab, Utah. Powell then spent the summer of 1872 on the Kaibab with Harvey C. DeMotte, also a professor in Illinois. Powell's experience that summer led him into ethnology, and he spent most of his remaining career as the first director of the Bureau of American Ethnology, which he founded. He served additionally as director of the U.S. Geological Survey from 1881 to 1894.

A variety of resource-utilization ventures had a relatively minor impact on the plateau and surrounding lands. Settlement around the

Grand Canyon was very slow until railroads increased access to the
isolated area in the 1880s. Even then, the North Rim remained hundreds of miles from any sizable community and could be reached only
by rough trails. The few hunters and trappers in the area found plentiful wildlife, but their efforts probably had little effect on the deer.
Policies to protect big-game animals were largely unknown. Deer,
elk, moose, and even bear were food sources for settlers, not mere
sporting targets or objects for public viewing.

Cattle and sheep ranching on areas north of the canyon increased as
settlers moved south from Utah in the 1850s and 1860s. A series of companies grazed livestock on lands surrounding the Kaibab Plateau, and
ranchers moved their stock onto the plateau to graze on the meadows in
the summer.[10] These private operations continued into the early 1890s,
when President Benjamin Harrison established the Grand Canyon Forest Reserve in 1893. This designation had little meaning for the local livestock companies, however, since there was no government bureau to administer the land or enforce grazing limits. Even when it was placed
under the jurisdiction of the General Land Office in 1897, permits for
grazing far exceeded the availability of land or livestock at the time: up to
twenty thousand cattle and two hundred thousand sheep.[11] While cattle
numbers may have reached several thousand at times, there were never
more than a few thousand sheep in the area. Given the extent of livestock
grazing in the area, mountain lions, wolves, and coyotes faced constant
persecution from ranchers. Just as exact figures for livestock were not
kept during this period, no one recorded the numbers of carnivorous
animals destroyed. In such a remote area, mountain lions and wolves
would certainly have eluded ranchers' rifles, but later reports greatly exaggerated the prevalence of predators.

Towns that grew up around ranching operations were built from timber cut in the Kaibab forest and nearby Mount Trumbull. Loggers operated a portable steam sawmill at Big Springs beginning in 1871. Mining
operations had an even less direct effect on the wildlife and habitat of the
Kaibab, but they did lead to the establishment of more-or-less permanent camps in the area. Prospectors built copper mines near Jacob Lake
around 1900, and a smelter went into operation near Ryan, on the west
side of the plateau. These never produced much ore, but permanent
roads in the early 1900s began to replace the rough tracks that early ex-
plorers had used.

When mining efforts failed around the turn of the century on the
South Rim of the canyon, prospectors turned their claims into primitive

resorts. A few early entrepreneurs had served with Theodore Roosevelt in Cuba and borrowed on his influence to ensure claims for land in the area. Separated by hundreds of miles of rocky roads, tourism developed slowly on the North Rim. Few travelers made the trek merely to see the sights. The first automobile reached the canyon from Kanab as early as 1909, when a party embarked on a three-day drive that required gasoline caches at thirty-mile intervals and road repair en route. The forest reserve offered a seemingly pristine environment to turn-of-the-century conservationists. Apart from the few entrepreneurial souls who eked out a living, distance isolated the Kaibab Plateau. Railroads, the lifelines of Western commerce, and cities like Phoenix, Salt Lake City, and Flagstaff, were too far away for the resources of the plateau to be anything but an undefined wilderness. Official designation as a forest reserve, game preserve, and national park had little effect on human activities there, at least for a while.

THEODORE ROOSEVELT'S KAIBAB

Teddy Roosevelt's commitment to protecting wildlife for future generations earned him great distinction even before he became president. He enjoyed an extended involvement as a sport hunter, a leisure activity that emerged slowly in the years after the Civil War. Journals devoted to sport hunting also began to appear regularly in the late 1860s. In eastern states, Roosevelt and other wealthy sport hunters organized game-protection societies to defend against perceived excesses in hunting. In journals and game societies, writers and organizers preached moderation in hunting. With its slow growth and limited participation, sport hunting itself posed little threat to game species in the West.

As hunters became increasingly involved in wildlife conservation, their roles varied considerably. The role of wildlife protector was adopted primarily by wealthy sport hunters. Market hunters, people who bagged birds by the wagonload for sale on the open market, could ill afford to consider protecting game. Among subsistence hunters, Native Americans had no voice in the creation of game-protection laws. Their ways of living and hunting had changed dramatically during the nineteenth century. Removal to reservations usually meant the end of access to traditional hunting grounds. Wealthy conservationists established game preserves and lobbied for legislation at the state and federal levels to protect game for future generations. They proudly, and somewhat naively, assumed that if human hunters could be controlled, nature would find its own balance as it had in generations past. Game shortages due to causes other than hunting by humans were exceptional, and conservationists blamed uncontrollable factors such as harsh winters for these rare events.[12]

As a big-game hunter and champion of broadly defined conservation policies, Roosevelt deservedly garnered enormous attention. Even before his first trip west in 1883, which took him as far as what is now North Dakota, Roosevelt combined hunting and natural history collecting. In the Dakota Territory, he witnessed the slaughter of big-game animals, particularly the American Bison. Eastern species of big game had grown scarce in recent years, and Roosevelt immediately foresaw a similar fate being repeated on lands that most people considered an inexhaustible frontier. When Roosevelt returned from the West, he wrote *Hunting Trips of a Ranchman*, an account of his hunting experiences. He included descriptions of white- and black-tail (mule) deer, elk, grouse, mountain sheep, buffalo, and grizzly bears, along with accounts of cowboys and stock raising.[13]

Roosevelt's essay caught the attention of George Bird Grinnell, nationally known naturalist and editor of *Forest and Stream*. Grinnell wrote a critical review of Roosevelt's piece for the magazine. Upon seeing the review, the young hunter-naturalist went directly to Grinnell's office, asking for clarification of those comments. The two soon realized their common goals and concerns, especially with the rapidly changing fate of wildlife in the western territories. Roosevelt recognized the value of Grinnell's broader experience in these matters. Soon after, they proposed a national organization devoted to hunting; members must be committed to preserving their sport for future generations. At a dinner party in 1887, the suggested organization met with the approval of several prominent sport-hunting friends and soon after they prepared a constitution for the Boone and Crockett Club.[14]

The Boone and Crockett Club was among the earliest of a proliferation of groups concerned with outdoor recreation, including fishing, camping, hiking, nature study, and ornithology. All of these activities, and their corresponding local and national interest groups, contributed to the early conservation movement. Almost all of these groups became involved in the protection of various forms of wildlife. Through his intimate involvement with the Boone and Crockett Club, Theodore Roosevelt was uniquely qualified as the leader of American conservation when he became president of the United States in 1901.[15]

Creation of federal game preserves was a new process. In 1903, Pelican Island in Florida became the first. The Kaibab Plateau was particularly unique in that lands formerly designated as a forest reserve received the additional designation of game preserve. In practical terms, the significance of this was not clear at the time. The newly created Forest Service would retain jurisdiction of the land and forest resources, meaning that livestock grazing and logging would continue. Protection of the game and scenery of the region took a back seat until the years 1910–19, when the National Park Service came into existence and took administrative control of sections of the plateau near the canyon's North Rim.

Roosevelt visited the Grand Canyon in 1903 and reported that it was "the most impressive scenery" he had ever seen. His famous advice regarding the protection of the canyonlands has been often quoted: "Leave it as it is. You cannot improve on it. The ages have been at work on it, and man can only mar it. What you can do is to keep it for your children, your children's children, and for all who come after you, as the one great sight which every American . . . should see."[16] Roosevelt united his passion for big game with his deep admiration for the Grand Canyon itself in 1906 when he established the Grand Canyon National Game Preserve in Arizona Territory. The president's proclamation exercised his authority to "set aside [lands] for the protection of game animals and be recognized as a breeding place therefor" in the Grand Canyon Forest Reserve. Congress had granted that presidential authority just five months earlier.

Senator Reed Smoot of Utah introduced the bill providing authority to the president in January 1906. Smoot served as chair of the Committee on Forest Reservations and the Protection of Game, but he had a more specific interest in the land north of the Grand Canyon. Smoot's efforts represented the widely held opinion that the Colorado River should form the southern boundary of Utah. In proposing the bill, Smoot actually foresaw Roosevelt's creation of the game preserve in Arizona Territory. He hoped the preserve would strengthen Utah's claim to those lands, which were much more accessible to the Utah towns of Kanab and St. George than to Flagstaff or any other settlement south of the canyon.[17] Introduction of the bill in the U.S. House of Representatives included an extended comment—made by Representative Joseph Howell from Logan, Utah—on the suitability of the area as a game preserve and the expectation that the lands of the Arizona Strip would be annexed by Utah. Without any congressional representation from Arizona Territory, the plan seemed likely to work. The bill passed in both the Senate and the House and was signed into law in late June.[18] No change in state boundaries was made at the time of the preserve's creation, and the boundary remained unaltered when Arizona became a state in 1912.

Roosevelt's interest in creating the Grand Canyon National Game Preserve was perhaps more of a response to the entrepreneurial designs of Charles J. "Buffalo" Jones. According to one account, Jones developed a plan to create a ranch in House Rock Valley adjacent to the Kaibab Plateau, where a hybrid stock of bison and Scottish Galloway cattle could be developed. When Jones first visited the area north of the Grand Canyon, he encountered the breathtaking vistas, endless forests, and deer streaming across the meadows. He was reportedly unable to decide where to locate his ranch. As a solution to this quandary, the game entrepreneur proposed the idea of having the entire plateau set aside as a game refuge, where his buffalo would be allowed to range freely. Secretary of Agriculture James Wilson granted Jones a permit to graze cattle and other big game in the forest reserve. Such a permit undoubtedly came by way of a special arrangement with President Roosevelt.[19]

Roosevelt's proclamation established virtually the entire forest reserve as a game preserve, rather than merely designating only certain sections within the original reserve. The president hoped to extend this ambitious approach more widely on federal lands. The Kaibab could be a starting point. His continued concern for decreasing game in the West led him to suggest the following: "The national Government could do much by establishing its forest reserves as game reserves, and putting on a sufficient number of forest rangers who should be empowered to prevent all hunting on the reserves." Yellowstone National Park presented a similar example of federal protection.[20]

Imagining game preserves simply as lands where hunting would be prohibited missed the question of predators that eventually became so important. Roosevelt despised the toll taken by cougars and wolves, which grew fat in areas where deer were still abundant, but the president and his contemporaries did not conceive of cougars and wolves as predators in this period. Only a handful of government biologists used this concept between 1905 and 1920. Like farmers and ranchers, hunters readily assumed the common-sense connection—where abundant, cougars and wolves destroyed deer, elk, sheep, and cattle. The connection was complicated, however, because deer and other game species competed with livestock for grazing range, so ranchers did not necessarily welcome the preservation efforts of sport hunters. When push came to shove, ranchers wanted livestock ranges free of carnivores and game, while hunters preferred game preserves free of carnivores and livestock. When Roosevelt established the Grand Canyon National Game Preserve, he made the assumption, mostly correct

at the time, that ranchers had already minimized the carnivore presence on the Kaibab. Only regular maintenance of the cougar population by sport hunters like Roosevelt himself would be necessary. Thus
the preserve was created, for all intents and purposes, in the absence
of predators.

EARLY ADMINISTRATION OF THE PRESERVE

When Arizona became a state in 1912, its boundary with Utah remained
unchanged. Lands north and south of the Grand Canyon fell wholly
within the jurisdiction of the new state. Arizona senators Henry F.
Ashurst and Carl Hayden left their marks on the state's conservation history by leading the effort to make the Grand Canyon a national park. The
National Park Service was created in 1916, and Ashurst and Hayden
pushed for congressional approval to establish Grand Canyon National
Park on February 26, 1919. Establishment of the park meant that the
many tourist facilities and concessions already in operation on the South
Rim would finally be administered consistently. On the North Rim, almost no development had taken place, so Park Service officials assumed
that implementing new policies would not be problematic. One of the
primary features of the legacy of the Kaibab deer, however, was the ongoing dispute over the different administrative philosophies of the National
Park Service and the Forest Service, which continued to oversee all but
the southern reaches of the preserve.

The only regular Forest Service employee on the game preserve between
1906 and 1918 was a former Yellowstone game warden named James T.
Owens. Owens was well known on the Kaibab as "Uncle Jim," and his duties
there had almost nothing to do with forestry, as was often the case on western federal lands during that period. He worked for a time with Buffalo Jones
to establish the bison ranch in House Rock Valley. Owens also guided hunting parties in the area, taking numerous mountain lions in the preserve. In
later years, he reported killing over six hundred mountain lions during his
tenure there. This number was unconfirmed, although subsequent reports of
the deer situation often regarded Owens's feat as factual. As a consequence,
later foresters often attributed the increase of the deer herd to a shortage of
their natural enemies. Uncle Jim's credibility was supported by his interactions with the likes of President Roosevelt, who hunted mountain lions on
the Kaibab in 1913, and Western novelist Zane Grey, who wrote of his experience roping lions in the Grand Canyon in 1908. Both benefited from hir-
ing Owens as a guide.[21] Whether his estimates were reliable or not, Owens
killed six hundred cougars—more or less—over a twelve-year period on an

area of hundreds of square miles, and not only in the game preserve. He undoubtedly strayed far from the Kaibab lands in his pursuit of the big cats in
northern Arizona and southern Utah. He was never explicit about how many
lions he took in different areas. A quick calculation places his hunting success at one lion per week, perhaps less. This would reveal little about the
resulting changes in predator-prey relations that received so much subsequent attention. Whatever the numbers, early game protectors did not set out
to kill the predatory animals in game preserves. On the contrary, conservationists, naturalists, and biologists initially showed little concern over the relationship between carnivores and game. Local ranchers undoubtedly practiced regular predatory animal control, but not in an effort to protect deer.
The U.S. Bureau of Biological Survey began systematic predatory animal control in the West after 1915, but not on the Kaibab Plateau. Control efforts
were closely tied to livestock ventures, which were in decline north of the
Grand Canyon by that date. One observer at the time suggested that wolves
in particular followed cattle operations, thus their presence on the Kaibab
may have been an anomaly in nature created by the rise and fall of ranching
in the late nineteenth century.[22]

Constant domestic grazing on the forest reserve had long affected the
size of the deer herd, although little attention was paid to the deer prior
to creation of the game preserve. The Forest Service allowed livestock
companies to run their stock on federal lands, but by the early twentieth
century few profited from keeping animals on the Kaibab. Due to changes
in the market, the cost of transporting animals from that remote part of
the country, and the reportedly declining condition of the range, the
cattle and sheep companies diminished their holdings in the area until
no large commercial herds remained. Local residents continued to run
livestock on the Kaibab for decades, and the question of how their presence impacted the deer remained a point of contention.[23]

The factor that has probably received the least attention in accounts of the
Kaibab situation concerns changes in the way American Indians lived around
the plateau. Establishment of the game preserve meant a prohibition of
hunting for whites and Indians alike. The restriction was undoubtedly
difficult to enforce, but unlike such park areas as Yellowstone, the remote-
ness of the Kaibab made it less attractive to poachers. This was one of the
considerations that made it "ideally adapted as a game preserve," according
to its earliest proponents. In addition, the creation of separate reservations
for the Kaibab Paiutes and Navajos meant that their ability to move freely
about on traditional hunting grounds was severely limited.[24]

Steady tourist traffic on the North Rim did not begin until the 1920s. A visitor camp was opened in 1917, but travel was arduous until railroad development around Bryce and Zion National Parks made the North Rim reachable. By 1922, National Park Service Director Stephen Mather had made every attempt to put the North Rim on the map as a destination equally worthy for the traveler to Grand Canyon National Park.[25] He combined his influence with railroad developers and a national public relations machine to draw attention to the unique forests surrounding the canyon. In a series of articles for the *Saturday Evening Post*, journalist Emerson Hough described the virgin forest of the Kaibab as an increasingly rare and valuable American spectacle. Mather arranged Hough's visit and accompanied him on a tour across the plateau. Hough's article on the Kaibab Plateau marked a crucial juncture in the game preserve's history. With the creation of Grand Canyon National Park and the depletion of the range, the deer took on new meaning for the preservation of the area's resources. The economic value of the land for ranching, while never substantial, seemed now insignificant in comparison to the recreational possibilities for the nation's greatest "virgin pine forest."[26]

Just as Hough was describing the limited value of the range for livestock, he also noted the potential danger for wildlife if the preserve continued to be overstocked with cattle and sheep. The journalist opposed ranching in such a place and noted the need for unified jurisdiction of the plateau. The multiple practical uses of the Forest Service would conflict with the preservation and recreational goals of the National Park Service. Logging, grazing, and mining could not coexist with tourism, especially if tourists came to see untouched wilderness and abundant wildlife. Disagreement over the aims and jurisdiction of the plateau escalated in the midst of uncertainty over conditions and the future of the preserve.[27]

Before attempting to explain the tumultuous events on Buckskin Mountain during the mid-1920s, a look beyond the scene in northern Arizona reveals broader questions about the activities of ecologists, mammalogists, and government biologists in establishing new research programs on novel government preserves. In addition, the local and national audiences for this work increasingly demanded simultaneously conflicting answers to questions of land use and the meaning of wildlife.

2

Beasts in the Garden

GOVERNMENT BIOLOGIST VERNON BAILEY

Vernon Bailey was only six years old when his family moved to Elk River, Minnesota. In those days, the town was perched on the edge of the north-western frontier, thirty-five miles upriver from Minneapolis along the Mississippi. Bailey taught himself taxidermy as a teenager, and by 1883 his work had attracted the attention of C. Hart Merriam, one of the nation's leading naturalists. Bailey trapped gophers and sent them to Merriam in Washington DC. Merriam was impressed with the young man's skill in identifying different species, describing variations in individuals, and preparing the specimens. Merriam eventually hired Bailey as a government field naturalist in what became the Bureau of Biological Survey. The young naturalist began work in the Great Plains and Rocky Mountains. Bailey subsequently spent his "whole life on biology and study of animals," focusing especially on animal habits, distribution, abundance, and economic relations.[1]

One of Bailey's earliest field studies took him through northern Arizona, where in December 1888 he learned firsthand about the Kaibab Plateau. Because of deep snow, Bailey was unable to examine conditions there directly, but he talked with local settlers, who at the time told him that game was getting scarce as livestock numbers increased.[2] This brief mention of the Kaibab marked the earliest reference to the area's natural history by one of the government biologists who became intimately involved in the later controversy. Bailey did not return to the Kaibab for many years, but his work in the intervening period helped shape federal biological policies that created problems in northern Arizona.

Bailey's introduction to biology was not unique among his late-nineteenth-century peers. Young men and women interested in nature vigorously read the growing literature of natural history in the United States, taught themselves collecting and preserving techniques, apprenticed with established naturalists, and enrolled in colleges and universities to study such topics as zoology, botany, ornithology, and geology. These young naturalists entered the world of science at the same time the country was undergoing a change in its perspective toward its western territories and newly formed states. This new generation of scientists faced new social and political pressures, and to some extent they created new principles and techniques to cope with those pressures. At the same time, naturalists in the late nineteenth century perpetuated the established traditions of natural history. They continued naming, describing, collecting, and observing the plants and animals they found. They continued to organize the information they gathered systematically and to travel through every imaginable habitat in search of more representatives of known species as well as unknown specimens.[3]

Bailey joined Merriam as a government scientist during a period of significant flux. While farmers and ranchers increasingly demanded practical advice, the Department of Agriculture responded to scientists' calls for bird protection by creating a division that would address problems in "economic ornithology." Merriam headed this division from the start, but he hoped to maintain a comprehensive natural history focus and immediately worked to have the word "economic" stricken. He succeeded, and the office became known as the Division (and still later the Bureau) of Biological Survey. Merriam's investigations included the creation of floral and faunal distribution charts for much of the country. By the turn of the century, the demand for practical results from government science forced the Biological Survey to focus once again on problems that had a bearing on the nation's agriculture. The Biological Survey was called upon to investigate crop damage caused by insects and rodents, as well as livestock damage caused by carnivorous animals.[4]

Even before the nineteenth century, local governments had established bounty systems in the eastern United States to protect livestock from wolves and other carnivores. Such bounties were implemented in the colonial period. Eastern farmers and hunters exterminated the animals that killed their cattle, horses, and sheep.[5] The same system met with only limited success in the West, due in large part to the vastness of the range. Livestock grazed over enormous tracts of sparsely inhabited public land. Bounty hunters managed to kill only a fraction of the animals that threatened ranchers' stock. Administration of ineffective bounty systems became a great burden to local officials. As an alternative, ranchers increasingly called for a coordinated attack against wolves, mountain lions, coyotes, bobcats, and bears through a large-scale coordinated system managed by the federal government. By the 1890s, ranchers were more convinced than ever that the federal government should administer such a system. Before long, demands from livestock owners shifted the focus of the Biological Survey to make control of livestock enemies one of its highest priorities. By 1905, the bureau established a program for predatory animal control. This program catered to Western ranchers, but it also gave the Biological Survey a stronger role in what most taxpayers could identify as an important public service. Compared to efforts that supported agriculture, the basic natural history work of the bureau seemed superfluous. The program set up by the Biological Survey became a sort of centralized bounty system, where federal taxes paid hunters and trappers regular salaries in addition to individual bounties. These government employees would track down livestock killers and any other carnivores. Annual reports partially took the place of animal pelts as evidence of the program's success. However, more comprehensive scientific studies did not completely disappear from the agency.[6]

The Biological Survey fulfilled the charge set by the ranchers and at the same time conducted fundamental scientific investigations. Government naturalists blurred the line between practical results and fundamental data by going into the field with a broad agenda. Their reports ultimately contained a mixture of information that would satisfy a variety of audiences. In 1907, Vernon Bailey, still working as a field naturalist with the Biological Survey, reported on the habits of wolves. His mission was to help ranchers and government agents trap and kill the animals more effectively. Bailey's practical explication of how to control wolves included additional information on their habits and their effect on other species. He recognized the "enormous losses" on the Western cattle ranges and the "destruction of game" on forest reserves, game preserves, and in national parks "through the depredations of wolves." In cooperation with the Forest Service, government biologists worked to ascertain the best methods for destroying these pests. Efforts to destroy wolves, Bailey insisted, could not be undertaken haphazardly or without long-range planning. Whenever ranchers or federal agents undertook half-hearted or short-term wolf poisoning, trapping, or hunting, more wolves could restock the range from neighboring areas within a year or less.

Based on this assumption, wolf numbers could be kept down sufficiently to prevent serious depredations "only by constant and concerted effort." Even with such commitment, Bailey did not expect complete "extermination" of the wolf in the near future. As long as wolves continued to roam the grazing lands of the West, ranchers would consider the program unsuccessful. For many government biologists, the practical impossibility of exterminating wolves meant job security and the opportunity to pursue their more fundamental studies. The two goals of control and investigation were not really in conflict, as long as ranchers were content to let federal naturalists handle both simultaneously. It became the field naturalist's job to satisfy ranchers' needs and scientific curiosity by explaining their findings with an emphasis on practical applications. For this reason, the majority of Bailey's 1907 report focused on the specific methods of poisoning, trapping, and hunting that would be most successful in exterminating what he called the "cattle wolf."[7]

The next year, Bailey described the government campaigns to kill wolves and other livestock enemies, and for the first time he used the term "predatory animal." The Biological Survey apparently standardized this phrase with the creation of programs for control and destruction of predatory animals. This usage did not become commonplace in scientific literature until the 1920s, when it was shortened to "predator." Earlier references to wolves and other predators typically were made as "carnivorous animals" or "carnivores."[8]

Bailey enumerated the wolves and coyotes killed in or adjacent to national forests. The total might have been twice the official estimate, considering the number of animals in surrounding areas. Official estimates also varied from state to state. The government biologist used Wyoming as his example because the Biological Survey had more systematic data from that state, although it was hardly typical. He reported over one thousand wolves killed and almost two thousand coyotes destroyed. Twelve states participated with active campaigns in thirty-nine national forests. The Forest Service conducted these campaigns on lands under its administration. Bailey reported, "The Forest Service has made vigorous efforts to destroy wolves and other predatory animals on or near the national forests, and through its force of forest rangers has carried on the most systematic war on these pests ever undertaken." The federal government's mission was taking shape. It would destroy wolves and other predatory animals throughout the western United States and its territories using the federally coordinated bounty system. Government bounty hunters killed over eighteen hundred wolves (mostly in Wyoming) and twenty-three thousand coyotes in 1907. This resulted in an estimated saving to the livestock industry of $2 million. Despite these reports, Western ranchers soon grew critical of the bounty method of destroying livestock killers. They realized that even with federal administration, fraud was undermining effective extermination. Bounty collectors duped government officials with doctored-up skins and often collected multiple bounties. Livestock owners again called for a federal program to take over the extermination efforts more directly and systematically.[9]

The demand for additional government participation meant an increase in the Biological Survey's involvement, both in administration and as a source of scientific expertise. Congress granted a small appropriation for "experiments and demonstrations" in the control of animals that endangered livestock. This outlay of funding for scientific study placed the bureau directly in charge of more practical work: the destruction of wolves, coyotes, and other injurious animals. Studies of "food habits" directly fulfilled the agency's mandate to study the "economic relations" of animals that affected human activities. The situation became even more urgent with the involvement of the United States in the war in Europe, when food conservation became part of national defense. Concern for livestock continued to be the primary argument for ongoing predatory animal control. The Biological Survey would expand control between 1915 and 1930 with the use of poison. This work, less directed toward understanding life histories of predatory animals and thus of significantly less scientific value, became the focus of criticism from scientists outside the bureau.

Game protection played virtually no role in justifying predatory animal control. Vernon Bailey's early report on wolves contained only passing references to the threat they also posed to game animals. The government biologist used the protection of deer hunting grounds in the Upper Midwest as an excuse to promote wolf control for the protection of livestock more generally. He believed that if hunters left wolves "unmolested" in certain areas, the livestock killers could potentially repopulate much larger regions of livestock country. No one at the time explicitly called for destruction of predatory animals in order to protect big game.

HORNADAY AND LEOPOLD

Nationally renowned naturalist William T. Hornaday expressed the most extreme fears of early-twentieth-century wildlife enthusiasts. He focused particularly on protecting game from wasteful and unethical hunters. Sport hunters supported game protection as a means of propagating their sport, but Hornaday went even further. He wrote several books on game protection and the need to preserve wildlife, which he believed was "vanishing" across the country. Human hunters posed a far greater threat to game species than wolves or coyotes. He did not support predatory animal control as a means of wildlife propagation. In most areas, livestock interests already reduced the danger of predatory animals, so game conservationists gave the issue no thought. According to Hornaday, protection of game from animal enemies was needed only in certain areas. The Kaibab Plateau was one of those areas. In describing the situation on the Grand Canyon National Game Preserve in 1913, the nationally recognized wildlife protector noted that the forest was "not the finest place in the world for the peaceful increase of wild game." The canyon itself contained only a few mountain sheep and mule deer. He added, "Buckskin Mountain, on the northwestern side, is reeking with mountain lions and gray wolves, and both those species should be shot out of the entire Grand Canyon National Forest."[10]

Hornaday's work deeply influenced Aldo Leopold. Leopold read Hornaday's books on the potential extermination of wildlife and immediately began arguing that income on federal lands would increase if the forests were stocked with—rather than depleted of—wildlife resources. As a New Mexico forester from 1909 until 1924 and an avid hunter since childhood, Leopold became concerned about game conservation and the potential role of the national forests in preserving wildlife. Hornaday's message instilled in him a sense of urgency.[11] Leopold helped organize local sport-hunting groups around Albuquerque and occasionally lectured on wildlife protection around New Mexico. The ambitious young forester established and served as editor of the Carson National Forest *Pine Cone*, a newsletter wherein Leopold found another outlet for his early ideas on game conservation. In the first issue of the *Pine Cone*, Leopold voiced his interest in game conservation, and where necessary he supported "the reduction of predatory animals." To expand his interest in game, he wrote an article on "varmints" wherein he attempted to enlist the support of the livestock industry. Since cattle and sheep growers had a history of exterminating wolves, mountain lions, and coyotes, Leopold proposed that ranchers join sport hunters and other game conservationists, who shared the same antagonism toward predatory animals, at least in certain regions.[12]

Allying ranchers, sport hunters, and conservationists was a novel approach to game conservation. In addition to extending Hornaday's comments about lions and wolves on Buckskin Mountain, Leopold suggested a partnership with ranchers. Previously, ranchers attempted to save rangelands for exclusive livestock growing. If game species had a place at all, ranchers believed, it should be confined to small preserves. In 1915, Leopold asked livestock owners to consider game conservation as an allied effort in range management. He wrote, "It seems never to have occurred to anybody that . . . the stockmen and the game protectionists are mutually and vitally interested in a common problem. This problem is the reduction of predatory animals." At this time, he saw wolves and coyotes as enemies to both livestock and game because of the value of ranching and sport hunting, respectively. According to the young forester, predatory animals were guilty of "continuing to eat the cream off the stock grower's profits" and also of depleting the already low game supply. He observed that, in spite of the best efforts of the Biological Survey, varmints continued to thrive. Game animals did not stand a chance without the coordinated efforts of humans. Leopold advanced this coordinated effort a step further. He convened informal meetings with government predatory animal inspector J. Stokely Ligon and president of the New Mexico Wool Growers Eduardo M. Otero. Both the Biological Survey and the Wool Growers offered support for predatory animal control, now for the combined good of sport hunting, game conservation, and the livestock industry. Ultimately, Leopold hoped, this support would translate into funding and increased action against predatory animals. The Biological Survey did step up efforts toward predatory animal control after 1915. Federal funding increased dramatically during those years, and trapping and hunting efforts gave way to widespread use of poison because it was considered more effective in eliminating predatory animals.[13]

From his early work in New Mexico, Leopold's interest in wildlife deepened. Part of his novel approach to animal life in the forests probably derived from his early training in forestry. He used forestry techniques as a kind of model for wildlife.[14] In the late 1920s, he undertook an ambitious survey of game conditions that served as the basis for the first textbook on the subject, *Game Management*, published in 1933.[15] In that book, for the first time, Leopold attempted to describe systematically certain principles of management that would improve game populations. Far from being the result of one man's genius, *Game Management* integrated the experiences of mammalogists, entomologists, botanists, foresters, and ecologists. Those experiences, including efforts to protect and control the game on the Kaibab Plateau, provided a set of questions on which to base new management principles. Leopold and his colleagues were perhaps more baffled and intrigued by the complexities of game management in the 1930s than they had been in the early years of protection and administration of game on western preserves. Developing an appreciation of those complexities occupied game administrators as completely as developing new principles of management.[16]

FOREST SERVICE ADMINISTRATION ON THE KAIBAB

The increasing predatory animal control efforts in the West reverberated on the Kaibab Plateau, where game protection was just beginning to raise new questions. Those questions became particularly difficult when the National Park Service gained jurisdiction over the southern portion of the Grand Canyon National Game Preserve in 1919. Systematic, federal predatory animal control efforts did not begin any earlier on the Kaibab than elsewhere, and the intended effect was primarily to protect livestock. Ranchers undoubtedly killed coyotes and wolves there in the last decades of the nineteenth century. Sport hunters took mountain lions off the plateau before 1916, including Zane Grey in 1908 and President Roosevelt in 1913.[17] Official destruction of predatory animals began sometime after that, but later Biological Survey and Forest Service reports offered only vague statements regarding the beginning and duration of control activities on the preserve. The Forest Service began preparing reports of wildlife conditions on the Kaibab Plateau in 1920. With the emerging interest of the National Park Service in tourism around the Grand Canyon, emphasis on the preserve turned toward creating a spectacular deer display. More significant than predatory animals for the deer, livestock numbers on the Kaibab dwindled as profits dropped due to the declining condition of vegetation. Local foresters wrote the first reports of the change in vegetation, describing the conditions of the deer and the range. There, they raised concerns about management and expressed hypotheses and opinions about the role of predatory animals. While these early reports were not based on data gathered systematically in controlled situations, they reflected years of local foresters' experience on the plateau. Their points of view dominated perceptions of conditions for the readers of those reports, as well as for wildlife biologists who conducted studies of the Kaibab for decades to follow.

In 1920, forest supervisor J. C. Roak prepared a report on the status of the Grand Canyon National Game Preserve. He indicated that the numbers of deer were increasing and called the current estimates of fifteen thousand to twenty thousand deer conservative. If the estimates reflected inaccuracies, however, the supervisor did not believe a more systematic count of the deer justified the expense of sending more foresters into the field. Roak argued that with no plan of management in the works, an accurate count served no purpose. Roak may have based his findings on a separate report prepared at about the same time by another local forester.[18]

Forest examiner S. B. Locke showed a strong interest in wildlife. He signed his report, which described the range conditions in more detail, "In Charge, Game and Fish." Locke noted that conditions varied considerably. Despite the damage to vegetation evident in some areas, he reported that the deer were in excellent condition. In addition to praising the condition of the deer, Locke recommended no change in the policies toward their protection. He strongly opposed an open-hunting season for

Small-scale livestock operations have long been a part of the history of the Kaibab National Forest, as evidenced by this corral at the Ryan site, in the northwestern corner of the forest. Photo by the author.

the simple reason that because of the large number of deer, hunting in the preserve "would hardly be a sporting proposition." Unlike Roak, Locke favored a careful count of the deer. He wrote, "In order that we may have a definite basis for our plans in handling the situation it is necessary to know as closely as possible the number of deer on the Forest. I believe an attempt should be made to get an accurate estimate."[19]

Roak and Locke arranged their priorities for the forest differently. Roak thought a plan of management that included the deer should precede any expensive studies. Until the Forest Service established a plan, he recommended continuation of the current policy of protection. Locke, on the other hand, believed the Forest Service needed immediate studies so that a plan could be developed. He advocated the commencement of efforts toward managing the deer rather than simply protecting them.

Roak and Locke both commented on predatory animals in their reports, speculating on the relationship between these animals and the deer. Roak noted that Biological Survey hunters killed only a small proportion of the estimated one thousand mountain lions on the plateau. In his opinion, the growing deer population had enabled the lion population to increase over the past few years. More deer simply meant more food for lions. He also noted that the Biological Survey would take charge of any controversy over predatory animal control, so the Forest Service should not get involved. Locke commented more extensively on this issue. He assumed the number of mountain lions to be as great as at any time in the past on the Kaibab Plateau. As evidence, the local forester cited the legendary lion hunter, Uncle Jim, who reported killing two hundred lions in a single year. Locke concluded that at present lions might be responsible for killing hundreds of deer. In his opinion, predation could account for the continued health of the deer herd and the absence of starving deer. Locke spoke for both Forest Service officials and "local people familiar with conditions," writing that the number of deer on the game preserve had not increased within the past three years. He found no evidence of losses from starvation and concluded that "the natural increase must be taken up principally in an overflow and those destroyed by predatory animals." According to Locke, the latter source of loss was difficult to determine but must have been "very considerable." Locke's observation that the deer population seemed stable suggested that the Forest Service was succeeding in its administration of the deer. The overall goal of the preserve, however, was to protect and encourage deer, not to allow predatory animals to kill deer. Stability was not a Forest Service objective. Whatever role mountain lions played in preventing increase of their prey, Locke suggested that the lions should be reduced. Instead of falling prey to predatory animals, deer would be encouraged to migrate off of the preserve when they became more numerous. The Forest Service would also endeavor to prevent excessive concentration of deer during the winter. Locke made these plans explicit, writing, "The proper management of the game preserve requires action along three lines: the destruction of predatory animals, the encouraging of drift to other areas, and the prevention of extreme concentration during the winter."[20]

The details of Locke's suggestion included encouraging liberal predatory animal hunting by the Biological Survey. He also hoped the construction of deer trails would encourage game to move north in greater numbers. Deer had become more common in Utah as far as seventy-five miles from the Arizona state line. The Forest Service presumed this to be the result of migration from the preserve. Locke recommended experiments to test the effect of creating disturbances among the deer in areas where they concentrated during the winter. In order to track the success of these efforts, the local forester favored a careful count of the deer. He wrote, "In order that we may have a definite basis for our plans in handling the situation it is necessary to know as closely as possible the number of deer on the Forest. I believe an attempt should be made to get an accurate estimate." Locke's interest in limiting competition between deer and cattle was not explicit in his report. In later controversy over how many deer were on the range, the Forest Service would never forget the assumed fact that more deer meant fewer cattle.

In the summer of 1920, Locke's superiors clearly wanted to maintain the range for cattle. In forwarding Locke's report to the chief forester in Washington, District Forester Leon F. Kneipp further stressed the necessity of controlling predatory animals. Kneipp emphasized control because he saw the additional advantage of pleasing local ranchers. Increasing the deer would be a secondary effect of protecting livestock interests on the plateau. Competition between deer and cattle might pose a problem eventually, but only if the Forest Service first succeeded in keeping mountain lions from killing livestock. Kneipp, who served previously as the chief of grazing for the Forest Service, clearly preferred the scenario where his agency would decide between game and livestock, rather than letting predatory animals destroy both options. The grazing official inferred that the increasing deer herd on the Kaibab might eventually "become so extensive as to interfere with the grazing of local stock." Such a conflict did not exist at the present time, according to Kneipp's sources, but he wanted to prepare for such an eventuality. He explicitly referred to the shared jurisdiction of the Forest Service and National Park Service for the game preserve. His concern, as district forester, was to manage the game preserve and protect the interests of local ranchers at the same time. Kneipp detailed the efforts needed to remove predatory animals, primarily mountain lions. The matter, he concluded, should be taken up with the Biological Survey, perhaps because the Forest Service could not directly influence management on lands not under its jurisdiction. The Biological Survey might recommend to the National Park Service, for example, that lion control be extended into the park. Local Forest Service officials would offer to oversee the implementation of Biological Survey suggestions.[21]

The Forest Service forwarded their concerns to the Biological Survey. One Forest Service official in Washington DC noted that most mountain lions in the preserve lived along the North Rim of the Grand Canyon. The Biological Survey had practiced virtually no predatory animal control on the south end of the plateau in recent years. The forester reported, "For the last four or five years, no mountain lion hunting whatever has been done in that region except in one or two instances where [Uncle Jim] Owens has brought out from the [E]ast, parties of sportsmen whom he took into the country to have a lion hunt." Those hunts served merely for sport, not to protect livestock or wildlife. Officials in the Washington Forest Service office agreed that predatory animal control should be handled by the Bureau of Biological Survey. This route of action enabled the bureau to make arrangements with the National Park Service and keep the Forest Service out of the fray. The Biological Survey began planning for action almost immediately. Acting Chief A. K. Fisher thanked the Forest Service for its information. He added, "We have already arranged to put hunters on the Kaibab National Forest during the coming fall and winter with a view to destroying mountain lions to protect livestock and game." The bureau's predatory animal inspector, George E. Holman, would supervise the control work directly.[22]

THE NATIONAL PARK SERVICE AND ITS DEER SPECTACLE

Just as the Biological Survey increased its predatory animal control activities and the Forest Service reported an increase in the deer, a new government agency had come into the picture on the Kaibab Plateau. Although the Grand Canyon had been designated a national monument in

1908, there was no federal agency to administer the surrounding lands. With the establishment of a National Park Service in 1916, and the creation of Grand Canyon National Park three years later, new concerns for the use of the canyon's North Rim emerged. The park's northern boundary was established about fifteen miles north of the North Rim, near DeMotte Park. The boundaries of the Grand Canyon National Game Preserve did not change. This meant a significant area of the game preserve was now administered by the Park Service, with regulations pertaining to wildlife that differed dramatically from those of the Forest Service.

Stephen Mather, the Park Service's first director, was particularly excited about his agency's new acquisition. He quickly recognized that along with the spectacular views of the canyon's South Rim, the forests and wildlife along the North Rim would also attract tourists by the thousands. Accounts of the abundant wildlife, particularly the mule deer, multiplied in national magazines and newspapers. Beginning in 1920, Mather took it upon himself to promote the Kaibab deer as an attraction, accompanying journalists on tours of the park, writing essays of his own for the national press, and even taking a Kaibab mule deer fawn on tour with him back East.[23]

Journalist Emerson Hough wrote two installment articles for the *Saturday Evening Post* that brought nationwide attention to the Kaibab Plateau. Hough hoped the plateau could be continuously preserved for use by the general public and administered by a single, federal agency. Such a forest would stand as a tribute to democracy in contrast to "Old World" forests, which had been reserved for the exclusive use of royalty in many European countries. The Kaibab Plateau qualified as such a place, according to Hough, where "nature's fences" kept wilderness wild. Roosevelt had created the game preserve, and the deserts and canyons had kept it isolated from development. Hough wrote, "So there we have a marvelously beautiful wilderness, the least known wilderness in the United States, already fenced off, already appraised, and already set aside." While the national forest, game preserve, and park each protected the plateau, Hough hoped that an unprecedented move toward preservation would unite jurisdiction of the area. When he drove up onto the plateau, accompanied by Mather, Hough reportedly exclaimed, "We were in the President's Forest!"[24]

According to Hough, the Kaibab consisted of no less than "the greatest remaining pine forest of the United States." Mather and the group's driver told Hough they might see several hundred deer in a day, standing in full view of the road. Hough and his companions were skeptical and made jokes, but by the end of their day's drive they had seen sixty-nine deer themselves. He concluded that estimates of over ten thousand deer on the preserve must certainly be accurate and probably conservative. At the same time, the journalist remarked that many of the deer he saw were in "very low flesh," while cattle in the area were also in "very poor" condition in general. Hough concluded, "It is admitted—and any stockman tourist cannot fail to see it anyhow—that this forest is very badly overpastured—so much so that the grazing permits have now no value, and it is a losing venture to range cattle here."[25]

THE ECONOMICS OF CONTROL

Although Forest Service officials no longer had the same unquestioned authority over policies on the game preserve, they wanted to increase mountain lion control in order to make the range more appealing to ranchers. Some areas, where sheep and cattle had caused severe damage to vegetation in the past, had recovered to the point that grazing might again be profitable. An assistant regional forester, Ernest Winkler, visited the Kaibab in the summer of 1921 and reported on the recovery of the vegetation. Winkler found that unlike typical livestock ranges, deer appeared to be causing damage on the Kaibab now. He described the injuries to trees between two and six feet tall. Sheep would not reach that high, and cattle generally did not browse on trees. Only deer could be blamed. Even the ponderosa pine, a valuable timber species, showed damage from some animal. Winkler considered the possibility that horses or squirrels might be eating the pine buds, but he concluded that such widespread injury must be from the deer. The damage seemed greater nearer the canyon rim, where the Forest Service allowed little sheep grazing, but deer were numerous. Grazing officials would need to find a way of reducing the deer if ranchers were ever going to bring their livestock back to the Kaibab.[26]

While the Biological Survey increased pressure for predatory animal control on the Kaibab, mammalogists began questioning the effect of these activities on other animals. The organization of a professional society for mammalogy in 1919 meant that government biologists had to answer to a more diverse scientific audience than they had faced in earlier years, when most serious mammalogy was done within Merriam's Biological Survey.[27] The focus on predatory animal control, in particular, had broadened. The demands of the livestock industry, meanwhile, remained virtually unchanged. Ranchers still longed for the day when predatory animals would be unknown on grazing lands and even on federal forests. Joseph Grinnell and Joseph Dixon at the University of California became critical of the Biological Survey's divided allegiance to zoological studies and predatory animal control. Grinnell, a founding member of the American Society of Mammalogists and director of the Museum of Vertebrate Zoology in Berkeley, worried that poison in particular killed indiscriminately and depleted the nation's stock of zoological specimens. In 1921, Dixon, who described himself as an "economic mammalogist," made an effort to tally the Biological Survey's success in exterminating mountain lions on the Kaibab, among other places. That success could be measured in dollar amounts by estimating the value of livestock saved from depredation. On the Kaibab in particular, the Biological Survey could not provide complete information since everyone familiar with the area knew that most of the mountain lions killed there had been taken for sport by Uncle Jim Owens or hunters guided by him. The bureau officially employed Owens for only fifteen days in November 1919 and beyond that could offer no figures on his activities. The same was true of most predatory animal hunters at the time, as Dixon learned from acting bureau chief W. C. Henderson. Henderson wrote, "It is hardly practicable for us to furnish you a statement as to the catch of mountain lions by our various hunters as most of them take lions in connection with their hunting operations against other predatory animals." Dixon received more definite—but not necessarily more accurate—reports from predatory animal inspectors in the region.[28]

Dixon relied especially on information from George Holman, who was a Biological Survey predatory animal inspector. Holman worked as part of the Cooperative Campaign for the Destruction of Predatory Animals in Utah, a joint effort of the Biological Survey and the Utah State Livestock Board. As a government scientist working cooperatively with the livestock industry, Holman defended the recent expansion of predatory animal control in the region, pointing out that earlier bounty hunters had overstated the success of their efforts. He explained to Dixon, for example, that the Biological Survey had employed Jim Owens only briefly. Holman commented: "Statements made to the effect that Mr. Owen[s] has killed 1,100 lion in sixteen years are very much exaggerated." A more accurate estimate might be extrapolated from the sixty-seven lions that Owens killed in a five-year period, as reported to the Forest Service some years earlier. Holman concluded that the number was somewhat less than two hundred, adding, "Mr. Owen[s] is one of the few old plainsmen still living in this country, and is frequently called on by tourists and people whom he meets to recite stories of his past and his hunting expeditions and I fear that through the frequent telling of these stories he has continued to exaggerate on the facts until the figures you have heard of have been given publicity." The figures were clearly untrustworthy. Dixon appreciated the inspector's frankness and immediately requested more information. The zoologist wanted to know how many lions a hunter *could* kill in a year. Holman explained that the current record came from the Kaibab Forest the previous winter. Two men working with dogs over a period of four months killed twenty-three lions, presumably all on Forest Service land north of the Grand Canyon. In less rugged country and without severe weather, they might have killed more, but Holman would not offer specific numbers. He also informed the zoologist that so far that winter, hunters on the Kaibab had found no fresh sign of lions, adding, "Apparently the work done last year in this locality was very effective and nearly cleaned up the situation."[29]

On the economics of control, Holman added that working with dogs was relatively expensive and that the Biological Survey planned more experimental poison use to determine the effectiveness of that method against lions. To balance the ledger, Dixon hoped to establish the value of livestock killed by mountain lions. Holman did his best to calculate the damage in Utah, where he had better estimates. On average, each mountain lion caused between five hundred dollars and one thousand dollars worth of damage to livestock every year. A wolf also caused one thousand dollars in damage, while coyotes and bobcats annually caused at least fifty dollars each. The exceptional predatory animal, prone to kill livestock exclusively, might cost ranchers many times these amounts. Dixon found these estimates far above averages in California, where he calculated the damage done by a lion to be about one hundred dollars per year. Exceptional cases sometimes reached six hundred dollars. Dixon concluded that although Holman's figures were much lower than Owens's tall tales, the Biological Survey inspector continued to use "extreme or exaggerated" estimates, rather than offering "actual conservative figures."[30] These differing opinions of exaggeration and estimation would echo for years to come.

By the end of the winter, Forest Supervisor Roak reported the Biological Survey had not fulfilled Holman's desire to clean up the mountain lions. Roak himself examined numerous cougar kills, where what he called "young" and "thriving" deer fell prey to mountain lions. Older deer became "easy prey" to what Roak described as "an unbelievable number of coyotes." Rather than suggest that deer should be protected from depredation, Roak's primary message was that the Forest Service needed to dispose of some of the deer. He noted that if vegetation ran short, deer might suffer, but cattle would be the first to starve. The forest supervisor insisted that the deer currently had adequate food, and while he supported removal of some deer, he opposed suggestions from the Biological Survey that called for hunting in the preserve. He enthusiastically supported "a very careful study" of the situation before any action was taken. Roak recommended that the person to do those studies must spend a considerable time in the forest and must rely on local foresters for a complete description of the conditions. Biological Survey field naturalist Edward A. Goldman was already scheduled to spend part of the fall and winter in the preserve studying the conditions of both the vegetation and the deer.[31]

Just as the Biological Survey faced increasing pressure to end its predatory animal control program, administrators of the Grand Canyon National Game Preserve encountered a similarly mounting conflict. Kaibab officials in the early 1920s found that the fate of the deer was joined to broader national visions of game protection and management. Many demands and uncertainties clouded the meanings of successful protection or proper management. To allow increase or not to allow increase of the deer herd was the basic dilemma.[32] Many believed the initiation of careful research and the implementation of scientific expertise could solve this dilemma. Each side, however, involved new and complex questions, so that neither side would appear to be the clear choice, seemingly regardless of the amount of research conducted or expertise provided.

3

A Deer Dilemma

In the early 1920s, the Kaibab Plateau attracted attention from the federal government's most experienced and highly placed biologists. Corroborated by the observations of local foresters, the findings of Biological Survey field researchers pointed to an unprecedented dilemma. On one side, efforts to protect the deer had succeeded and any policy change in the preserve might contradict its original purpose. On the other side, a new picture was emerging, one that suggested that the continued increase of deer could soon jeopardize the future of the preserve. With or without human intervention, the Kaibab deer seemed on the brink of a crisis. In the face of this dilemma, the eventual outcome seemed undetermined, but with both public and private interests at stake, the matter could not be left to chance. It fell to government biologists to make the first crucial choices. They would first attempt to decide how many deer inhabited the plateau and how fast the number might increase. They would also consider the factors that influenced the increase. In neither case were the answers available as matters of scientific fact. In the absence of scientific fact, simple estimates and untried actions achieved the status of management goals and principles. Acknowledging such uncertainty in the context of this dilemma provides a better historical backdrop for the activities of government biologists on the Kaibab in this period. This approach contrasts with the more common tendency to see with hindsight that poor choices were made for purposes of political expediency or as a result of ignorance. Seeing the dilemma first, the estimates and actions of early game managers can be appreciated as illustrations of the best of human effort.

GOVERNMENT BIOLOGISTS

Edward W. Nelson became the head of the Biological Survey in 1916. Trained initially as a teacher, he abandoned that career to conduct surveys of natural history in Wyoming, Utah, and Nevada. Nelson's only academic training in biology came in a special course at Johns Hopkins University, which he dropped before the end of his first year to join a research expedition to Alaska. As a result of these retreats westward for scientific research, he became one of the most respected naturalists of his day. He served as chief of the Biological Survey for eleven years. In addition to his research, he also provided on-the-job training for younger naturalists, much like that which he received in the 1870s and 1880s. Nelson's mentoring particularly influenced Edward A. Goldman. While on an expedition in California in 1891, a broken wagon wheel forced Nelson to stop for repairs at the Goldman family farm. In addition to finding help with his wagon, Nelson found Goldman, then eighteen years old. From California, their lifelong collaboration took them throughout the United States and Mexico, as well as into parts of Central America.[1]

Both Nelson and Goldman commented repeatedly on the situation in northern Arizona during what became a turbulent period for government biologists, but only Goldman conducted extensive fieldwork there. Beginning in September 1922, Goldman joined S. B. Locke in investigating the conditions of the deer, the range, and the forest on the Kaibab Plateau. They came to be regarded as the first "experts" to comment on the situation, and they made explicit their concern over the declining conditions of the game preserve. The need for "expert" advice and "expert" study was expressed throughout correspondence relating to the Kaibab deer beginning around 1922. More often than not in this period, references to experts were references to Goldman. His observations carried weight within the Biological Survey, and his work with local foresters gave him credibility within the Forest Service. In Goldman's first report on the Kaibab deer, coauthored by Locke, the condition of the food plants soon became the primary issue. The remaining livestock and the increasing deer had thinned the vegetation.

Goldman and Locke expressed their concern over the vegetation with reference to the concept of carrying capacity, which was developed in the late 1890s by ranchers and Department of Agriculture researchers. Carrying capacity referred to the number of animals a certain piece of range could support without deterioration. In response to widespread concern about the reported deterioration of range conditions, ranchers and government scientists hoped to establish management plans for livestock on the range using the concept. Damage caused by big game had not concerned government scientists previously, except for recent problems with elk around Yellowstone National Park. Aldo Leopold was in close touch with the concerns of livestock owners. He worked briefly in the Forest Service's Office of Grazing in Albuquerque, and in early 1915, he report- edly first came across the term "carrying capacity" in connection with range science. Both Leopold's timing and location in New Mexico make it likely that he was the first person to recognize the implications of carrying capacity for wildlife management.[2]

Goldman and Locke, using the term in 1922 on the Kaibab, extended its meaning in important ways. It took on significance beyond the economically driven world of cattle or sheep ranching and ultimately helped transform simplistic wildlife protection efforts into a form of scientific management. Goldman and Locke spent two weeks studying the plateau. Based on this investigation, they wrote a report for the Biological Survey in fulfillment of three goals. They hoped to determine the abundance and condition of the deer, as well as the condition of the ranges, and to identify any measures that might relieve the overstocking that the forest supervisor had recently reported.[3]

Forest Service estimates of the wildlife in the preserve in 1922 suggested there were at least twenty thousand deer. Goldman and Locke ranked themselves among the few who had "an intimate knowledge of conditions." Anyone with such knowledge would use this estimate as the minimum number. They reported that the deer were "everywhere abundant" and "exceedingly abundant in certain localities and abundant over large areas." They supported these statements with comments about the heavy browsing of trees and shrubs. For better or worse, the deer population could now increase by several thousand animals per year due to their high reproductive success. Unlike Ernest Winkler from the regional Forest Service office, who compared deer and livestock in terms of "damage" to vegetation, Goldman and Locke compared the effects on the range by distinguishing between deer and livestock eating habits. Generally, they understood that cattle "graze" on ground vegetation, like grass, while deer "browse" on shrubs and low trees. Grass was abundant in many areas, but except early in the spring deer did not eat grass. By contrast, cattle preferred grass and ate very little of the shrubs and tree branches that were preferred by deer. Because grass was heavily grazed, especially near water holes, the experts concluded that the capacity of the range for cattle had been reached. Continued forage destruction would lower the carrying capacity of the range for both livestock and wildlife. They recommended immediate cattle reductions. Deer reductions might yet be needed in the near future.

MANAGEMENT PLANS

Reducing livestock and reducing wildlife were dramatically different issues, however. Reduction of cattle simply meant the Forest Service could issue fewer grazing permits for the next year, a system worked out partly in response to range management research done in the first decades of the twentieth century. Ranchers would have to find other places to graze their cattle or ship them to market. Reduction of deer, particularly on a national game preserve, had never before been contemplated. The conservation-minded public increasingly treasured this preserve and generally opposed government actions that might harm its pristine character. Thanks to the efforts of Stephen Mather and Emerson Hough, the Kaibab deer had received too much attention to be "reduced" discreetly. Goldman and Locke recognized these difficulties and did not make hasty recommendations. They suggested further studies to ascertain the carrying capacity and how it could best be reached.

Any serious examination of the preserve would have to consider the seasonal migrations of the deer, which were well known to local experts. Those same experts, however, were unsure of the implications for management of those movements. Deer apparently had different needs during different seasons of the year, and these needs would have to be considered. On the Kaibab Plateau, the higher elevations lay along a ridge running the length of the preserve generally from north to south and provided essential summer range for the deer. In the winter, the deer moved down toward the edges of the plateau, some to the east and most to the west of the north-south ridge.

By 1922, Goldman and Locke, like Roak, wanted to be certain that the Forest Service had a larger plan of game management in place. Game management at this point in time referred to explicit administrative goals. These goals would establish priorities for maintaining deer in large numbers for visitors and wildlife enthusiasts to enjoy. Management would also aim to protect the deer from starvation should they destroy too much of their own food supply. In every case, the health of the forest and suitability for livestock grazing would receive due consideration. Under the heading "Necessity for Game Management," Goldman and Locke summarized that the deer had reached the limit of "grazing capacity" and further increase would result in destruction of the forage most palatable to the deer accompanied by "a lowering in the carrying capacity of the range." If the Forest Service allowed the deer to increase without control, the animals would overstock the range and "suffer losses due to overutilization of the forage and very likely suffer from some epidemic disease as most commonly occurs when any wild animal becomes excessively abundant in any region." Goldman and Locke believed these suggestions were novel in game management. The means they proposed were not novel, however. They hoped hunting activity would provide a triple solution. In addition to killing deer, hunters would reduce overconcentration of the deer by scattering them in certain areas. Hunters would also encourage the deer to migrate off of the plateau. Goldman and Locke referred to these actions as "principles" and looked forward to testing their principles. They concluded: "Since this is in a way a pioneer effort to apply such principles of management to game, detailed information regarding the conditions present at the beginning and at various times after action is taken will be particularly valuable." The experts hoped the Forest Service would take these actions—especially hunting— only after further study had shown them to be absolutely necessary.

Although Goldman and Locke considered that predatory animals play some role in the management of the deer, no one could have anticipated later events. The experts stated that "the proper protection of the deer must consider [predatory animal] destruction." Due to the large size of the preserve and the great distances predatory animals might travel in order to reach it, Goldman and Locke believed only continual control would keep predatory animals from increasing beyond restraint. They hoped the deer could be managed and that predatory animals would only disrupt deer management. In fact, many officials in the Biological Survey and Forest Service considered hunting of both deer and predatory animals to be the only reasonable management approach. Further reduction of livestock would mean the end of ranching there and would not prevent what they saw as an impending deer crisis.

By November 1922, the Forest Service and Biological Survey began to implement a "plan of management" through a "constructive program of utilization of wild life on the Forests." It would be the first such program initiated by the Forest Service, and officials feared opposition from people who saw game preserves as a final and scarcely adequate haven for big game. Based on Goldman and Locke's report and a discussion with Locke, Forest Service grazing inspector Chris Rachford predicted conflict. He explained to Chief Forester William B. Greeley that they faced "a very big problem" of administration. Rachford cited "experts" from both the Biological Survey and the

Forest Service who had examined the situation. Removal of some deer
would be necessary in order to prevent serious future losses and to
maintain a reasonable and permanent number of deer. He anticipated a potential public relations crisis if the Forest Service did not
handle the problem with all possible tact and ingenuity. Rachford
suggested that the Biological Survey continue to provide "expert advice." The Forest Service would coordinate publicity in support of
management actions and would undertake those actions. He also informed forester Greeley that Aldo Leopold, whose reputation as a
game expert was growing steadily within the Forest Service, had examined the plans.[4]

By the end of the year, the Forest Service and Biological Survey agreed
that deer hunting would take place on the Grand Canyon National Game
Preserve. Of the estimated twenty thousand deer on the plateau, Goldman
recommended removal of about two thousand. He hoped this modest 10
percent removal would curb future increase without arousing insur-
mountable protest. The secretary of agriculture could authorize hunting
under authority of the original congressional act that created the preserve. The federal government preferred to secure the cooperation of the
state for this action. Assistant Forester Will C. Barnes advised the chief
forester that hunters from outside Arizona, particularly Utahns, should be
allowed to hunt on the Kaibab for not more than ten dollars. Out-of-state
hunters would undoubtedly be attracted to the northern Arizona forest in
greater numbers than Arizona hunters, given the long trip around the
Grand Canyon that took in-state hunters either through California or
Utah to the Kaibab. At the time, Arizona law set the fee for out-of-state
licenses at twenty dollars. Since the Forest Service would charge an additional amount to cover the cost of administering the hunt, Barnes hoped
reducing the out-of-state fee would balance that cost. The Arizona legis-
lature could "get the ball rolling" when it convened that winter. As it
turned out, Arizona took no action on the proposal that year. The two federal agencies would first have to find ways of convincing the state and the
public that the need for hunting on the Kaibab was becoming urgent.[5]

Because Edward Goldman did not spend the entire winter on the preserve, he returned in early spring to meet Locke and other Biological
Survey and Forest Service officials. The group visited the winter range of
the deer, notably Jumpup Point and Sowats Point on the west side of the
plateau and south of House Rock Valley on the east side. Goldman and the
party found the winter forage to be in good condition for deer, particu-

larly in the lower canyons. Deer had heavily browsed in some places, decimating the preferred cliff rose plants. Overall, the biologist concluded that deer and livestock together had lowered the carrying capacity of the winter range. Goldman referred to what range managers called "period overgrazing," meaning that cattle overutilized the range early in the spring, the most critical season for its annual growth. Cattle tended to graze at the lowest elevations in the winter. Compared with deer, cattle then moved to higher elevations earlier in the spring. This caused greater damage on the summer range as well. Even though livestock and deer had different grazing preferences, their combined effect on both summer and winter ranges accelerated vegetation damage.[6]

As for the condition of the deer, Goldman reported that they looked excellent. This description may have been somewhat at odds with the reports of "cow boys" in the area who noted that a few deer appeared to be suffering from "pink eye," an eye disease that sometimes partially blinded the animals. Goldman also noted that the deer foraged heavily in concentrated areas when they might easily have spread out, particularly around Jumpup Point and Sowats Point. He could not explain this behavior. Localized concentration caused great damage to forage in those areas. Possibly as a result of the concentration, more deer seemed to be distributed farther to the north and west than in previous years. According to descriptions solicited from local observers by Goldman, the number of deer west of the plateau, beyond Kanab Canyon, had doubled in the last ten years. Nevertheless, the biologist obtained no information to justify a revision of the estimate of twenty thousand deer on the plateau, as reported in his previous memorandum. He did not think it practical to undertake a special count of the deer at that time, although ranchers who saw grazing lands increasingly threatened applied pressure to do just that. Goldman noted, "Owing to the rough country occupied and the growth of cedar and pinyon or brush, it is clearly impractical to attempt a count of the deer even when concentrated on the winter ranges."

The Biological Survey planned an expansion of efforts to control mountain lions and coyotes on the plateau, but Goldman found little evidence of depredation on the deer. The biologist recommended controlling deer in order to protect the range. He did not want to interfere in whatever plans the predatory animal control division might make. Most importantly, Goldman recognized the intertwined effects of the deer on the separate winter and summer ranges and the corresponding effects of those ranges on the deer. He began to realize that seeing one range without seeing the other could easily lead to widely diverging opinions of the overall conditions in the preserve. Goldman hoped that year-round study would give a better picture of conditions as a whole. At the very least, such intense scrutiny might expose the complexity of comparing different ranges within the same preserve, since that complexity escaped the grasp of most casual observers.

DEER UTILIZATION

Later that summer, Edward W. Nelson, chief of the Biological Survey, prepared a memorandum on the conditions of the preserve and suggested methods of "utilizing" the surplus deer. Nelson conducted no study of the plateau himself but relied on Goldman's reports of the conditions. The survey chief's plans embodied the best of a philosophy that maximized human benefit from efficient use of natural resources. He worked with numbers and production goals, apparently with little thought for practical and aesthetic considerations. Taking the estimate of twenty thousand deer in the preserve as conservative, Nelson suggested the herd might increase by nearly eight thousand additional deer per year. This increase would quickly bring the range to a critical point, if such a point had not already been reached. To minimize damage in the event of such an increase, Nelson foresaw the need for hunting in the preserve. His was one of the first such official recommendations for hunting. The Biological Survey chief outlined his plans, proposing a hunt of up to two thousand deer per year in congested areas. This would limit the increase in deer numbers and would serve to correct what he saw as an uneven distribution of the deer. The activity of hunters in these areas would be critical in getting the deer to spread out. Nelson believed that removing two thousand deer would barely make a dent in the projected increase, but the redistribution would alleviate severe range damage on overcrowded areas.[7]

Nelson presumed that if the deer browsed on a wider variety of locations, increases of eight thousand to ten thousand deer per year might be acceptable and even desirable. The possibility of actually increasing the number of deer in the preserve excited the bureau chief because more deer ultimately meant more resources available on government land. He wrote, "If the deer can be scattered to cover the preserve more fully than at present the number of breeding animals the range will support can be increased and later the annual surplus would correspondingly increase."

Nelson suggested that the Biological Survey first needed to understand the uneven distribution of deer. If vegetation on the entire preserve could be uniformly browsed, increased production of deer could be expected. Expanded hunting would become the means of harvesting the surplus. Certain areas would be kept free of hunting, particularly along the highway and near the national park boundary. The details, Nelson admitted, would have to be worked out in "actual practice." Eventually, the deer could provide a valuable commercial commodity. He wrote confidently that the "peculiar location and boundaries" of the Kaibab Plateau made it the kind of game preserve that would "continue to produce a large surplus of deer, most of which must be disposed of commercially." He concluded by commenting on the uniqueness of his proposal and the kind of ongoing investigations that would be needed to make it prosper. "Nothing of this kind has ever been attempted heretofore in America," Nelson noted. "The successful perpetuation of deer here on such a scale will depend on the intelligence with which the Preserve is handled. The beginning is simple but the successful perpetuation of this Preserve will require careful study of the main factors affecting the deer both for good or ill."[8]

Nelson's proposal included one especially remarkable feature. He wanted a cold storage plant built on the preserve to hold "three thousand or four thousand deer carcasses" as they waited for transportation. A central contractor would coordinate plans for refrigeration and transportation. At the same time, Nelson reiterated his recommendation for more forage studies, more fawn studies, and more predatory animal studies. He believed full and detailed notes on these topics would "furnish the foundation of facts from which a definite knowledge of the deer and the range can be built up." This kind of information would soon make possible a situation, he concluded, where "the deer on the Kaibab can be handled with all the certainty of a regular live-stock business." At some point the chief hoped the Biological Survey could employ a full-time game expert in the preserve, but daily observations by forest officers could provide valuable information, if properly directed. Nelson's enthusiasm for building up the deer population for commercial game hunting found almost no support elsewhere in the federal government, and he had not even considered the opinion of the state of Arizona.

In order to set hunting plans in motion, with whatever level of support he could muster from the Forest Service, Nelson talked to the Department of Agriculture's solicitor in the U.S. attorney general's office, R. W. Williams. Williams had specialized in game law since

1902, and he assured the Biological Survey chief that killing deer in order to protect federal lands from damage fell clearly within the Department of Agriculture's rights as holder of "absolute title" over those lands. The real problem, particularly for Nelson, was that the federal government could do nothing less than kill the deer outright. It could not open the Kaibab to public hunting. The state of Arizona, like every other state, retained the constitutional right to administer its own game. Thus, Arizona—and not the Department of Agriculture—held the authority over open sport-hunting seasons within its borders. In order to allow hunting, the state game warden needed authorization from the governor to open the season. Moreover, hunters could not transport deer out of the state without a special permit. Given the scope of Nelson's proposal, to kill over two thousand deer, the state's usual open season would have to be extended. In addition, because of the proximity of the Kaibab to the main population of Arizona, federal officials would have to encourage hunters from Utah, and possibly Nevada and California, to participate. Additional fees would create obstacles to out-of-state hunters. The urgency of the situation, as Nelson described it, suggested that a legal agreement could easily be drawn up between Arizona and the Department of Agriculture. This agreement, in recognition of the exceptional situation at hand, would allow both governments to cooperate in temporarily circumventing state law. Solicitor Williams cautioned that any action taken by the federal government that did not consider the need for "complete harmony" in this matter would undoubtedly invoke the wrath of the state. He offered his legal opinion only with the understanding that Nelson did indeed seek a harmonious solution and would consult with the state authorities before proceeding with these recommendations. Nelson, duly warned, made no further push for hunting on his own.[9]

Nelson undoubtedly recognized that other federal officials—those who championed the concept of a game preserve—would consider hunting in any form anathema to preservation. In late 1923, Secretary of the Interior Hubert Work, National Park Service Director Stephen Mather, National Parks Association President Robert Sterling Yard, Chief Forester William B. Greeley, and Secretary of Agriculture Henry C. Wallace exchanged views on how they could maintain the preserve and protect the deer. Yard first asked Interior Secretary Work what specific plans were in place. Yard

The Snake-Kanab road runs through Snake Gulch toward Kanab Creek in the northwestern section of the forest. The vegetation on the slopes is typical intermediate range. Photo by the author.

believed he spoke for "the man and woman on the street" who might object to the hunting of deer in a preserve or national park.

Secretary Work replied that the Department of the Interior had no direct jurisdiction over the administration of the Kaibab National Forest, but he acknowledged that the lands under its control in the Grand Canyon National Park would certainly be affected by the Forest Service activities.[10] Work then informed Agriculture Secretary Wallace of his explicit opposition to hunting on the preserve. He worried that nearly two decades of protection efforts would be wasted if hunting began. The Department of the Interior and the National Park Service by then recognized the unique value of the deer. Hunters allowed on the Kaibab might "get a taste of hunting this noble animal, [and] it may be years before [hunting] can be stopped." Work spoke for his department and the National Parks Association when he cautioned that "years of work in protecting this herd may be wasted and the attraction of the deer lost to the thousands of tourists who are bound to get into this section which is just now being opened up to travel."[11]

At the same time, Work feared that any statement against Forest Service plans for management of the deer might be construed as the interference of one department with another. He hoped his concern would be seen only as an attempt to preserve "the deer as an object of natural interest." Work soon received assurances from Wallace that a decision would not be reached until the situation was thoroughly studied. Chief Forester Greeley attempted to calm Yard's concerns over the hunting question. Greeley's review of the reports of "game experts" from the Biological Survey and local foresters, particularly Goldman, indicated that the increase of the deer accelerated with each passing year. Greeley considered the problem a perplexing one, since his agency had actively protected the deer from a number of conditions, "including the very aggressive extermination of predatory animals." Nevertheless, he did not believe any change in policy should take place without considerable study. The forester concluded, "I will not approve any change in the present policy until the general plan of management of the Kaibab, including the herd as one of its major features, has been worked out to our satisfaction."[12]

These opinions ultimately created more problems than they solved. Other than Nelson, no one suggested any specific means of reduction, which according to Goldman and other local observers would have to take place in the near future. Each official hoped to see additional studies conducted, and these would take time. In an effort to expedite the study process, several of these departments and organizations agreed that they should assemble a committee to examine the situation. A joint committee would propose a practical and feasible solution. With their diverse backgrounds, they would attempt to consider both the warnings of the game experts and the attitudes of the man and woman on the street. Once the Department of Agriculture and the Forest Service agreed upon the proposal to appoint a committee of experts, Secretary Wallace took responsibility for inviting members from a variety of conservation organizations and governmental departments. In his invitation, he described the history of the Kaibab deer. He noted that the deer increased after having been "completely and successfully protected from any form of killing." This protection primarily consisted of the prohibition of hunting, but Wallace made it clear that other factors contributed to their increase. Most significantly, the secretary described the assumed effect of predatory animal control undertaken for the protection of livestock, not deer. Even though little mountain lion hunting had actually taken place on the Kaibab in recent years, Wallace recalled how employees of the Forest Service and the Biological Survey had "vigorously exterminated" predatory animals throughout the West. He went on to suggest that the normal loss among the Kaibab deer from lions had "undoubtedly been greatly reduced." Efforts to preserve the deer amounted to "double protection" from hunters and lions and led to the great increase.[13]

The solution to the problem, as Secretary Wallace envisioned it, was to end the double protection. A committee of experts should decide whether hunting could reduce the deer numbers sufficiently. They should also consider the role of predatory animals in the future maintenance of the deer herd. Wallace was not the first to recognize the potential role of predatory animals in limiting the increase of prey species. In this setting, however, he seemed to forget that predatory animal control was primarily intended to protect livestock. The fact that he had so clearly stated this relationship with regard to the Kaibab deer in early 1924 indicates that the common-sense connection between predatory animals and prey could be made by almost anyone. Since mountain lions eat deer, removal of mountain lions would mean more deer. This hardly represented the dawning of a new ecological awareness. Given that experts drew no definite conclusions on the need for hunting or the role of predatory animals, Wallace was merely speculating. Whatever the secretary's motivation, numerous experts participated on the committee because they hoped to resolve the practical challenges of how to preserve the Kaibab deer. At the same time, they hoped their examination would contribute to fundamental knowledge of deer and other large game species.

Predatory Animal Control

The difficulty of satisfying academic scientists and ranchers intensified in the early 1920s. Professional mammalogists formally opposed predatory animal control, particularly the use of poison, while ranchers continued to lobby for a predator-free range. The Biological Survey was caught in the middle. Many survey officials were themselves mammalogists, but they could not or would not abandon their support of predatory animal control for the simple reason that control activities justified their existence as government biologists. This period marked the beginning of a change in the "value of a varmint." Previous accounts of this dispute over predatory animal control assume that the mammalogists eventually won by pointing out that "predators" had value in natural communities. This assumption overlooks the fact that both professional mammalogists and government biologists were struggling to identify the *role* of predatory animals. Until they did, they could not come to grips with the potential *value* of that role. In the early 1920s, they operated without a coherent concept of a predator.[14]

During this period, many scientists believed arguments over predatory animal control could be resolved through ongoing field research. The Kaibab provided a common testing site for unanswered questions, but the situation there generally created new questions and sometimes showed the old ones to be misguided. In the summer of 1924, the secretary of agriculture's investigating committee opened a more public debate over the place of predatory animals in game management, but the terms were uniquely defined by the somewhat peculiar situation on the Kaibab. Mammalogists had initiated a more limited debate several months earlier.

In early 1924, the American Society of Mammalogists formed the Committee on Wild Life Sanctuaries, which was to "make a study formulating policies for the preservation of predatory animals and to recommend the location of certain wild life preserves suitable for the preservation of such animals." Charles Adams chaired the committee and was joined by Vernon Bailey, Joseph Dixon, Edward Goldman, and Edmund Heller. Joseph Grinnell's efforts had led to the creation of the committee. The mammalogist questioned the Biological Survey's efforts to eliminate a number of species. As a naturalist and scientist with a strong interest in conservation, Grinnell was dismayed by the enormous energy being directed toward extermination and the missed opportunity to study these animals.

Chief of the Biological Survey Edward Nelson consistently acknowledged the validity of Grinnell's concern, but clearly stated the Biological Survey's practical mission with regard to predatory animals. Nelson wrote: "The Bureau expects its hunters to devote their entire time to the capture of predatory animals and does not wish them to take over any work which would seriously interfere with their effectiveness." When Nelson referred to his employees as hunters, he clearly admitted that not all workers in the Biological Survey were biologists. In fact, Bailey, Goldman, and Nelson himself were somewhat exceptional. Trained in the field and lacking academic credentials, they nevertheless undertook expansive research projects, surveying numerous species in large regions of North America. These men published their findings and enjoyed a respected status among their academic peers. Most employees of the Biological Survey, as Nelson implied, worked at more practical tasks deemed important to the public good but of minimal scientific value. The primary duty of most Biological Survey workers was to protect agricultural enterprises in the most effective way possible. For the control of predatory animals, that meant poison, as Nelson explained. Grinnell had suggested that certain predatory animals might actually provide a practical service in limiting rodent populations. Nelson responded that a Biological Survey poison crew could destroy more rodents in a week than coyotes would destroy in a year. For Nelson, this served as evidence that humans had permanently upset the balance of nature, first by establishing agriculture, then by promoting agricultural practice through further tinkering with natural populations. The best course of action now was to attempt to control nature through human effort. Although rodents were never the issue on the Kaibab, the role of predatory animals was always of concern—the only question being whether they were essentially good or bad. Long before the question arose in this context, people had wondered whether humans should rely on balance rather than exerting their own control of nature. This question emerged in various guises on the Kaibab and became part of the legacy of its lesson.[15]

While these discussions continued over the next few years, and the situation on the Kaibab Plateau became widely known, Nelson's agency faced increasingly difficult questions regarding the role of predatory animals and the balance of nature. Edward Goldman often took the brunt of criticism. Grinnell, along with students and colleagues at the University of California and other scientists around the country, built their case against the Biological Survey based on the belief that a moratorium on extermination efforts was needed while further studies of predatory animal life histories could be completed. Some mammalogists believed the government was bending to the wishes of special interests, including the livestock industry and the game-hunting industry. Their point was not to condemn Biological Survey activities, but to question the motivations behind predatory animal control. Grinnell and others were convinced that the government destroyed potentially valuable animals in deference to a few narrow interest groups. These mammalogists succeeded in passing a resolution outlining their demands at the 1924 meeting of the American Society of Mammalogists.

The mammalogists' resolution pointed to the Biological Survey's "propaganda" for predatory animal destruction and the financial motivation of arms and ammunition manufacturers in causing "serious injury" to

wildlife conservation. The American Society of Mammalogists insisted,
"[T]here exists no real occasion for a nationwide campaign for the destruction of predatory animals, and that this is particularly unwise because it furnishes a pretext for illegal hunting out of season." The mammalogists resolved to counter propaganda by forwarding their opinion "to
other interested organizations, game and protective associations, and to
all Federal and State agencies concerned."[16]

The Kaibab deer figured significantly as several members of the mammalogists' newly formed Committee on Wild Life Sanctuaries presented
papers at the 1924 meeting as part of a symposium entitled "The Scientific and Economic Importance of Predatory Mammals." These papers
included a defense of Biological Survey programs and policies by Edward
Goldman. He pointed to the destructive role of predatory animals and
reinforced Nelson's claim that humans had overturned the balance of
nature. Goldman's arguments were rebutted by two academic mammalogists. First, Joseph Dixon, a student of Grinnell, used stomach-content
analyses to paint a more complex picture of predatory animal food habits. Second, Charles Adams, the first American to earn a Ph.D. in ecology,
suggested that a new balance of nature existed on the public lands of the
United States. The symposium helped define the scope of discussions
regarding predatory mammals for the rest of the decade.

Edward Goldman placed the situation on the Kaibab Plateau at the
forefront of many discussions of predatory animals. Goldman defended
policies of control on the Kaibab and elsewhere. While many biologists
insisted that the Biological Survey should first study the life histories of
predatory animals before exterminating them, Goldman attempted to
convince society members of the necessity of immediate and ongoing
government control efforts. The government biologist pointed out that
nature was complex, and complexity led to differences of opinion concerning predatory animals. The Kaibab example in particular demonstrated to Goldman how difficult it would be to unravel the combined
influences of predation, livestock, grazing, and protection from human
hunting. He explained that his opinion differed from that of many others due to his deep understanding and full information regarding the status of predatory mammals. He called for consideration of the problem "in
its true bearings" or in its complex and diverse settings.

Goldman's attitude toward the balance of nature was similar to
Nelson's, and it signified an important shift in the thinking of many
scientists and naturalists. He maintained that although balance had

long been considered a fundamental feature of nature, in the twentieth century balance could only be considered "hypothetical." The
notion that species remained in balance, neither increasing nor decreasing, could not be supported, particularly when observing the
many changes in population taking place as a result of the activities of
humans. Goldman suggested that before the so-called discovery of
North America, large game animals across the continent were limited
by large carnivores and what he called primitive human tribes. Europeans bearing firearms then "violently overturned" the balance of
nature, and it could never be reestablished. By 1924, humans had
confined game animals to the western mountains, particularly in
parks and national forests. Predatory animals had followed their prey
and now threatened to destroy the few game animals that remained.
Moreover, those predatory animals often turned to livestock for food.
For a variety of reasons, predatory animal control served the purposes
of "practical conservation." In Goldman's view, control provided a
simple solution to an otherwise impossibly complex problem.[17]

Goldman intentionally stacked the evidence for the destructiveness of
predatory animals. He dismissed the proposition of Grinnell and others
by directly addressing the notion that predatory mammals might serve a
beneficial role in limiting populations of rodents in certain areas. This
suggestion, Goldman insisted, belied the fact that food supply and diseases more commonly reduced rodent numbers. He pointed to a few
notable cases where rodents had increased tremendously in the presence
of predatory animals, suggesting the ineffectiveness of those predatory
animals in limiting the increase. Goldman then noted the greater effectiveness of human efforts in reducing these rodent populations with poison. He insisted that to allow predatory animals to persist, expecting
some benefit to humanity, was to miss the point of civilization. In his
view, "civilized man" had overturned the balance of nature by creating
"artificial conditions and contacts throughout his sphere of influence."
For this reason, practical considerations demanded that humans assume
effective control over wildlife everywhere. All animals, Goldman suggested, "must be checked wherever they become too numerous or too
injurious to human interests." Humans needed to control nature in the
absence of a primeval balance. This rhetoric helped justify the existence
of the Biological Survey by offering effective results.[18]

As particular evidence of the destructiveness of predatory animals on
deer, Goldman cited a predatory-animal hunter on the Kaibab Plateau

(no doubt Uncle Jim Owens) who found nothing but deer remains in the stomachs of mountain lions he killed. The heavy toll these predatory animals exerted on the deer population directly opposed the stated purpose of the preserve. For Goldman and many others who believed that the balance of nature no longer functioned even in remote parts of the United States, destruction of the mountain lions, initially practiced for the protection of livestock, now constituted a sensible step toward "effective control of wild life everywhere." This would be true not only on the Kaibab Plateau, but throughout the West. The destructiveness of only a few predatory animals, for example, could quickly "threaten the extermination of the game upon which they must necessarily live."[19] In a sense, predatory animals must be controlled for their own good, as well as for the more obvious good of human society, which preferred to see deer and antelope at play on the range. For this reason, Goldman stated that even in the parks where policies protected wildlife, the destructiveness of predatory animals would have to be minimized.

The difficulty of the choice of killing off predatory animals did not escape Goldman. "As nature lovers we are loathe to contemplate the destruction of any species," he noted, "but as practical conservationists we are forced by the records to decide against such predatory animals as mountain lions, wolves, and coyotes. We cannot consistently protect them and expect our game to be maintained in satisfactory numbers."[20] Perhaps even more importantly, Goldman pointed out that any attempt to conserve wildlife without considering the economic realities of the western range might alienate the livestock industry. Failure to consider the interests of ranchers could arouse opposition to the establishment of game preserves. He concluded that *protecting* large predatory mammals, which endanger both livestock and game, would discredit "practical conservationists" and "risk through prejudice the defeat of measures which may be vital to the future welfare of our country."[21] As his use of the Kaibab example betrayed, even such an isolated place would be too close to human "civilization." Goldman's call for practical conservation emphasized economic justifications for control. Most members of the American Society of Mammalogists, however, did not share his view. They saw other ways of ensuring practical conservation and viewed the economic argument differently.

Joseph Dixon made a more complex case that included beneficial contributions of predatory animals and offered a conclusion comprehensively different from Goldman's.[22] The California zoologist studied the stomach contents of predatory animals and furbearing mammals for three years. Ornithologists and mammalogists investigating the economic relations of birds and mammals used this technique extensively. Dixon followed procedures established by Biological Survey scientist A. K. Fisher, who determined the economic value of hawks and owls using stomach-content analysis. Fisher judged that if birds of prey ate harmful rodents, they were beneficial.[23] A beneficial role for predatory birds diverged from the notion that hawks and owls were harmful because they destroyed songbirds. Dixon hoped to make a parallel argument for the beneficial role of predatory mammals using the Biological Survey's practice of stomach-content analysis. He claimed that while predatory mammals sometimes ate valuable livestock and game, most of their depredations served to financially benefit human activities in a number of ways. Dixon first listed the "general economic status" of predatory or furbearing animals. He divided this status into two lists labeled "Credit" and "Debit." Under credits, he listed the value of animal pelts or furs, destruction of harmful rodents and insects, and so-called recreational value. Under debits he listed the destruction of game and domestic animals, as well as the transmission of disease. Dixon argued that since food was the primary issue in the majority of these items, stomach-content analysis served as the most reasonable method of investigation into the general economic value of predatory animals.[24]

Based on examination of thousands of stomach remains corroborated by other investigators, Dixon offered numerous examples of the complex role predatory animals played in human economies. Coyotes, for instance, scavenged for a large proportion of their food. This meant that often their stomachs might contain the remains of a cow, even though the coyote had not killed that cow. Mountain lions, on the other hand, generally ate only prey they killed themselves. In the wildcat, about 45 percent of the remains came from "harmful" animals, predominantly rodents. Another 20 percent represented remains from "beneficial" animals, including game, livestock, and birds.

From the percentages of harmful and beneficial animals in the stomachs of predatory animals, Dixon drew only broad conclusions about the potential role of the carnivores. He therefore called for further study of these biological and economic relations. Given the need for ongoing research, Dixon concluded that extermination of predatory animals would be putting "the cart before the horse." He believed that more "facts" were needed as a basis for "sane" administration of animal assets (or liabilities). Dixon did not state that predatory and furbearing animals should be preserved and protected in the same way humans protected game and livestock, but he believed his evidence supported the American Society of Mammalogists' broader resolutions suggesting that predatory animals should not be exterminated before scientists could determine their role in natural systems.[25]

Ecologist Charles Adams challenged Nelson's and Goldman's argument that the balance of nature had disappeared when Europeans arrived in North America. Describing changes in the balance of nature since the arrival of Christopher Columbus in 1492, the ecologist stated that thousands of years earlier, nature maintained a "relative" balance of species. Adams acknowledged that American Indians had been a part of that relative balance. Recently, the changes begun by "adventurers and trappers" had accumulated to the point that the former balance of Pre-Columbian days was indeed gone forever. With the activities of humans in the last few centuries, Adams claimed, nature had begun to adjust toward a "new balance." That new balance in North America included the establishment of a vast public domain, which Adams believed was being foolishly wasted. While wildlife thrived on that public domain, the future value of this wilderness was being spent rapidly. Adams continued, "We have now largely disposed of this great bounty and have begun to feel the pinch of need and are beginning to come to our senses." The national conservation movement required scientific management to match the new balance of nature. Scientists should carefully consider the place of wildlife problems within a broader economic and social system. They should also conduct research that would contribute to the solution of wildlife problems. Finally, Adams suggested the scientists should formulate definite ideals and policies that would guide naturalists, conservationists, and policymakers.[26]

From this general statement of the need for scientific management and far-reaching conservation efforts, Adams went on to describe the particular status of "predacious animals." These animals faced immense pressure from human intervention. The relationship between predatory animals and the balance of nature, according to Adams, suggested that conservation of wildlife necessarily depended upon a better human understanding of all animals. He also acknowledged that because predatory animals presumably played an important role in preventing overpopulation of prey species, they were worthy of study. Furthermore, wild specimens were required to understand that role fully. All that remained for Adams was to decide how predatory animals would be conserved. Conservation depended upon a basic understanding of the relationship between the land and its people. The ecologist recommended that studies of predatory animals be conducted on urban lands, agricultural lands, and wild lands in the national and state parks and forest systems. On agricultural lands in particular, Adams noted the tremendous lack of support for such studies in the past, despite millions of dollars spent on the extermination of predatory animals. He suggested, "Some of this [extermination] money, as there has been relatively no lack of it, should now be diverted into scientific studies, and to the formation of wise public policies, if we are to achieve real, not apparent, success."[27] This comment struck raw nerves among officials in the Biological Survey, but Adams stopped short of accusing the government of buckling to pressure from livestock owners.

Adams agreed with many other observers, such as Emerson Hough, that a pristine preserve should be maintained on the Kaibab Plateau and other suitable, large public refuges. There, a sizable wilderness area could be completely isolated, and wildlife (including predatory animals) could be managed. Other parks might also be established, although Adams singled out the Kaibab as the most suitable. He added, "It would be worth years of effort to secure such preserves or sanctuaries, where all control measures were *absolutely prohibited*."[28] The public education necessary to support this plan would be considerable, but education would contribute to one of the greatest needs for understanding wildlife in America. Adams insisted that parks would have to preserve such animals as wolves and mountain lions, although such a claim might not apply on forestlands, where economic considerations were paramount.

Adams argued that in order to preserve wildlife, particularly large species such as deer, elk, and even cougars, forward-thinking conservationists would need to establish larger refuges like the Kaibab. These would serve scientific, educational, recreational, and economic purposes and would necessarily include large predators. Attempts to include predatory animals in these refuges safely, Adams cautioned, would require an understanding of the relationship between predatory animals and prey. The ecologist wrote, "For this reason it will require considerable study to determine just how many predators are necessary to maintain the normal balance in these almost wild preserves." Along the boundaries of these

preserves, administrators should expect some overflow of mountain lions, coyotes, and wolves. Proper control would be needed in these areas,
but control could be done "wisely only as a result of careful scientific
studies, such as we do not now have."[29] What Adams did not fully appreciate in distinguishing between lands where control of predatory animals
could continue and lands where they might be preserved was that in
many cases, such as on the Kaibab, those lands lay adjacent or had over-
lapping administration.

Edward Nelson, Edward Goldman, Joseph Dixon, and Charles Adams
represented the range, if not the entire spectrum, of attitudes toward
predatory animals among scientists. Mammalogists interested in studying the life histories of all mammal species hoped to preserve, at a minimum, samples of predatory animals in order to examine their food habits. Even more important, many hoped to study predatory food habits,
especially with rodents and game as prey. Ecological studies of predator-
prey relations were unknown at this time.[30] Most ecologists in the early
1920s focused their research on plant relations. Others initiated studies
on insects and entomological relations. They examined and tested ideas
like succession and the effect of climate on soils and organisms. Of
course, it only occurred to mammalogists and ecologists that predator-
prey research might be useful in wildlife conservation after questions of
game management arose—and they arose with the deer dilemma on the
Kaibab as early as anywhere. Scientists confronted the complexity of the
Kaibab deer situation, and they needed to invent methods (such as game
survey techniques) and define concepts (such as carrying capacity) that
might begin to answer rapidly mounting questions in this unique context.
Those questions involved relationships between deer, mountain lions,
coyotes, livestock, and other factors in the preserve. Because these questions fascinated people with widely ranging interests and practical concerns, scientists were not allowed the luxury of conducting their studies
in seclusion. Even the relative isolation of the Kaibab proved no match
for ever-mounting national interest in conservation and predatory animal control. Government biologists and mammalogists would soon join
representatives of diverse organizations from the forestry, livestock, and
tourism industries, as well as conservationists and sport hunters.

4

Getting to the Bottom of Things

The events on the Kaibab Plateau in 1924 produced fundamental and profound changes in wildlife biology. That year, the plateau hosted a national wildlife investigating committee, as well as a widely publicized deer drive and its first deer-hunting season. Each of these events failed to provide a clear way out of the deer dilemma, and the legacy of those failures convinced many observers that an appropriate solution would depend on greater scientific knowledge and administrative authority that would respond to that knowledge. Such an ideal solution, however, required a denial of the natural and human history of the game preserve. The committee's recommendations, the goals of the deer drive, and the difficulties of the first hunt—all less than ideal—did open new questions for wildlife biology far beyond the Kaibab Plateau.

THE KAIBAB INVESTIGATING COMMITTEE

Early in 1924, Secretary of Agriculture Henry C. Wallace convened the investigating committee. In August, the group traveled widely across the Kaibab forest and park lands along the north rim of the Grand Canyon. Members of the committee were not all scientists and their knowledge of wildlife issues on the preserve varied. Most, including John B. Burnham, the renowned conservationist who chaired the investigating committee, knew of Stephen Mather's efforts to promote the Kaibab as a "President's Forest." Other members of the committee included Heyward Cutting of the Boone and Crockett Club, T. Gilbert Pearson representing both the National Association of Audubon Societies and the National Parks Association, and T. W. Tomlinson, a member of the American National Livestock Breeders Association. To varying degrees, they agreed that this unique wilderness setting should include spectacular wildlife displays. During their two-week visit, however, local foresters and ranchers made a point of familiarizing committee members with the diverse and, in many places, lamentable conditions of both the deer and the vegetation. The committee recognized the dilemma of promoting further increase in the deer herd when the current state of affairs already presented unanswered questions. Thus, rather than offer its hoped-for expert solution, the committee served primarily to publicize the uncertainty of the situation.

Committee members acknowledged that any proposed solution would have to meet the goals of both the Forest Service and National Park Service, which shared jurisdiction of the preserve. Local foresters wanted to see the deer reduced immediately to save some vegetation for what remained of local livestock ranching. Park officials were just beginning to see the fruits of promoting the Kaibab Plateau and the North Rim of the Grand Canyon to tourists. The committee report served the interests of neither agency, noting both the great abundance and deplorable appearance of deer. The great numbers of deer served the interests of the National Park Service, while their poor condition favored Forest Service hopes for reduction. The committee attempted to find neutral ground by describing what was known about the events that led to the dilemma. The isolation of the preserve and the inability of animals to migrate contributed substantially to the problem. The committee attributed some of the increase to a lack of limiting factors. Although lacking specific details, a common-sense formula accounted for present conditions and future increases. The report stated, "The natural checks on the excessive increase of the deer, such as predatory animals (mountain lions, wolves, coyotes, and bobcats), have been reduced. It is certain that the number of deer must eventually increase far beyond the limits of adequate food supply." Recognizing that the deer would increase perilously, the committee recommended that "artificial checks" would be needed to "reduce them to the numbers which the range can properly support in a thrifty condition." The artificial checks the committee recommended were shipping the deer alive or shooting them. These actions—and not any form of natural predation—should be part of efforts to establish so-called scientific management on the Kaibab Plateau.[1]

Scientific management of game, as proposed by the Kaibab Investigating Committee, would include human control of an increased number of factors. It would differ from current policies, which left too much to chance. Merely protecting wildlife seemed to produce undesirable results. Recognizing that game protection based on negative and arbitrary restrictions had failed, committee members on the Kaibab called them-selves "modern conservationists" and wrote, "Game Management is the scientific balancing of all that concerns the numbers and welfare of game on a given area." Identifying the problems of conventional game protec-tion became an important step for the committee. The report stated that game management should consider "the food supply, the distribution, the ratio of sexes, the maintenance of an adequate breeding stock, the absolute number that should be removed annually, the control of preda-tory animals, the places where game may or may not be shot, and pre-eminently the creation and maintenance of game preserves."

In the past, game protection had been limited to closed hunting sea-sons and bag restrictions. Most importantly, the committee opposed the prevailing philosophy that protection was the key to game abundance. "Such a comprehensive scheme is a matter of positive administration and not merely a question of negative restrictions," they insisted.[2] Although from a practical standpoint this statement did not offer guidelines for actions, it was exactly the kind of solution Secretary Wallace and others expected from an expert committee at the time. The effectiveness of such a solution relied on constant efforts by state and federal officials to moni-tor and balance these factors. The committee's expansion of game man-agement consisted of listing a wider range of contributing factors. List-ing, however, remained a long way from actually implementing scientific management plans.

The committee members offered estimates for the deer population that ranged from twenty thousand to fifty thousand animals. In their re-port, they compromised, reducing the estimates to a single figure and agreeing on twenty-five thousand as a conservative current estimate. Such a compromise proved extremely problematic. They offered a rec-ommendation based on this compromised estimate that immediately intensified controversy. They suggested a dramatic reduction, proposing that "one-half of the existing herd be removed and that this removal be accomplished as quickly as possible."[3]

Given varying initial estimates of the deer numbers and the recom-mendation to remove half of the deer, the committee implied that this removal could involve as few as ten thousand or as many as twenty-five thousand deer. The larger number represented more than the total actual number that several experts believed to be on the plateau. More signifi-cantly, to remove even ten thousand deer would require a small army. The committee recommended three primary means of reducing the deer:

trap and ship the deer to areas where game was scarce; allow limited sport hunting; and, only if absolutely necessary, allow officially sanctioned killing by government hunters. Trapping and shipping deer had never been attempted on such a scale. Bringing hunters to a game preserve hundreds of miles from the nearest population center posed legal and logistical obstacles that the committee never considered. Yet, they hoped that an initial reduction would allow biologists and government experts to study the situation further without causing additional damage to the range.

Forest Service officials reviewed the report first and turned to the United States attorney general in search of some legal means of initiating sport hunting without further delay. The likelihood of significantly reducing the herd through trapping and shipping the deer seemed slim, so the Forest Service hoped to open its lands to hunting as soon as possible. Sport hunting would be more efficient and less controversial than sending in government hunters to kill large numbers of deer. Using language adopted from its range management policies, an assistant forester in Washington DC, E. A. Sherman, explained that the Forest Service could hope to reduce the herd to the appropriate carrying capacity of the plateau. Acknowledging the advice that half of the estimated twenty thousand to fifty thousand deer should be removed, Sherman wrote, "It seems that the situation which Government experts had predicted, but which we had hoped could be prevented through regulated hunting on the area, has come about much sooner than we anticipated." The Forest Service official blamed a protracted drought for the "grave nature" of the range and the deer. He did not relish "the wholesale killing of the deer by Federal officers" and hoped that "this method of reducing the herd to the proper carrying capacity of the range" would only be used as a last resort.[4] Sherman wanted legal advice on how to proceed. Chris Rachford, a grazing administrator for the Forest Service, agreed and took the matter personally to Assistant Attorney General R. W. Williams.

OPPOSITION FROM THE NATIONAL PARK SERVICE

The Kaibab Investigating Committee's report met with public opposition from Park Service director Stephen Mather. Mather made it clear that the committee's recommendations would not be acceptable on the national park or on lands adjoining it. The reason, according to the director, was that the preserve and the park existed to provide an opportunity for Americans to see abundant game. Killing deer on a preserve amounted to nothing short of slaughter. He disagreed with the argument that protecting the deer for the long run justified the slaughter of deer in the present. Mather's opinions about the Kaibab deer appeared in *Outdoor America*, the magazine of the Izaak Walton League. Editor Will H. Dilg agreed with the director and hoped the article would raise opposition to the proposal to kill deer on the Kaibab. In an editorial, Dilg asked readers to get involved in offering alternative solutions to the problem, stating, "The columns of this magazine are open to anyone who can suggest a plan that will save this marvelous remnant of outdoor America made possible by that far-sighted sportsman and conservationist, Theodore Roosevelt." Dilg and Mather insisted that some plan other than killing the deer outright must be initiated. Mather rejected the destruction of deer partly on the basis of a lack of precedent. He wrote, "No more drastic measure in the history of game conservation in America than this has ever been proposed."[5]

While Mather opposed the committee's recommended solution, he did not suggest that the committee mistook or exaggerated the seriousness of the situation. The Park Service director recounted the history of the deer in much the same way others had. The preserve was established when the deer numbered as few as three thousand. Unlike deer in other parts of the country, these few had survived "hunters and predatory animals owing to favorable geographical conditions." Protection from hunters, along with "the killing off of predatory animals within the preserve," had enabled the herd to increase dramatically. Mather nevertheless accepted only the lowest estimate of approximately twenty thousand head. The Park Service also recognized that vegetative conditions had declined. Despite his agreement with this basic statement of facts, Mather did not agree that killing the deer was the solution. He feared that even the most carefully supervised hunting would destroy the tameness of the deer and wipe out the years of work devoted to protecting the herd. Not only that, but the present tameness of the deer would make hunting a less-than-sporting endeavor, like approaching a herd of tame cattle and shooting them. In addition, Mather's opposition to killing seemed related to his insistence that the role of predatory animals had not been thoroughly appreciated. He referred to the destruction of "nature's own means of balance" as "man's mistake." The park director believed that mountain lions "would have kept the increase of the deer down to a safe margin that the preserve could have carried." They were also destructive to livestock, and Mather implied that man's mistake was actually the fault of the Forest Service.[6]

This observation derived from Mather's desire to preserve all manner of native wildlife in the parks. He did not possess an understanding of predator-prey relations, nor did he argue for the existence of the balance of nature as Charles Adams had at the mammalogists' meeting. Mather's preservation impulse and his disdain for ranching around his parks, not an enlightened game management technique, led him to oppose killing deer.[7] His use of the phrase "balance of nature" was an exercise of logic, and while others agreed with Mather on this point, no one at the time knew whether predatory animals could be used effectively as a means of game management.

As Mather's involvement increased, so did the visibility of the deer situation nationwide. He brought a fawn from the Kaibab east to Washington, where it attended a gala dinner at the Willard Hotel and reportedly browsed on President Hoover's salad.[8] *Outdoor America* published a number of letters from readers supporting Mather's views. They included an editorial reprinted from the *Phoenix Gazette*, which predicted outrage among sport hunters if the government carried out its plan to slaughter the deer. In another letter, New York conservationist Stephen S. Johnson agreed particularly with Mather's interest in predatory animals. The current conditions there differed from conditions in the past, he insisted, due to the lack of predatory animals. Johnson had visited the Kaibab Plateau several times, most recently the previous summer, and he described nature's ability to adjust to change, stating, "Nature supplied the predatory animals for the purpose of keeping down an over-production." Humans had destroyed those animals, and as a result, "nature will produce the great herd of deer." Having established the logical role of predatory animals in the past, however, Johnson made no recommendation for their role in the future.[9]

Outdoor America also published correspondence from Arizona governor George Hunt, who unequivocally opposed the "slaughter." A letter from Secretary of Agriculture Wallace expressed his distress but general agreement with the recommendations of the committee. Arizona rancher Charles McCormick wrote to recommend a change of boundary lines between park and forest lands. Both game and livestock easily crossed the current east-west line. McCormick wanted a boundary that would divide the plateau along natural barriers. Such a border would give the Park Service greater jurisdiction over the deer, while the Forest Service could allow more complete utilization of the range by livestock. The rancher's proposal, like all boundary disputes concerning the preserve, received no further comment, no doubt because it looked like a land grab for the ranchers.[10]

As McCormick's proposal illustrated, a continuous obstacle in the emerging controversy was the divided jurisdiction of the preserve between the Forest Service and the Park Service. The Biological Survey nominally served as a source of expert biological advice to both federal services, but that advice was neither internally consistent nor consistently compatible with the different missions of the Forest and Park Services. The Biological Survey also continued predatory animal control campaigns in the area. As each department attempted to plan for the future management of the deer, leading bureaucrats began to position themselves at opposite poles. Forest Service efforts increasingly aimed at reducing the deer directly by sport or official hunting. Mather and the Park Service attempted to expand the boundaries of the park farther north in order to protect the deer. The Biological Survey was caught in the middle, on a line of scientific evidence that seemed as tenuous and chimerical as the boundary across the plateau itself.

In the midst of this repositioning, Mather discussed the role of predatory animals with his staff. One of his assistants, Arno B. Cammerer, described the gist of these discussions to Grand Canyon National Park Supervisor J. R. Eakin. Cammerer revealed Mather's desire to eliminate Biological Survey predatory animal control measures within the park. Mather wanted Eakin to take over mountain lion control and limit it to what was absolutely necessary. Getting the Biological Survey hunters out of the park would not only solidify Mather's power over the situation, but more importantly, it would allow him the opportunity to try a different approach to reducing the deer herd. Park Service officials hoped more exclusive control over management would allow them a chance to prove the park could regain its natural balance. They believed that success in this maneuver would end the controversy. Their solution to the controversy included the remarkable suggestion of allowing predatory animals to coexist with the deer. Mather thought that mountain lions might limit the deer population. Assistant Director Cammerer sought Eakin's advice on the question of whether lions would serve the park's goals, asking, "[W]ould you favor nature retaining its own balance for a couple of years at least to test this situation out?"[11] Mather and Cammerer were prepared to reexamine conventional protection methods to see what animals could and should be controlled in the park. Ideally, any control work would be done by park employees. Ending predatory animal control specifically to limit deer numbers would have been an unprecedented move. The potentially revolutionary idea did not receive any further attention at that time, however, due to ongoing divided jurisdiction of the preserve and planning of a different set of herd-reduction methods.

IMPLEMENTING REDUCTION PLANS

Early in the fall of 1924, George McCormick, the brother of outspoken rancher Charles McCormick, suggested that some of the deer might be rounded up and driven off the plateau to an area where deer were scarce. Both McCormick brothers were experienced cattle ranchers, and George had a particularly strong entrepreneurial spirit. He offered to lead the deer drive himself, for a fee, and claimed that he could move thousands of deer down from the east side of the plateau, into the Grand Canyon, and across the Colorado River. From there, the deer could be distributed to parklands on the South Rim, forestlands, and the Navajo Reservation. The plan seemed destined for failure to people who knew that deer did not commonly herd and move like cattle. McCormick, however, was both optimistic and desperate. Optimistic in the sense that he believed that large numbers of seemingly tame deer could in fact be driven like livestock; desperate in the sense that the deer had already cut too deeply into the available grazing lands for his family's livestock.[12]

Novelist Zane Grey was optimistic for different reasons. When he heard of the proposal, Grey promoted the drive in hopes of writing a book and producing a motion picture based on the effort. He imagined filming footage of the actual event for the movie. State game officials likewise believed against all available evidence that the deer would fall into line and move like cattle across the plateau and down the narrow trails into the eastern end of the Grand Canyon. Governor Hunt himself endorsed the effort as a solution—preferable to slaughter—to the apparent overpopulation problem on the North Rim and also as a step toward repopulating the diminished herd on the South Rim of the canyon where tourists rarely saw much wildlife. The state authorized McCormick to drive between three thousand and eight thousand deer and promised to pay $2.50 per head, delivered safely to the South Rim.

McCormick, Grey, and state officials offered no solutions to the logistical problems they would encounter along the way, even if the deer did move in an orderly fashion off of the plateau. Provisions would have to be made to keep the deer overnight during the course of the long drive. Many Forest Service officials considered the deer drive impossible from the outset. Deer would not behave like domestic livestock, they argued. Others in the Department of Agriculture tempered this opinion somewhat, claiming the drive might be possible, but would be entirely "impracticable." In Washington, Forest Service officials urged John Burnham to write Governor Hunt on behalf of the investigating committee to put an end to the plans. Regional Forester R. H. Rutledge believed the Forest Service should "call the governor's bluff" by meeting to discuss the details of the drive. On that occasion, foresters could challenge the optimists with questions about deer behavior, logistics, and liability. Rutledge would also point out that the ranchers involved in planning the "scheme" were "not the most reliable."[13]

Governor Hunt would not agree to a special meeting. He continued to insist that the plan was "both possible and practicable" based on the recommendation of McCormick, whose twelve years' experience as a rancher in the area provided adequate credentials for Hunt. Holding the deer overnight would present no problems since they would be confined in the canyon. The governor did not bother with the question of food or water for the deer. Once on the South Rim the deer would find "more than ample" forage. In addition, Hunt knew that "wild horses" had been driven along the same route in the past and used this as evidence of the plan's viability for driving "tame deer." Even the strongest critics hoped that the drive might produce some relief in the situation. Many believed it was worth a try, in any case. With the governor's insistence, the Forest Service finally decided it would be prudent to give the plan a "fair trial."[14]

Secretary of Agriculture Wallace, who had convened the Kaibab Investigating Committee, favored novel solutions such as this deer drive. He seemed reluctant to promote hunting, and Governor Hunt lobbied him to support the drive. Wallace, however, died unexpectedly in late October, leaving his assistants to promote the governor's plan. Acting Secretary C. F. Marvin explained the situation to the president of the Arizona Game Protective Association. The association had offered its service in order to serve "the purpose intended by Theodore Roosevelt." Marvin wrote, "Experts of the Department agree that the driving is worthy a trial rather than resort to the last of the three plans suggested by the committee of experts who recently visited that area; namely, deliberate slaughter by Government hunters." With that, the Department of Agriculture offered the

cooperation of the Forest Service and Biological Survey in the hope of assuring success for the plan. Marvin also thanked the Arizona association
for its offer of help, assuring them that the Department of Agriculture
fully supported the preservation of the deer through the reduction of the
herd "to about fifteen thousand head."[15] With that, the Forest Service and
the Arizona game warden began to work out details for the plan. Rutledge
soon discovered what he had suspected all along, that McCormick had
little idea of how to insure success in the drive. Rutledge had more faith
in G. M. Willard, the state game warden. Willard acknowledged that Governor Hunt was endowed with an unrealistic attitude regarding the potential for success of the drive. In no position to argue, however, Willard
acquiesced to McCormick's scheme; they should at least give it a try. The
Park Service, on the other hand, seemed convinced the drive would fail
and wanted nothing to do with the effort. Park officials attempted to distance themselves from what they saw as a public relations nightmare. In
the end, they decided to allow the drive to pass over park lands, but left
the administrative details to the state and the Forest Service.[16]

Just about the time all the involved parties and government agencies
found ways to reach a consensus, the Forest Service initiated a dramatically different solution to the problem of how to limit the deer herd. In a
surprise move, the Forest Service opened the Kaibab Plateau to hunting
at noon on November 15, 1924. Forest Service officials, who felt they were
humoring the governor by participating in plans for the deer drive, had
grown impatient and exercised their power to protect forest lands from
the overabundant deer. The legal justification and approval for the hunt
apparently came through Chris Rachford's discussions with federal attorneys. Hunting lasted only eight days, during which the state of Arizona,
under the direction of Governor Hunt, arrested hunters who attempted
to take their quarry off of the plateau.

The governor's betrayal was manifest in the quick arrests he ordered.
With these arrests, the focus of the controversy suddenly shifted from
disagreement between federal agencies over the proper means of deer
removal to an even more pronounced battle over game laws and states'
rights. The hunt violated state game laws and initiated a serious battle
between the federal and state governments. Not only did the federal
agencies differ in their ideas for management of the deer, but simmer-
ing disagreements between federal and state authorities now exploded. In
the process, new alliances were being forged. News of the hunt reached
Stephen Mather in Washington via telegram from Park Superintendent

Eakin. Mather had convinced Governor Hunt that tourism in the national park was more important to the state's economy than hunting in the national forest. The states' rights issue at first provided leverage for Mather. When the controversy later became an issue for the Supreme Court, game leaders in other states saw that the laws might be interpreted in their favor. The case became a precedent for the many legal battles over game that followed.[17]

By the end of November on the Kaibab Plateau, the immediate problem of reducing the deer herd remained unsolved. Hunters killed only a few hundred of the thousands of excess deer. The herd still faced disaster in the eyes of most observers. Rutledge wrote a letter to the editor of the *Arizona Republican* to describe the ongoing need for deer removal. The brief hunting season, he said, had not changed plans for a deer drive. The drive would take place on the east side of the preserve and would not alter conditions on the west side, where the Forest Service had tried hunting. Given the poor condition of the range everywhere, the drive would hopefully remove deer from areas otherwise inaccessible to hunters and those who would attempt to capture and ship the deer. The situation seemed grave, since hunting had been minimal and the success of the drive seemed uncertain. Rutledge concluded, "It is obvious that heavy losses from starvation are bound to occur."[18]

ZANE GREY'S DEER DRIVE

Zane Grey, the acclaimed Western novelist, provided the most complete first-hand account of the attempted deer drive. His tale, although accepted largely as fiction, resulted from the novelist's direct participation in the actual planning of the drive and corresponded closely with reports from official participants in the event. One such official, M. E. Musgrave, leader of predatory animal control for the Biological Survey, recounted how men began to gather in a camp on the east side of the Kaibab Plateau on December 12, 1924. Over the next few days, it became apparent to Musgrave and others that the drive would be impossible. Several inches of snow had already fallen; the terrain was extremely rough; the crew lacked sufficient "manpower"; the deer seemed skittish; and George McCormick showed a complete lack of organization. The Biological Survey leader later reflected that with enough men they might have succeeded in driving the deer from one part of the range to another. Realistically, however, the attempt to drive them over a narrow trail or into any place where they would be crowded would prove impossible.

In 1925, after participating in the failed deer drive, Zane Grey wrote The Deer Stalker, in which a forest ranger champions deer conservation, but efforts to save the deer are thwarted by natural barriers and human conspirators.

Attempting the impossible, then, the men—whether on foot or on horse-back—found that the deer ran and jumped right past them. Musgrave concluded, therefore, that shooting the deer in congested areas would be "one of the best possible solutions."[19]

Zane Grey was on the scene both to witness the event for use in his next Western novel and to secure movie footage to accompany the story. The narrative, first published serially in *Country Gentleman* in 1925 and titled *The Deer Stalker*, became the unofficial source of information on the failed drive.[20] Grey's fictional account, however imaginative, is firmly grounded in the actual events of 1924 on the Kaibab. His main character, Thad Eburne, represents an amalgam of the young foresters on Buckskin Mountain. Grey also infuses an extra dose of conservation ideals in this character, enough to make the fictional forester unpopular with other Forest Service officers in the story. These ideals undoubtedly reflect Grey's own feelings toward the wildlife of Arizona and the West. Eburne becomes a hero in the story by rescuing a damsel in distress, avoiding the pitfalls created by political tensions between government agencies, and correctly predicting the ultimate failure of the deer drive.

Another character, Jim Evans, fills the role of real-life lion hunter Uncle Jim Owens. Grey knew Owens personally from many trips through Arizona, beginning back in the days when Uncle Jim and Buffalo Jones began their bison ranch in House Rock Valley. These events play in the background of *The Deer Stalker*. Evans declares that humans have upset the balance of nature by "killin' off the varmints, specially the cougars." The fictional hunter continues, "These heah deer ain't had nothin' to check their overbreedin' an' inbreedin'." The hero Eburne agrees wholeheart-edly, as does Zane Grey. A character named Bill McKay represents George McCormick as the man who came up with the deer drive idea. McKay convinces the governor of the feasibility of driving the deer off Buckskin Mountain. The governor is "agin' the shootin' of deer" and dislikes the federal agencies arguing over his state's wildlife. Eburne pitches the idea to the Forest Service with considerable conviction and surprising success. In the story, most of his colleagues are "favorable disposed" to the propo-sition. Grey explains, "They spoke of it as preposterous, yet undoubtedly were intrigued by the originality, the audacity of the idea."

In Grey's novel, as was the case in real life, there is desperation to see the situation resolved before winter. The investigating committee—Grey quotes directly from their final report in the book—did not offer solutions but created an atmosphere of urgency. The Western novelist adds to the suspense by focusing attention on a large cattle company (ostensibly the Grand Canyon Cattle Company), which had forced smaller operations out of the area but subsequently had to remove its own stock from Buckskin Mountain when quality grazing range became scarce. In the story, greedy ranchers want the deer killed to make room for more cattle. They oppose the deer drive, and Eburne suspects that the ranchers are actively undermining his own and McKay's efforts to organize the event. These suspicions go unproven in the book, and there was no corresponding evidence of a conspiracy in actual fact. Grey's notorious distaste for the Mormon ranchers of southern Utah undoubtedly led him to sensationalize that drama. The feature of the controversy that Grey captures best is how the urgency of getting deer off of Buckskin made otherwise unlikely proposals appealing, for ranchers, foresters, and conservationists alike.

The idea that deer could be trapped and shipped by truck or railway to other parts of the region, or even across the country, intrigued many bystanders as a particularly humane solution. In Grey's book, however, the unpleasant details of terrified deer captured in small traps highlight the gruesome reality of such efforts. Of trapped adult deer, more die of accidental, self-inflicted injuries than survive to reach a new home on distant ranges. Eburne repeatedly lobbies for the deer drive on the grounds that trapping is much more dangerous to the deer. Killing the deer outright is equally abhorrent to the hero. The thought of hunting on Buckskin Mountain makes Eburne "feel so helpless and hopeless that I became almost physically ill." He compares it to the kind of legalized murder only a government-authorized army can perform during wartime. When hunting begins, as described by Grey, the hero is caught in a bind. He championed the governor's opposition to the hunt, but his duty to the Forest Service requires him to prevent the state from arresting hunters. The operation had been planned in secret, to catch the state off-guard—an accurate portrayal of exactly what had happened in November 1924.

After the substantial failure of the hunt and the unresolved legality of the state's arrests, the deer drive seemed to be the only option left to get the deer off of the mountain before winter. Grey describes numerous delays in obtaining funds for the operation. Some of those funds were to come from a motion picture company that hopes to film the event.[21] The delays make skeptics of the drive even more pessimistic. In the novel, McKay experiences difficulty moving supplies from Flagstaff to the North Rim. Grey adds drama by repeatedly suggesting that the cattlemen, who would rather see the deer killed than driven, are behind these logistical problems. Once the deer drivers are assembled, they find the animals surprisingly scarce and skittish, possibly the result of more agitation by uncooperative ranchers. Grey tells of reports that a few men heard gunshots over the previous few days, which apparently made the deer even more wary.

When the drive finally commences, the hero Eburne has resigned from the Forest Service to take a more active part in the drive. A first attempt at keeping the deer in front of a line of men on foot and on horseback proves that the deer will trot unconcernedly along, then jump through even the smallest opening. In larger groups, the deer make like a stampede, reverse directions, and soon disappear into the forest behind the men. A second attempt to drive the deer a day later coincides with the winter's first blizzard. The men are blinded by the snow and frozen by the wind. Worst of all, the motion picture company fails to get a single frame of the deer. Grey's hopes for the drive are dashed. In his book, the denouement involves only a happy ending for Eburne, who finds himself unhindered by his Forest Service job and is able to go to work for the wealthy woman from New York who buys a ranch near Flagstaff and marries him.

Back to Reality

Zane Grey's fictional novel corresponds closely with the official reports of local foresters, including details of organizational problems, the skittish deer, the line of men on foot and horseback, and the snowstorm. In short, the deer drive was attempted, and it did fail. But however much Grey's account was based firmly in the actual events as he observed them, his interpretations of how the problems on the plateau arose out of administrative inadequacies and natural complexity were less consonant with the views of other participants.

Grey's repeated comments in the book about the balance of nature and the problems caused by removing cougars reflected his real-life insistence that the Forest Service had mismanaged the preserve by killing the predatory animals. The author told Biological Survey predatory animal leader Musgrave in 1924 that he had taken the matter up with the federal government years earlier. According to Musgrave, "[Grey] recommended that they allow the lions to increase in order to hold a balance of nature." This was a dangerous idea for a government predatory animal hunter to consider because there would be no direct control over the deer herd. Musgrave wrote that "if the lions were allowed to increase and anything

should happen to a part of the deer [the lions] would practically exterminate them before the lions could be gotten under control." Musgrave remained committed to the Biological Survey's policy on predatory animals.
He concluded: "We also explained to [Grey] that it would be much better
for people to be allowed to eat the meat of excess deer rather than to feed
mountain lions."[22]

Grey used the plight of the Kaibab deer to suggest to the broader public
the potential role of mountain lions in the balance of nature. He received
no satisfaction from the Biological Survey, so he wrote an article that appeared on the front page of the *Arizona Republican*. There, Grey recalled
his advice to the government a full fifteen years earlier, that mountain
lions not be exterminated. He added, "It is a fact that man cannot destroy
the balance of Nature without dire results." He concluded: "This whole
matter of the deer situation on Buckskin Mountain proves how futile it is
for men to interfere with the laws of Nature."[23]

In February 1925, the *New York Times Magazine* published an article by
William Du Puy describing the plight of the Kaibab deer. The deer, completely isolated on the Kaibab Plateau, multiplied unchecked by hunters
and predatory animals alike. The story explained that the balance of nature was upset by government hunters killing mountain lions in the
woods during the same period when deer hunting was prohibited, giving
the deer an "unusual opportunity to multiply."[24]

The spirit and even the wording of this article reflect the influence of
Mather, who was publicizing the plight of the deer across the nation.
People like Mather and Zane Grey, not the biologists, were concerned
about the "balance of nature" and the role of predatory animals in maintaining it. Mather, unlike the "game experts" of the Biological Survey,
believed that such a balance could and should still be established on wildlife areas. Unlike many mammalogists at that time, he did not follow the
accepted wisdom that nature's balance had been upset by human activities in the late nineteenth century, and he believed it was up to progressive scientific management to establish a new nature based on scientific
principles. Mather was an idealist and even a sentimentalist, but he was
not alone in his beliefs. As Du Puy and other journalists at the time
pointed out, a broad sector of society believed the Kaibab deer should be
saved from hunters' rifles. Alternatives to killing deer, although impractical, might be a step toward restoring balance. The Forest Service and
Biological Survey recognized this public sentiment. Consequently, they
embraced publicity that demonstrated the severity of the problem. This

pointed to the absolute necessity of reducing the deer herd through hunting. Mather's own attempts to publicize the desperate plight of the starving deer ironically gave the Forest Service a stronger argument for management, by hunting if necessary.

Mather realized too late that this overly pessimistic notoriety weakened his position. The article in the *Times* went too far in insisting that all the deer would starve on the Kaibab by the time spring arrived. As a result, Mather feared, people would not even come to the North Rim the next summer if there would be no chance of seeing deer. Stephen Johnson, the New Yorker who had previously written to *Outdoor America*, explained to Cammerer that he did not believe the herd was as near extermination as Mather had claimed. Based on his own observations of the deer, he wrote, "I would be willing to bet the great deer herd is not any where near extermination. Some may die, possibly from extreme weather and starvation but there will be plenty left." Furthermore, the New Yorker believed that it was "not too late to assist Nature to help herself."[25] Mather jumped at the opportunity to get Johnson's help in clarifying the situation by giving an alternate view to Du Puy's. "Would it not be a good idea," Mather asked insistently, "for you to write a note to the editor of the *New York Times* protesting against such statements as were contained in the article?"[26]

Johnson immediately wrote just such a letter explaining in more detail his view of the situation, not only with regard to the conservation of the deer, but also—reminiscent of Grey's opinion—the motives behind the movement to kill them. He agreed that the herd had multiplied, but insisted that the deer were not in such a dire condition. Furthermore, he suggested that those who hoped to limit their numbers by claiming they would starve anyway had other designs for the plateau. The New York conservationist insisted that "a great many people do not wish to see the deer roaming the Kiabab [*sic*], eating a range that might be used for cattle and sheep."[27] Those who stood to gain from livestock grazing promoted deer reduction for their own "selfish motives," according to Johnson.

Johnson also noted that suggestions for trapping and shipping the deer to other preserves were destined to fail. He believed that nature should be allowed to take its course. Mather had hoped Johnson would defend the Kaibab deer against claims that they were doomed, and he had every reason to be pleased with the first part of Johnson's letter. In the end, however, Johnson suggested as part of the solution exactly what Mather had been campaigning against—government killing of deer. At the same time,

Johnson proposed that predatory animals were also part of the solution, not the problem. He wrote that "if nature is allowed to take its course," by saving predatory animals from destruction, the Kaibab deer "will live in peace and plenty for a great many years to come and will be one of the interesting sights to the tourists driving through this wonderful virgin forest." As part of letting nature take its course, however, Johnson argued that a certain amount of hunting would be necessary.[28] This letter to the editor illustrated the extreme difficulty of finding ideological allies. On the one hand, Mather and Johnson agreed that the Park Service should encourage tourists to visit the North Rim and even to restrict further predatory animal control. On the other hand, Mather hoped to prevent the death of any deer.

Conservationists, government leaders, and biologists alike found the situation increasingly complicated. Recommendations, often of a most simplistic nature, came out of the woodwork. In an effort to resolve the controversy, one man offered his services to President Calvin Coolidge as an "unbiased" expert. The man, Louis A. Wagner from Prescott, Arizona, asked the president to appoint him as "a U.S. Game Warden with special orders to investigate the conditions of all game in the Grand Canyon National Park, and any other of the National Parks." Wagner would attempt to answer the critics who he said believed that "the deer were not starving at all and that it was just another grab of grazing lands for cattle interests." Coolidge's staff stamped the letter: "respectfully referred for acknowledgment and consideration." Wagner's offer was first referred to the secretary of the interior, then to the secretary of agriculture, and finally to the Forest Service, where Chris Rachford replied to the Prescott man. Rachford informed Wagner that the deer situation "was thoroughly investigated during the past season by a committee selected by the Secretary of Agriculture." Without acknowledging the subsequent controversy, he concluded by saying that the Forest Service had already prepared and initiated a plan.[29]

Park rangers inspecting the North Rim of the Grand Canyon and surrounding park areas that winter reported that the deer were generally in good condition. According to Chief Park Ranger E. T. Scoyen, two rangers who spent five days in mid-February traveling through areas north of the canyon "did not find any dead deer and all seen were in good condition." Scoyen noted that some Forest Service officials reported seeing "very few" dead deer in other areas. Foresters and park rangers seemed to agree, however, that during the mid-winter of 1925 the deer were not "on their usual winter range." This was just the kind of report Mather wanted to see. Even if conditions were a bit unusual, by summer the deer would be back in the high meadows. He used this report to help convince people that the park continued to be a place of tremendous interest to tourists, not only for viewing the Grand Canyon but also to see abundant wildlife. Mather forwarded a variety of these kinds of materials to the editor of *Outdoor America*, Will Dilg, including comments by local residents like James DeLong, owner of the Kanab Café, who wrote that next year's forage crop would be better. Mather encouraged Dilg to send Donald Hough, a reporter and naturalist, to the Kaibab to give a longer account of the conditions that would contrast with William Du Puy's *Times* article and serve to correct Johnson's conclusions. Mather would concede that "there are more deer than should be in the Kaibab Forest," but he believed yet another study of the situation would show that the great bulk of the herd came through the winter in good shape. He insisted that "there is no basis for such conclusions as reached by Mr. Du Puy in his article." Mr. Hough would not find any real "tragedy" on the Kaibab.[30]

PONDERING THE NEXT STEP

Given the differing opinions of administrators on the preserve, there existed real confusion over what should be done for the deer generally. More specifically, conservationists disagreed over the role predatory animals might play, if any. Longstanding Forest Service and Biological Survey policies would answer this latter question. Both agencies favored predatory animal destruction, and they were prepared to justify those policies. As the national press raised this issue, Chief of the Biological Survey Edward Nelson made his view of the predatory animal issue quite clear to Chief Forester William B. Greeley. Nelson believed that mountain lions should be prevented from increasing in numbers. Allowing them to increase would set up a situation that would require great efforts to control later. The Biological Survey chief worried that an uncontrolled lion population on the Kaibab "would invade the surrounding stock country and necessitate the employment of men to get rid of them."[31]

The Forest Service and Biological Survey would work together to institute a plan for continuous studies of the Kaibab Plateau. These studies would include monthly rides to "check the distribution of the deer and the effect of changing conditions through the various seasons." Nelson hoped for significant data for the administration of the preserve. Plans for monthly inspections of deer stomachs from various parts of the preserve would also supply data on the food preferences and condition of the deer. Finally, sample plots were being built to protect vegetation from deer browsing, and more importantly, to secure information "needed in connection with restoring the forage-carrying capacity of the Kaibab area." The Forest Service continued to expand similar studies throughout the country during this period. Nearby sites in Utah represented the state of the art in range science at the time.[32] Edward Goldman would coordinate the activities on the Kaibab beginning in June. In the meantime, Goldman was preparing a paper describing the administrative problems surrounding the Kaibab deer that had created a condition of "surplus game."[33]

By the late spring of 1925, Chief Park Ranger Scoyen confidently reported that the crisis had passed, and the herd had not met with destruction. The enormous numbers of deer estimated on the plateau must have included "phantom herds" that existed along with the actual herds to create inflated public perceptions of game problems. Perhaps the Kaibab herd had never been as large as some suggested, therefore few deer actually starved. Journalist Donald Hough, knee-deep in reports that the once-overpopulated herd had not starved but had somehow disappeared, drew his own conclusions. In an article for *Outdoor America*, which was titled "The Phantom Herd of the Kaibab," he reasoned that a moderate-sized herd suffered only moderate losses. Hough's visit to the Kaibab, along with information outlining conditions there, convinced him that visits to the North Rim would include substantial wildlife viewing opportunities. Mather was undoubtedly gratified.[34]

Debates on the national level by this time overshadowed local studies on the Kaibab. Scientists, along with state and federal officials, had plenty more to learn from examining existing conditions. Local researchers began to recognize the broad implications of their findings. Expertise took on new meaning as parties interested in local findings expanded to include hunters, conservationists, nature lovers, game officials, and ranchers across the country as well as scientists around the world. These groups all hoped to gain a better understanding of relationships among animal species, between animals and vegetation, and between humans, plants, and animals. The Kaibab did not offer ready answers to questions about these relationships, but it showed the urgency of finding such answers. Each attempt to study the situation to date had fueled disagreements between government agencies and among scientists. New research on the plateau could perhaps at last aim toward quantifying the conditions of the deer and forage. Fieldworkers began to monitor vegetative recovery stations. They looked forward to a time when researchers would not face constant political tension. As the tumultuous events of the previous year—the brief hunt, the controversial arrests, and the failed deer drive—became secured in the collective memories of wildlife scientists and officials across the country, local observers began to hope effective management could begin in earnest.

5

Taking Notice of the Kaibab Deer

[On the Kaibab] it was clear that the absence of their usual
enemies was disastrous to the deer . . . for the deer as a
whole depend on [cougars or wolves] to preserve their optimum numbers and to prevent them from over-eating
their food-supply.

CHARLES ELTON

NEW VIEWS

By the spring of 1925, neither the cynics, who predicted thousands of
deer would starve, nor the boosters, who confidently expected a healthy
herd equal to previous years, could point to clear evidence in support of
their prognostications. The winter range, while more denuded than in
years before, was not covered with the carcasses of starved deer. As spring
turned to summer, however, deer numbers appeared to be down dramatically, and the animals exhibited behavior that was notably different
from what experts considered normal.

Unprecedented efforts to describe and improve conditions on the
Kaibab began that year. The Park Service brought in a new superintendent who would tirelessly promote the deer for many years to come. The
Forest Service appointed a supervisor with little game experience, but
whose efforts to manage the deer by forestry standards provided the first
quantitative studies of wildlife in the preserve. Broader national interest
also brought expanding requests for information and unsolicited advice
from all quarters. In addition, the Kaibab deer became an increasingly
common point of reference for ecologists, game officials, and conservationists alike.

While park officials publicized the survival of the deer in preparation for the summer tourist season, Edward Goldman found new problems on the Kaibab in early June. The depletion of forage on the summer range was causing abnormal distribution of the deer just as it had on the winter range several months earlier. Instead of moving directly to the higher elevations, deer lingered on the intermediate range. Whatever their numbers, these changes in behavior reflected the poor state of the habitat. In Goldman's view, problems appeared increasingly complicated for the deer. In the summer of 1922, the biologist had observed few deer on the brushy slopes of the intermediate range, but in 1925 they were common among the oaks there. Most of the young aspen on the summer range were defoliated or dead, and the older trees had no leaves within reach of the deer. Soon, Goldman predicted, the forage producing capacity would be reduced on the previously undamaged slopes of the intermediate range as well.

Along with declining vegetation, he commented that the Biological Survey had undertaken no predatory animal control in the previous two years. Even without control measures, he found evidence of very few mountain lions and no evidence of deer killed by the big cats. These observations contributed to his belief that predatory animals would have little effect on the deer now. Goldman's view that humans had upset the balance of nature contributed to his continued support for control, even as the deer increased. He also noted that coyotes were numerous, and he believed these smaller predatory animals had killed a large number of yearling deer. The bureau planned to begin a poisoning campaign against the coyotes in the fall when hunting made deer entrails available for bait. Goldman supported poisoning these vermin without commenting on their potential role in preventing expansion of the deer population. He believed that hunting would prove far more efficient than allowing lions or coyotes to roam federal lands. Besides, the government biologist could not determine whether deer found dead on the winter range had been killed by predatory animals or died of starvation. In either case, coyotes had scavenged the carcasses and scattered the bones.

In describing the conditions on the plateau, Goldman compared the current situation to that of the year before. In 1924, he had seen many fawns and expected the herd to increase rapidly. In 1925, however, few yearling deer were seen. The biologist tried to quantify the scarcity: fewer than a half-dozen yearlings among groups of fifty or more deer. Throughout the preserve, Goldman noted that he saw relatively few deer. He commented repeatedly that it was the time of year when deer were widely scattered and least often encountered, but he reported with surprise their rarity in what he considered to be their usual haunts. At the same time, deer were relatively abundant in areas where they had not congregated in previous years, particularly in the intermediate range. Deer were also especially abundant in the open meadows of VT Park, where they were unquestionably in worse condition than the year before. Goldman suggested that the unfit appearance of the deer could merely be a perception created by greater numbers in the meadows, but he was convinced that the deer looked worse for the simple reason that conditions were bad.

Goldman's conclusions ultimately supported the observation that many deer had died of starvation during the previous winter, even if no one found their carcasses on the rugged terrain. In spite of the starvation, he maintained that damage done to the vegetation meant that the number of deer remained far in excess of the forage producing capacity of the range. Goldman advised: "The deer reached the maximum number last summer. Nature has begun to take her course, but further extensive reduction is necessary until the deer have been decreased to a point that will permit restoration of forage." He supported the Forest Service in attempting to capture fawns and ship them elsewhere but emphasized that an increased reliance on hunting was needed in the coming months. The biologist recommended that "suitable arrangements should be made in agreement with the state to have the hunting season begin earlier and extend longer than the open season for deer applicable to other parts of Arizona." Previous observers had not suggested hunting as a primary option on a large scale, particularly not the report of the investigating committee. Only Biological Survey Chief Edward Nelson had advocated hunting on a commercial scale. Goldman himself had never strongly supported hunting in the past himself, but he now asserted that solution above all others.[1]

In addressing the American Society of Mammalogists on the topic of "surplus game" earlier that spring, Goldman had reiterated his conviction that conservation and "practical game management" required a thorough understanding of forage conditions. After witnessing conditions on the Kaibab during the summer of 1925, he became more convinced than ever that "nature lovers" and "persons with a sentimental interest in wild life" needed to be awakened to the realities there. In preparing an article for publication in *American Game*, the bulletin of the

American Game Protection Association, Goldman described those realities. Although the Kaibab was not his only focus, four photographs illustrated the heavily browsed and dead vegetation left on the preserve. The
government biologist noted that protection from predatory animals and
disease would fail "through ignorance in providing an adequate supply of
the prime requisite—food." He added that proposals to use "large predatory animals as a counterpoise to excessive numbers of large game" were
unacceptable in light of the fact that "human interests are paramount,"
and therefore, predatory animals must be kept under rigid control
through proper management, which meant poisoning coyotes and killing
big cats. He cautioned that those who failed to understand the significance of shortages in vegetation had clouded the issue by offering a wide
range of opinions on the problem. Goldman concluded that what the
situation demanded was "less misdirected sentiment, less politics, more
team work, and clearer vision from a wider viewpoint in carrying out
game conservation programs." Such a solution would be especially effective if the sentiments, politics, teamwork, and vision could be united by
an unequivocal scientific understanding of the situation. For the government biologist, acknowledging this was to realize that the problem lay not
in the number of deer on the preserve, but in the disparity in sentiments,
politics, and the like.[2]

Goldman also spent part of that summer introducing E. Raymond Hall
to the problems on the Kaibab. Hall was a graduate student at the University of California and worked that summer for the Biological Survey conducting a study of the deer and vegetation of the preserve. As a bureau
employee, he learned of predatory animal control efforts dating back several years. As a student of Joseph Grinnell in the Museum of Vertebrate
Zoology, Hall was also familiar with the recent debate over the potential
economic value of coyotes with regard to rodent control and the separate
scientific value of predatory animals.

Hall spent June and July of 1925 studying the preserve. For the first two
weeks Hall accompanied Goldman as a field assistant. In a comprehensive report, Hall provided a complete list of vegetation eaten by deer, distinguished between preferred foods on the winter and summer range,
and also commented on the condition of each plant species. For example,
aspen trees were by far the favorite food of deer on the summer range.
The deer would stand on their hind legs to reach the higher branches.
When they had eaten all of the foliage within reach, the deer would push
against the flexible tree trunks, bend them over, and "ride" them down

to reach the leaves at the tops. Because of this heavy browsing, Hall estimated that aspen had not reproduced in the last five years. On the winter range, the hardy cliff rose bush was the overwhelming favorite of the
deer. Because of severe overbrowsing for several years, it appeared to the
young biologist that during the winter of 1924–25, cliff rose provided virtually no food for the deer and would need several years to recover. According to Hall, starvation had taken a toll on the deer. Without specify-
ing numbers, Hall reported finding many dead deer on the winter range
and also some on the summer range. The carcasses generally lay near
denuded and dead forage plants on the winter range. These dead forage
plants not only meant starving deer in the present, but less food for deer
in the future. Hall's descriptions of the conditions on the summer and
winter ranges were as complete as any compiled up to that time. In addition, he stated clearly that the deer had "gone beyond" the maximum capacity of the range in the past year. Because of this, deer had begun starving in large numbers.[3]

Although he had limited experience on the Kaibab, Hall linked the
increase in the deer herd to the control of predatory animals with a di-
rectness no biologist had suggested previously. He thought that ending
predatory animal control on the preserve and surrounding areas might
serve as a solution. Most importantly, administrators on the Kaibab
needed a detailed description of the biological features of the area. The
young biologist recognized, in traveling with Goldman and several forest
officers, that opinions about the conditions and the number of deer varied greatly. He hoped that the Biological Survey, the Forest Service, and
scientists like himself would coordinate and synthesize their information. Such a synthesis went beyond the scope of his own report, but he
believed greater coordination would provide solutions to the problem.
While Hall's methods resembled Goldman's, the young biologist drew
different conclusions about the apparent role of predatory animals. His
data, much less extensive than Forest Service or Biological Survey observations, did little to persuade more experienced men.

Chris Rachford of the Forest Service exchanged views with Hall that
summer as well. Rachford suggested that many observers had exaggerated
losses due to starvation, and he cautioned against hasty speculation. Before Hall's report became widely distributed, the grazing specialist
wanted additional and potentially more reliable information. Any new
plans should be based on extensive study. With Mather and other Park
Service officials increasingly opposed to predatory animal control, forest-

ers and Biological Survey biologists needed to justify control activities while at the same time limiting the deer herd through hunting. Rachford admitted that accurate estimates of changing deer numbers would be impossible to obtain and hoped to avoid confrontations with the Park Service. Using uncertainty as an excuse to maintain the status quo, he was one Forest Service official who did not advocate predatory animal control. First of all, Rachford wrote to the chief forester, "The country is so large, brushy, and cut up that in the absence of a very large patrol it would be difficult to get a fair count of the dead animals." He continued, in general agreement with Hall, "It is equally certain that predatory animals, especially coyotes and mountain lions, take a large toll of the deer." Rachford concluded that control could wait: "It does not seem that we should be particularly worried about predatory animals until we have succeeded in reducing the deer herd down to the permanent capacity of the range."[4] No one in the Forest Service or Biological Survey expressed a similar opinion. Perhaps as a result of his solitary stance, Rachford did not explicitly suggest adopting Mather's approach of seeing whether or not predatory animals would restore the balance of nature.

The Forest Service planned to permit hunting again that fall as a means of further reducing the deer. Since the hunting debacle the previous year, the Forest Service had learned that Arizona had a state law on the books since 1919 that allowed hunting of certain animals in order to protect agricultural lands or other resources. This law would allow the state to conduct a special hunt of the Kaibab deer by special agreement. The Forest Service immediately requested an agreement to extend the hunt in order to protect the plateau from further overpopulation.[5] Walter G. Mann, forest supervisor on the Kaibab since the previous November, went to work trying to convince the state that they needed a hunting agreement. Mann began by preparing the first in a long series of annual game reports. This game report provided only a sketch of his observations and suggestions. He reported that the deer were in far better condition than they had been in the previous year. The animals found abundant mushrooms on the summer ranges and many looked fat, according to Mann, after coming off the winter range "in very poor condition." The forest supervisor noted that there were fewer deer than last year, but he did not offer any actual estimates. He had to rely on other observers, since his own tenure began less than a year earlier. Coyotes seemed to be on the increase and were killing fawns at the "fawn farms," where the Forest

Service had begun raising young deer for shipment to other preserves.[6] Fawns could be captured and transported more easily than
adults, and their constant removal would limit the increase of the
deer. Mann's assessment here could serve only as a benchmark, but
as the years went by, his word became increasingly respected by local
observers, state bureaucrats, and national officials alike.

EXPANDING INTEREST IN KAIBAB REPORTS

Ecologist Charles Adams had argued for the preservation of predatory
animals for scientific study since the 1924 American Society of Mammalogists meeting, opposing Biological Survey policy and the stance of
Edward Goldman. As a member of the society's committee studying these
issues and helping to formulate policies, Adams was anxious to receive
input from as many sources as possible. He had visited the Kaibab himself during the summer of 1924 on a trip through the West. Then, after
reading Donald Hough's article in *Outdoor America*, he requested copies
of all available reports on the status of the Kaibab deer from the federal
agencies administering the preserve. He had seen enough of Goldman's
descriptions and wanted instead to see reports by local Forest Service
officials. He initially requested information from Park Superintendent
J. R. Eakin, but Eakin hesitated, not wanting to send any material received by his office without the permission of the Park Service director.
Eakin asked Mather for approval. Back in Washington, Mather and his
assistant Arno Cammerer decided against providing information to
Adams, who so vigorously opposed the Biological Survey. Cammerer told
Eakin to hold off, stating that "these reports [from the Forest Service] are
in the nature of a confidential communication to this office and should
not be published promiscuously." Recognizing that the reports might be
interpreted to favor Forest Service plans, he continued, "There are statements and observations that hold possibilities of a controversial nature
and we want to avoid that."[7] The Park Service was only beginning to see
the need to hold its cards more closely.

Eakin either did not appreciate the delicacy of the situation or thought
Adams should be trusted in this instance. He might also have wanted to
avoid a personal confrontation with the ecologist. Eakin asked Cammerer
to reconsider. Hough had already cited the reports in his article, so with-
holding them from Adams seemed unjustifiable. Not wanting to be the
one to disappoint Adams, Eakin wrote, "Dr. Adams will be somewhat dis-
pleased if these reports are not sent to him. Dr. Adams is inclined to be

rather antagonistic to the service anyway and this refusal would no doubt make him more so." The superintendent thought the reports provided "plain statements of facts and individual opinions are not expressed in them." With that, Mather sent a memo to another assistant, Arthur E. Demaray, agreeing that the reports should be sent to Adams as Eakin requested.[8] These hard-won reports became part of Adams's growing evidence regarding the need to preserve all animals for scientific study. At that time, however, Adams did not promote the protection of cougars for the purpose of regulating the deer herd.

The Park Service office in Washington received numerous requests for additional information on the Kaibab deer. In early 1926, C. L. Harrison—not a trained ecologist like Adams but a wealthy Cincinnati banker—asked Mather for data to help with a calculation of the connection between predatory animals and deer. The Cincinnati man was concerned that the Park Service's policy of not killing any animals on their lands might lead to the total destruction of the deer on the Kaibab. He suggested that by not controlling predatory animals the cougars would soon increase and kill all of the deer. Harrison supported this warning with a set of calculations. No one previously had used actuarial estimates of reproductive rates and predation. Harrison had his numbers tested by an assistant actuary in the War Department.[9] The calculations began with the following assumptions: suppose the Kaibab lands contained three hundred cougars of killing age and thirty thousand deer, and suppose the common estimate— that a cougar kills one deer per week—was correct. Next, consider a rate of cougar increase as observed by Sol Stephan, manager of the Cincinnati Zoological Gardens. Stephan reportedly had "known cougar in captivity to produce five young." This rate of five offspring per year became the standard in these calculations. Using "conservative" estimates, the increasing cougars—again killing just one deer per week—would kill 26,000 deer by the end of 1926. Of course, deer would also increase during the same period. By the end of the year, not considering cougar predation, Harrison and Stephan suggested that the 30,000 deer could increase to 70,000. Subtracting the number of deer killed by cougars would leave 44,000 deer for the next year. The following year, the surviving deer might then increase by 60,000 to 104,000. In the same year, the cougar population would have increased to an estimated 2,000 animals, each capable of killing one deer every week of the year for a total of 104,000, coincidentally eliminating the deer completely. By 1928, a population of 4,500 cougars would require 234,000 deer, but instead the actuary predicted the cougar would starve.

These estimates and calculations were admittedly "not in accord with the facts," the actuary stated, but the estimates suggested that the deer could easily be wiped out by cougars within a few years. In addition, many of the initial thirty thousand would die of causes other than cougar predation. The actuary concluded: "While these calculations are probably far from accurate, they seem to indicate quite clearly that with the very rapid increase in the number of cougar, the deer, if not entirely exterminated, will be greatly reduced in number in the next two or three years, and that they will no longer furnish an adequate food supply for the cougar."[10] The War Department actuary noted that the cougar had no enemies. The carnivores would have to find other sources of food before the complete destruction of deer occurred. Cougars "will of necessity be forced to eat less often and go farther afield to find deer of other herds, colts, and horses and cattle."

Back at the Park Service, assistant director Arthur Demaray offered no substantial response to this memorandum with its dire calculations for the future of the deer. He suggested that Harrison forward a copy to Will Barnes at the Forest Service.[11] The Park Service, after all, was simply not in the business of killing cougars; the Forest Service was. This actuarial argument would have no effect on Park Service policy.

When Will Barnes received a copy of the computations, he responded defensively to Harrison and questioned the purpose of the unsolicited calculations. Although the Forest Service generally regarded numbers as unassailable in the search for an objective way to determine management goals, the War Department figures struck the assistant forester as contrived. He wrote, "If it was intended to discredit or perhaps show the uncertainty of figures, no matter how carefully worked out, it certainly proves its case." Barnes was more inclined, however, to suggest corrections based on his own experience in the field. Before joining the Forest Service as a grazing expert, Barnes worked as manager of the Esperanza Cattle Company in Arizona. He therefore compared the potential for increase of the Kaibab deer, which had gone from about four thousand head in 1906 to somewhat over thirty thousand in 1926, with the kind of estimates he made in the cattle business in the 1880s. He explained the process whereby livestock owners calculated their potential future worth. Barnes wrote that, as a rancher, he "used to take a stubby lead pencil and figure out that by starting with a hundred cows, in twenty-five years we would have something more than a million head and still have sold nearly a million more." Those calculations were hopelessly optimistic. He continued, "As a matter of fact after getting down to actualities on the range, if we had good luck, with the one hundred cows at the end of ten years we would have only 200 or 250 head."[12]

According to Barnes, like cattle, the Kaibab deer never increased substantially. Prior to 1906 the deer were held in check by "indiscriminate and reckless hunting," largely by Indians with cougars playing a smaller role. Once hunting stopped, the cougar became more important. Still, even as the deer finally began to increase, he estimated that cougars took only a few hundred head each year. In general, Barnes was not impressed by any of the conclusions reached by the actuarial calculations, and nothing more came of them. For him, field experience showed that animal increases were more complex than the hard numbers offered by a desk-bound calculator.

During the spring and summer of 1926, New Mexico forester Aldo Leopold and S. B. Locke began corresponding regarding the fate of the Kaibab deer and efforts to manage them. Leopold was embarking on a book project to be titled "Southwestern Game Fields." He hoped Locke, the most experienced local forester on the Kaibab, could offer help in pointing out some of the key lessons learned in the previous half decade in northern Arizona. Leopold followed events on the Kaibab beginning as early as 1922. His correspondence with Locke in 1926 included several requests for clarification of data ranging from the density of deer in certain areas, to the acreage of deer range, to hunting success on the plateau. From these he created data tables, which he sent to Locke for review. By the end of the year, Leopold had completed his tables comparing the situation on the Kaibab to other deer ranges and asked Locke to meet him for an extended discussion. He wrote, "I wish you could stop over here sometime so that I could haul out my files and consult you on a lot of questions involved in my attempt to derive these game management ratios."[13] This meeting never took place, and Leopold did not visit the Kaibab himself until fifteen years later.

Leopold also kept in regular contact with Will Barnes, who in early 1927 wrote Leopold a long letter regarding the apparent role of predatory animals on the Kaibab. In that letter, Barnes suggested that the Park Service finally seemed to recognize that the questions surrounding predatory animals applied as much to parks as to forests. The reason for preserving those animals in the parks would be for educational value, although both Barnes and Leopold seemed to agree that beyond this, cougars, wolves, and coyotes should be eliminated from the parks as much as from the forests. Leopold later recalled this period of "trigger itch" in a famous essay. At the time, Barnes wrote, "As a matter of fact, I agree with you entirely that on hunting grounds we ought to exterminate some of these species." Particularly worthy of extermination were wolves and coyotes, the former being almost wiped out in the Southwest, while the latter were still on the increase.[14]

Independently of these statements, both Barnes and Leopold were prepared to make an exception when it came to the mountain lions on the Kaibab. Forest Service officials did not fully understand the situation there, and Barnes admitted it. He told Leopold that Stephen Mather had admitted that the Park Service would never allow lion hunting on its lands north of the Grand Canyon, or anywhere else for that matter. Mather wanted to let nature "take its course and let the lions have their way" in the hope that this would keep the number of deer down to a "reasonable size." Barnes recognized that this would furnish visitors to the park the added thrill that "they might some day run across a mountain lion killing a deer, or else see one of the lions skulking along some of the ledges." He even imagined that "it would have been absolutely right to have allowed the lions on the Kaibab Forest to increase could we have foreseen the complications that were to ensue within a comparatively few years through the rapid increase of the herd of deer."

Nevertheless, the forester suggested that whatever killing of lions did occur may not have increased the herd of deer to any appreciable extent. His summary of the imagined impact of lion hunting pointed out the enormous uncertainty of such activities and their eventual meaning. Barnes concluded, "We have been saying it did and of course nobody can prove to the contrary; therefore we shall probably keep on saying it, but as a matter of fact we have not killed in the last twenty years, by actual record, more than three hundred or four hundred of these animals at the very outside. Scatter that over twenty years and what has it amounted to? Ten or fifteen a year on an area covering over a million acres." This forester's account of the events on the Kaibab marked one of the earliest statements recognizing past errors and regret over disrupting what seemed like nature "taking its own course." Leopold undoubtedly pondered that humility and regret, tucking it away for explication in later writings. In concluding, Barnes agreed with Leopold that the whole idea of "the balance of nature" had been perpetuated by people—including themselves—who sometimes indulged in "a good deal of nonsense." The balance had long since been upset, but Barnes suggested that it should still be "borne in mind" when planning "raids on wild life of any kind."[15]

Charles Elton's Interest in the Kaibab

Efforts to understand the situation on the Kaibab necessarily began with research on the plateau itself. However, the continuing political controversy and the large number of complicating factors involved in the apparent plight of the deer mobilized scientists and conservationists around the world to contemplate the state of their knowledge. On the one hand, they imagined scientific hypotheses to explain the increase in deer numbers, and on the other hand, they sought solutions to the practical problem of deer management. Science and management did not remain separate in the minds of most observers for long. In fact, they went hand in hand, leading some conservationists to insist that the hypotheses would provide solutions, if only they could be put into practice. Others recognized that, just as hypotheses required supporting evidence, implementing them would transform their meanings. British ecologist Charles Elton attempted to address both theoretical and practical problems in ecology, realizing that management efforts in places like the Kaibab would not necessarily benefit from ecological theories developed in one place and subsequently applied to practical problems elsewhere. Scientists and fieldworkers interacting with one another in a variety of contexts might instead suggest appropriate directions for, and ultimately carry out, valuable research in ecology. Elton published *Animal Ecology* in 1927, and in that book he was acutely aware of the need for continued practical research in order to fill gaps in scientific theory. He actively supported bringing ecology to bear on economic and other practical problems, but he also acknowledged that such "application" demanded a two-way interaction between fundamental ecology and practical biology. The Kaibab deer served as a specific illustration of this interaction.[16]

Elton made a major contribution to animal ecology by describing the factors that seemed most important in determining animal numbers, insisting on "animal associations" or "animal communities" as the proper level of inquiry. He distinguished this ideal study from earlier natural history, wherein naturalists neglected animal associations while "swooping down" upon individual species of interest. Elton described certain components of communities for consideration. Among his examples of animal communities was that of "the deer in a sanctuary in Arizona"—the Kaibab deer. Herbivorous animal numbers, Elton suggested, would normally be kept down due to the pressure of disease and enemies such as carnivorous animals. For the Kaibab deer, he wrote: "Owing to the absence of their usual carnivorous enemies (e.g., cougars or wolves) they increased so much that they began to over-eat their food-supply, and there was a serious danger of the whole population of deer starving or becoming so weakened in condition as to be unable to withstand the winter successfully. The numbers were accordingly reduced by shooting, with the result that the remaining herds were able to regain their normal condition."[17] The way this account dramatically simplified the Kaibab situation between 1920 and 1927 made it all the more effective in illustrating Elton's point. The absence of the "usual enemies" had proven "disastrous to the deer," and those enemies therefore should be considered "hostile" only in the sense that "they are enemies to individual deer." As a population, the deer depended on their enemies "to preserve their optimum numbers and to prevent them from over-eating their food-supply." From this case, Elton began to build his argument that carnivorous enemies of herbivores—predators—were essential to animal communities and the regulation of animal numbers.

Describing the populations more generally, Elton noted that animal numbers increased with extraordinary speed, if unchecked. He suggested that the ultimate check on animal numbers was food supply, but other factors came into play before the food was exhausted. Foremost among these were animals that preyed upon others lower in what Elton called a "food-chain." Echoing Charles Darwin's example in *On the Origin of Species*, where the growth of clover was checked by "humblebees," which were in turn checked by field mice and so on up the chain to cats, Elton wrote, "Snails are eaten by thrushes, the thrushes by hawks; fish are eaten by seals, seals by sea leopards, and sea leopards by killer whales; and so through the whole of nature." In these food chains, the ecologist advanced the notion of a pyramid of numbers. The pyramid of numbers resulted generally from "two facts (a) that smaller animals are preyed upon usually by larger animals, and (b) that small animals can increase faster than large ones, and so are able to support the latter."[18] He noted that it was common for one species to prey exclusively upon another, but rare for a given species to be preyed upon by only one enemy. This led him to conclude that the food-cycle mechanism efficiently regulated numbers of animals as long as the environment remained fairly uniform.

Elton hastened to add that when the "balance" of the community was upset by a change in the usual order, numbers of predators and their prey often became highly irregular.

Returning to the issue of food supply, Elton suggested that the amount of food available set an "ultimate limit" on animal increase. As an ultimate limit, however, starvation seldom acted as a direct check on populations. More often, when food became scarce, Elton observed that "enemies of all kinds" would keep the numbers down. Starvation would not serve as a direct limitation because both food supply and requirements changed from season to season. Shortages would not necessarily last until starvation took a serious toll on the animal population. Again he cited the case of the Kaibab deer to make his point: "This can be well seen in the example of the deer in Arizona quoted previously, where increase during the summer imperilled [*sic*] the food-supply for the following winter." The ecologist concluded that other mechanisms must necessarily limit populations, but he admitted that exactly which mechanisms remained a mystery. Many complex interactions were not yet understood. As a first attempt at an answer, Elton described the way a number of carnivores and parasites seemed to regulate populations. In the end, he concluded only that it was "clear that variations in numbers play a very big part in the ecology of animals."[19] These included the individual characteristics of both herbivores and carnivores, and it also depended upon the various effects of seasonal and local conditions in the timing of their feeding.

In order to properly understand the factors that regulate populations and their powers of increase, Elton raised the question of the "desirable density" of animal numbers for different species in a community. This question resonated with the way ranchers and range managers determined carrying capacity, although Elton did not explicitly make the connection with range management.[20] The "unstable nature of the environment" and "the fact that practically no animals remain constant in numbers for any length of time" complicated any careful study of animal populations. In introducing the topic of animal numbers, Elton made it clear that neither theoretical ecologists nor practical field biologists knew much about populations. Such understanding was still in "an extremely early stage" that would require "biological surveys and study of animal communities, from the point of view of food-cycles and time-communities." Elton noted the great potential for populations to grow and eventually consume the earth, but he quickly added that such potential would never be realized due to the many factors that limit populations, particularly disease.[21]

Elton never formulated mathematical models for population change. He preferred to examine animals and their habits directly, rather than trying to model their potential for increase. This way of thinking was deeply affected by the notion of plant and animal interactions embodied in Darwin's "economy of nature." This phrase referred to thinking of nature as a system, not to making nature turn a profit in human terms.[22] Elton insisted on the practical importance of ecology. He was "chiefly concerned with what may be called the sociology and economics of animals." He recognized the importance of mutual exchanges between ecological research and the more "practical bearings" of these ideas. Ecologists would increasingly rely on the fieldwork of government biologists, range managers, and other observers in order to provide valuable theoretical and practical insights. It occurred to Elton that "the best observations have been made by people working on economic problems (most of whom, it may be noted, were not trained as professional zoologists)," especially since the principles of animal ecology were seldom if ever mentioned in university zoology courses. If training in this area was lacking, the whole field might suffer, since according to Elton "it is just such knowledge which is required by any one who is brought up against practical problems in the field, after he leaves the university."[23]

Ecology was the branch of zoology most likely to offer immediate help in solving natural dilemmas. In a number of places, Elton tied together the different strands of animal ecology that had developed over the previous twenty years or so. Theoretical and practical work, while ultimately interdependent, had separate traditions in the late 1920s. He perceived that the gap between them was widening—just when it ought to be narrowing—in the minds of many ecologists, mammalogists, zoologists, foresters, range managers, and wildlife biologists.

Going to Court

While local officials assisted a broad community of scientists and conservationists in assessing the Kaibab situation, political and legal matters relating to the preserve remained muddled. The dispute between the state of Arizona and the federal government, primarily the Forest Service, centered on the question of jurisdiction over management of the deer and grew most intense between 1926 and 1928. Arizona officials insisted that state control over wildlife was inviolable by federal ownership or administration of lands. Governor George W. P. Hunt led the complaint against the Forest Service and joined Stephen Mather in the belief that hunting would hurt tourism on the North Rim. So, when Arizona game wardens arrested hunters not holding state licenses in 1924 and 1925, they were enforcing state laws because the permits issued by the secretary of agriculture were inadequate without state licenses.

In order to get around this problem, the Department of Agriculture filed an injunction that would prevent enforcement of the state game regulations on the Kaibab in 1927. The Forest Service argued for the continuation of hunting by special permit on the Kaibab. In a special hearing, U.S. circuit and district judges attempted to decide who had the right to regulate deer hunting in the Kaibab National Forest. Since the federal government had the right to protect the vegetation on the preserve, and hunting seemed the most effective way of protecting federal lands, hunting by special permit in the game preserve could continue. The court's decision was based on evidence gathered in previous years, including scientific studies and official reports of both the state and federal government. In the court's view, these showed the acute need for reduction of the deer, dating back to 1922.[24]

The presiding judge wrote that several previous efforts to reduce the deer had either failed or proven inadequate. Action by the state prohibiting hunting had contributed to federal inability to manage its lands. In addition, the court recognized that the state had "canceled, revoked, or abrogated" earlier potential agreements with the Forest Service that would have allowed legal cooperative hunts. Rescinding those agreements led to the standoff. The judges thereby decided in favor of the Department of Agriculture, whose right it was to protect its lands. The special hearing did not answer the question once and for all, however. Immediately following the hearing, Governor Hunt filed suit against the federal government for the right to enforce state game laws on the Kaibab.

Even as Arizona appealed the case, the Forest Service sought the advice of solicitor R. W. Williams, who had advised Biological Survey Chief Edward Nelson and Forest Service Grazing Manager Chris Rachford on the same issue four years earlier. Following the decision, Williams advised Chief Forester William Greeley to expand efforts to abide by state laws. Blatant disregard for those laws would lead to disapproval in subsequent appeals. The reserve should not be opened for a hunting season "contrary to the laws of Arizona." Rather, in order to remain in the good graces of the courts, the federal government should increase efforts to reach a cooperative agreement with the state. Although the Forest Service had won the latest round, killing too many deer with an appeal pending would alter the evidence and likely lead to a reversal of the decision on the grounds that the herd had now been substantially reduced. If the justices in a higher court found there were no deer left to protect, or few deer left to hunt, they would almost certainly decide against the federal government's right to protect its lands. They would conclude that the Department of Agriculture had shown disdain for the state's right to appeal. Williams wrote that the Supreme Court might view "an extensive removal of deer as displaying a lack of deference for its appellate authority in an attempt to render futile the State's appeal." The federal authorities on the Kaibab could make the question of hunting "largely moot," since in the absence of abundant deer the court would have no opportunity to reverse the lower court's decision. The state could not regulate hunting after the animals were dead. Based on this legal advice, Forest Service officials agreed that killing would be kept to a minimum out of concern over the reaction of the public and the courts.[25]

While the Forest Service awaited the Supreme Court decision, local officials on the Kaibab continued studying the conditions and making plans. Earl Storm, a local forester, examined the estimated number of deer killed by predatory animals in 1927. He estimated that 1,000 deer were lost to predatory animals, including 2,500 coyotes, 1,000 wildcats, and 150 mountain lions; this number was nowhere near the number predicted by commentators like C. L. Harrison and his actuary. He also attempted—without much success—to discover the mortality rates of deer due to disease, starvation, and automobile collisions. In a more direct examination of the stomach contents of deer, cattle, and sheep, Storm found that deer ate mostly aspen and yellow pine on their summer range. On intermediate ranges they ate aspen, oak, and cliff rose; and on their winter ranges they ate mostly juniper, cliff rose, and sage. Cattle, by and large, ate grass, while sheep subsisted primarily on grass and weeds. These conclusions supported the assumption that deer and livestock did not compete for food.[26]

VERNON BAILEY RETURNS

Although Vernon Bailey participated actively in debates over predatory animal control and was familiar with the situation on the Kaibab, he had not visited the plateau since his first trip through the area in 1888. During the summer of 1928, the veteran field naturalist at last examined the preserve firsthand, accompanied by two Park Service officials, Superintendent M. R. Tillotson and ranger Edward Laws. In addition to reporting his findings on a variety of mammalian species, Bailey commented specifically on the condition of the deer. Several predatory animal species also received mention: mountain lions, bobcats, gray fox, bear, coyotes, and wolves. Of these, only mountain lions and coyotes functioned as enemies of the deer. Bobcats were the worst enemies to mountain sheep in the canyon, while fox were considered harmless. Bear were too rare to be of concern, and wolves were extinct in the area.

Bailey proposed solutions and suggested action based on expertise that came from wide experience with the Biological Survey. He demanded changes in the way the deer were studied. The biologist had more ideas for management than either E. Raymond Hall or Edward Goldman, and he discussed, in turn, all of the topics that had emerged up to that point: deer and range conditions, management, livestock, predatory animals, carrying capacity, and deer habits. The deer on the plateau could still be viewed in large numbers; Bailey himself counted 912 deer along the road through VT Park and beyond. Because he could not count fast enough to give an accurate number, he estimated there were over two thousand visible, which led to the conclusion that "the lowest estimate of twenty thousand or thirty thousand deer on the Kaibab is very conservative." The deer were very tame and could be seen grazing along the road. Among them were "literally hundreds" of spotted fawns, large, plump, and quick. The adult deer were no less impressive. Bailey wrote, "All of the deer were in prime condition, plump and smooth and heavily muscled if not fat." Based on this evidence, the range must be "well stocked," but not overstocked. The abundance of good food he observed seemed adequate for the current number of deer.[27] This report contrasted with observations made since 1924, but compared favorably with Goldman's earliest descriptions just two years before that.

With abundant food, however, came the threat that the deer would once again increase rapidly. Bailey estimated doubling in as few as two years, which was troubling, as the range would not hold much more than the current number, and the winter food supply was already questionable. In attempting to understand how rapidly the deer might increase in coming years, Bailey wrote: "A thorough study should be made of this deer herd to ensure its best welfare as well as to know how to handle other deer under similar conditions. The food most used at various seasons should be known and the carrying capacity of the range determined for both wet and dry years."[28] This comment pointed not only to his interest in the Kaibab situation for its own sake, but also as a test case for other preserves. Bailey was acutely aware of how carrying capacity could change under fluctuating conditions. Those fluctuations needed to be accounted for in the management plan.

In order to manage wildlife more effectively, Bailey believed the focus should be as much on minimizing domestic grazing as on predatory animal control. Park Superintendent Tillotson's goal of encouraging deer and other wildlife species all around the Grand Canyon for "display" purposes would be accomplished more readily by completely clearing both the North and South Rims of domestic livestock. He wrote, "If the accursed range cattle can be eliminated from the National Park there will be abundance of feed for antelope and deer all along the south side of the Grand Canyon." In addition to native food sources, Bailey suggested that certain species of vegetation could be introduced through planting or clearing ground of less-productive competitors in order to feed the deer more effectively. Finally, Bailey described the way deer had consumed virtually all of the vegetation within reach. He said that the aspens on the summer range had been "trimmed up to a fairly uniform deer line." This term was to become legendary in reference to the Kaibab deer, and the image of a deer line became a symbol of wildlife overpopulation as well as a hallmark for wildlife management disasters for decades to come.[29]

Back in the Courtroom

In the midst of further studies and awaiting a decision from the courts, the Forest Service faced new data that figured heavily in the fight over management of the deer. Hunters on the Kaibab had bagged few deer over the previous few seasons. Using these low success rates to argue that deer were scarce, the state complained that the herd had already diminished to numbers below what tourists, managers, and hunters all demanded. In response to apparently decreasing deer numbers, District Forester R. H. Rutledge prepared a memorandum describing his view of the subject. He stated that while 50 percent of the deer appeared to be in good condition, 50 percent were still in very poor condition. He noted that ribs and vertebra on the poorer animals could be seen from a distance of fifty yards. The Forest Service still had no way of getting an accurate count of the deer, nor did anyone else. Whatever their numbers, the food supply remained inadequate. Rutledge suggested that there might be 30,000 deer still in the preserve, and while 150 fawns had been hand-raised on farms for transport to other preserves and 600 adult deer had been killed in the previous year by hunters, these methods provided no substantial relief of the damage to vegetation. He concluded, "There seems to be no other solution to the situation than to, through some method, remove a large percentage of the deer," possibly as many as ten thousand head.[30] Other local foresters reported conditions as bad or worse than in 1925 for both vegetation and deer. One added, "If the oak brush and juniper is not in worse condition it is because all of it within reach was completely browsed three years ago."[31]

Rutledge also wrote to the chief forester, notifying him of a change that the Forest Service hoped would open better relations with the state. George Hunt lost the governor's race for the first time since Arizona became a state in 1912. His successor, John C. Phillips, would take office on January 1, 1929. Rutledge expressed hope that Phillips might not be in such tight agreement with Stephen Mather and the Park Service. This would offer the Forest Service some relief in managing the deer, but help from the U.S. Supreme Court came even before Hunt left office.[32]

When the case between George Hunt and the Department of Agriculture reached the Supreme Court in November 1928, state attorneys offered three different arguments. The first two arguments were based on states' rights: they argued that the injunction preventing the state's arrests of hunters with federal permits was defective, and they argued that the deer were the property of the state and that the federal government had no right to violate state law. The state's third and most significant defense went beyond the states' rights issue. They insisted that the deer were protected from hunting by the U.S. Congress since the Kaibab was, after all, a national game preserve. The Department of Agriculture defied a federal congressional mandate in addition to a state law when it allowed hunters on the Kaibab. The Department of Agriculture and the Forest Service argued that hunting had been and remained necessary to protect the preserve from destruction by the deer—that the preserve created to protect the deer from hunters now needed to be protected from the deer by hunters.

Despite the state's latest and most sophisticated legal case, the Supreme Court again ruled in favor of the federal government, upholding the decree that the state could not prevent the secretary of agriculture from allowing hunters to kill deer that posed a threat to resources on federal lands. The Supreme Court required only that all deer taken in these hunts be marked with special tags for transport off the preserve. In addition to protecting federal lands, the justices also showed concern for the deer herd. The case, as it had been described to them, led them to conclude that the deer were starving as a result of their own increase brought on by protection from hunting and natural enemies. The justices wrote: "During the last few years deer on these reserves have increased in such large numbers that the forage is insufficient for their subsistence. The result has been that these deer have greatly injured the lands in the reserves by overbrowsing upon and killing valuable young trees, shrubs, bushes, and forage plants. Thousands of deer have died because of insufficient forage."[33] Damage to vegetation gave the Department of Agriculture the right to allow sport hunting or even official killing, and many hoped these actions would save the remaining deer from starvation.

With this ruling, as far as the Forest Service was concerned, any population of deer that exceeded the carrying capacity was, literally, fair game. In a press release, the Forest Service explained the court's decision as follows: "A basis for efficient management of the game and other forest resources can be had only by working out and applying a feasible plan for removing each year the number of deer above the conservative carrying capacity of the available range." Forest Service officials estimated there was food available for between twenty thousand and twenty-five thousand head of deer, a figure that suggested an estimate of the preserve's carrying capacity. They also estimated that the herd, despite hunting in recent years, stood at thirty thousand head. They pointed out again that deer could not be expected to migrate nor could they be effectively transported. Hunters shooting for sport had removed a number of deer "small in comparison with the total number that needed to be removed." The Forest Service concluded that the only way to care for the range and the future of the deer was "to regulate the number of deer on the area in accordance with the carrying capacity of the range," which would have to include official government killing.[34]

For ten days in mid-December 1928, the Forest Service supervised killing of the deer by salaried government hunters. In a report of that hunt, Assistant District Forester R. E. Gery recounted the successes of men whose purpose was singularly to kill deer, saving them from starvation. The carcasses were given to local Navajo Indians. In the course of those ten days, the hunters killed 718 deer on the west side of the plateau and 216 on the east side. In general, Gery called the operation a success. Some lessons were learned, however. The Forest Service hoped to deliver all the deer either to local Indians or to charitable organizations in Arizona, but the logistics of such deliveries proved difficult. Many of the carcasses were spoiled by the time they were trucked off the plateau. Cleaning the carcasses for shipment and eventual use had created far more work than killing them in the first place. Gery wrote, "The men agree that if a man kills, cleans and snakes the carcasses to a point where they can be reached by the wagon, fifteen deer per day, he is doing a big day's work." A more efficient method would be for a hunter to simply shoot the deer, perhaps thirty per day, while a crew followed each hunter to clean and load the carcasses. With this method only four or five hunters would be needed. Forest Service officials never mentioned the most efficient method: simply killing the deer and leaving the carcasses where they fell. They had won their case in court and in the arena of public opinion. Their success relied on the claim that killing deer was preferable to letting deer starve. They did not want to go back to any option that left the deer, in a sense, unutilized. Protecting the deer had ironically come to mean protecting them from death by natural causes—predatory animals or starvation—even if it meant killing them outright.[35]

Systematizing Studies

In January 1929, Earl Storm and Walter Mann prepared a "progress report" for the Forest Service. In it, they provided information on the deer and range studies being conducted under their administration. They reported an increase in the total number of "exclosures" in the forest—fenced areas also referred to as "plots" or "quadrats" where the changes in vegetation could be observed in the absence of browsing by livestock or deer. No one referred to these comparative plots as "controls," as a sort of controlled experiment, but Forest Service officials clearly attempted to establish new evidence along these lines. Little had been written about these exclosures during the years when they were first erected in 1925. The plots provided long-range comparisons and by 1929 were showing initial results. Within the exclosures, which numbered forty-one by the end of the decade, local foresters kept careful records of plant growth. Storm and Mann tagged shrubs, conifer seedlings, and small trees, noting details of the size and condition of each. In addition to detailed notes kept on regular plot forms, they began to use photographs to set standards for comparison from year to year. These methods could be traced directly to forest management techniques in practice since the first decade of the twentieth century in the United States. Tagging vegetation to determine growth and damage by wildlife was an innovative approach to the problem. These techniques did not become common in wildlife biology until years later. Storm and Mann's report also included sections on vegetation and carrying capacity, tables of summary data from the exclosures on various ranges, the observed effect of deer browsing on timber and shrubs, and life history of the deer. It contained considerably more data than previous reports from any group of scientists or other organization. The sections of the report showed a clear evolution, based on earlier reports, with descriptions of various ranges and the seasonal effect of deer on vegetation, but with more detailed information and in some cases quantitative data.[36]

Another significant study underway at the time involved Aldo Leopold and S. B. Locke, whose continuing collaboration included efforts to understand deer ranges in general and the Kaibab in particular. Leopold asked Locke to write a chapter for his book on Southwestern game, focusing specifically on the Kaibab deer situation as local foresters currently understood it. Locke believed that the Kaibab deer illustrated problems faced by deer on Forest Service lands across the country, from Utah to Pennsylvania. He had agreed to write an outline of a chapter for Leopold. Among early drafts of Leopold's "Deer Management in the Southwest" manuscript, Leopold himself wrote an outline for what he hoped Locke would include in a chapter on the Kaibab situation. Leopold planned to send Locke a draft of the rest of the book in 1929, as he wanted the Kaibab chapter to include a comparison of Locke's experiences there with the experiences of other wildlife experts who would contribute to the book, including particularly J. Stokely Ligon and Fred Pettit. Ligon led the Biological Survey's predatory animal control program in New Mexico, while Pettit was a dentist by profession and a hunting partner of Leopold's.[37] Leopold hoped the Arizona chapter would include data from Locke on the composition of the Kaibab herd by sex and age classes, the proportion of does bearing fawns and the effect of range conditions on fawns per doe, additions to the food list, and an outline of salient points in the history of administration of the Kaibab herd.[38] Although Leopold never completed the manuscript for publication, he continued correspondence with Locke and other Forest Service officials on the Kaibab throughout his life.

Edward Goldman returned to the Kaibab Plateau in June 1929 to continue his comparative studies of the preserve. His report on conditions illustrated significant changes in his thinking about wildlife issues. He noted that the range produced only "ten per cent of [its] normal" vegetation. In this greatly depleted state, further pressure from the deer would severely damage the shrubs and small trees on the plateau. Although many observers reported the deer to be in "fair condition" or normally healthy, Goldman recommended "that the deer be reduced to a point that will permit the restoration of the range." As officials waited to take action and debated over the proper methods, delay was making matters worse. Each season that passed led to "a further reduction of feed producing capacity, further injury to the forest, and a lengthening of the period that will be required for restoration." Like Bailey, Goldman began to recognize the effects of changing annual weather cycles and fluctuations. Over time, an occasional wet year might provide temporary relief for an overstocked range. As the effect of repeated dry years multiplied, however, starvation of deer would begin to take its toll. The biologist wrote that observers unfamiliar with the history of the situation, who visit the area during periods of abundant rainfall, would be "deceived in regard to the true trend of conditions and assume that all is well with the deer and the forest." Light, irregular rainfall was the rule, making conditions during drought years "the true carrying capacity."

Starvation in drought years could be tied to other conditions on the plateau as well. When forage conditions were bad and deer began to starve, for example, predatory animals were also likely to make more "inroads" on the weakened deer. Hunger led to predation even more readily than it led to starvation. Goldman saw this as undesirable—a sign that proper care had not been taken to promote a balance between the deer and their forage supply. Although evidence of deer killed by mountain lions was lacking, Goldman believed that many carcasses probably lay hidden in the rough terrain of the preserve. The number of predatory animals should be kept to a minimum so the deer could be controlled by hunting and other means involving ongoing human intervention. He was not an advocate of letting nature take its course.[39]

If Goldman was not about to change his fundamental approach to control, he did continue to advance new ideas of how the situation could be described. In 1929, for example, the idea of percentage of normal served as a way of quantifying the condition of the range. This terminology became common in subsequent descriptions of the Kaibab Plateau. Goldman's quantification brought together the idea of carrying capacity and the need to reduce deer numbers, although it was still unclear what level of reduction would be justified by a given percentage. The biologist also emphasized the importance of considering dry years as the lowest common denominator in determining carrying capacity. The accumulated effect of drought years was important, he recognized, and previous

problems had resulted from oversimplifying assumptions about fluctuating climatic conditions. Wet years did not make up for dry years instan-
taneously. Finally, Goldman tied food shortage for deer to a possible increase of predatory animals. He reiterated that hungry deer made easy
prey for mountain lions and particularly coyotes. He concluded that efforts to control predatory animals should be ongoing, whatever the deer
numbers or conditions. None of Goldman's observations could rival the
changes taking place in the political arena, however.

Newly elected Arizona governor John C. Phillips appointed a new game
warden and a game commission. The warden was R. Lee Bayless, and the
commission included, among others, Homer L. Shantz and A. A. Nichol, both
biologists at the University of Arizona in Tucson. Forest Service officials in
particular had reason to hope that these changes would lead to easier agreement with the state over efforts to manage the Kaibab deer. In fact, officials
at most levels within the Park Service, Biological Survey, and state, as well as
various constituencies throughout the nation, shared the same hope.

Despite assurances that the deer would remain abundant in areas fre-
quented by tourists, certain Park Service officials did not easily fall into
line with these hopes for cooperation and in fact planned to increase
opposition to annual hunting on the plateau. Grand Canyon National
Park Superintendent M. R. Tillotson repeatedly frustrated the Forest Service and eventually the state with his demands. He began by recommend-
ing increased shipping of deer, despite a widespread awareness of the
practical problems involved in those efforts. Tillotson also opposed all
cattle grazing in or near the preserve. Admitting that destruction to the
range had occurred in recent years, he nevertheless insisted that the deer
themselves were much improved in 1929. Deer could be attracted to the
open meadows in summer by placing salt just beyond the shadows of the
trees, and regular counts of these deer would constitute the Park Service's
contribution to management studies. It appeared that the animals were in
good condition and hunting was unnecessary. Trapping and shipping
would be sufficient, according to the superintendent. Yet, in order to
keep up public relations, the Park Service would participate in cooperative studies of the deer and conditions for the time being.[40]

In the summer of 1929, a survey of the Kaibab was arranged to include
representatives from the various government agencies involved. It was
the first time since the 1924 Investigating Committee that such a survey
was organized, although its national significance was much more limited.
In preparation for this official survey, Biological Survey Chief Paul

Redington forwarded a copy of Goldman's latest report to the state game warden. Redington noted that this most recent report represented the culmination of field studies conducted by Goldman since 1922. The bureau chief added comments of his own on the steadily declining forage producing capacity of the range. Finally, he congratulated the state of Arizona for recent game-law changes and creation of the game commission. The new commission would have ample power to make the necessary changes to correct the persisting problem on the Kaibab. Redington concluded by suggesting that the state support efforts to remove deer alive whenever possible. The state should allow hunting of female deer, extend the season, and encourage both resident and nonresident hunters to "take as many deer as possible." He added, "It is sincerely to be hoped that with the full cooperation of the various agencies directly interested the problems of surplus Kaibab deer may reach a final solution."[41] Goldman and Bailey spent some time with the party, which included Rachford, Rutledge, and Mann from the Forest Service, Arizona Game Warden R. Lee Bayless, and Park Superintendent Tillotson. Their observations echoed what other reports suggested, but they focused more on actions to be taken. Cooperation, it was decided, would be essential. The Forest Service would be in charge of administering the hunting season and would ensure that state regulations be followed.[42]

To launch the official survey, a conference was held in Flagstaff on July 1. Participants discussed plans for the Kaibab deer and based their comments on recent studies and the occasion of the new state game commission. Governor Phillips spoke first, noting both that the game commission would have full authority to represent the state without his interference, but also that he personally hoped the situation would be worked out through the careful examination of the facts of the case. He wanted the commission to have autonomy, and he wanted the autonomous commission to provide a solution. Representatives of the Forest Service and Park Service alike described their desire to cooperate. According to the Forest Service's account of the meeting, written by Rutledge, Tillotson neither endorsed nor objected to killing deer. The park superintendent's view would become publicly known somewhat later. Rutledge concluded, "There is every reason to believe that [regular hunting] is only a question of detail from now on." The details included the length of the hunting season, the number of deer taken per person, the fee for hunters from outside Arizona, and the number of deer that could be trapped and transported.[43]

R. H. Rutledge inspecting heavily browsed forage on the west side of the plateau in June 1929. Photo courtesy of Kaibab National Forest.

A prominent member of the 1929 survey was botanist and president of the University of Arizona Homer Shantz. Shantz had visited the Kaibab many times throughout the 1920s and added to the survey's expertise by enlisting a number of noted university faculty members in entomology, botany, and range ecology. Three professors—Charles T. Vorhies, J. J. Thornber, and W. G. McGinnies—participated in the survey. Along with a group of eight students, these men examined conditions on the Kaibab independently of the government men. The university president himself was acquainted not only with the Kaibab deer and the plateau, but also with many of the personnel working for the Forest Service, Biological Survey, and Park Service there. Shantz presented a summary to Governor Phillips with two tables, one containing data demonstrating conditions on a "Normal Range" and one with actual data on the "Present Range" as he observed it on the Kaibab. Shantz concluded that the deer should be reduced. In addition, he suggested that juniper, which deer had browsed up to a level out of their reach, should be cut down. Since juniper was of no great value for other purposes, he believed this action would bring foliage to the ground and provide temporary relief for the herd.[44]

By the end of August, the state and Forest Service drew up an agreement that officially allowed regular hunting on the Kaibab Plateau on Forest Service lands. Hunters would be regulated in accordance with state law, which allowed each hunter to kill two deer, "only one of which may be a buck." The season would run from October 1 through December 15. In addition to the state license, hunters would pay a fee of $1.50 to the Forest Service. The document concluded, "This agreement should go a long way toward finding a solution of this very difficult problem." Announcement of the special hunting season made the front page of a Forest Service *Bulletin* in Washington DC in early September.[45]

Additional hunting, although an apparent solution to the problem, did not satisfy Park Service officials. Killing large numbers of deer while transporting relatively few alive contradicted all of Stephen Mather's efforts over the previous decade. As director of the National Park Service, Mather had ceaselessly promoted the expansion of federal lands for tourism in an era when outdoor recreation grew even beyond the pace of his extraordinary efforts. The North Rim of Grand Canyon National Park was no exception to Mather's boosterism. He had helped to create the legacy of tourists passing through the meadows of the plateau on summer evenings and seeing hundreds of deer munching on grass, clover, and mushrooms. Mather had retired as National Park Service director due to failing health and died in his sleep on January 22, 1930. His replacement, Horace Albright, exhibited identical devotion to promoting wildlife spectacles on the North Rim. Preserving Mather's legacy would prove to be one of his successor's major activities, but it would not be easy, as Albright soon discovered.[46]

6

Scientific Expertise in the Midst of Controversy

The Biological Survey Challenged

"We have several problems relating to Grand Canyon National Park which can hardly be solved without information and advice from the Biological Survey," wrote Horace Albright in late 1929. Among his earliest actions as director of the National Park Service, Albright asked Biological Survey chief Paul Redington for help in establishing policies that would further protect the Kaibab deer as a tourist attraction in spite of Forest Service hunting. Like Stephen Mather and Park Superintendent M. R. Tillotson, the new director wanted to ensure that sufficient herds would be visible from the main road into the park. Albright requested reports and information that might shed additional light on the situation. Redington, however, was not about to choose sides in the ongoing controversy, nor did he want to get caught in the middle. He eventually provided reports both to Albright and to the Forest Service. The Biological Survey chief declined to make specific recommendations and wrote to Chief Forester R. Y. Stuart that "the Forest Service must be the judge of the degree by which the surplus should be reduced." Redington knew that hunting that fall for the first time had been quite successful—some 2,372 hunters entered the forest during the hunting season in 1929—but he was unprepared to have his agency serve as a mediator.[1] Indeed, Redington and the Biological Survey were more concerned about a related controversy over predatory animal control.

In late 1929 and into 1930, the debate over the use of poison for predatory animal control reached a fever pitch. Harold E. Anthony, curator of mammals at the American Museum of Natural History in New York, led the American Society of Mammalogists' Special Committee on Problems of Predatory Mammal Control. In his appointed society role, Anthony explained the concerns of certain mammalogists regarding poison use to the Biological Survey. This meant attempting to keep the peace with Redington and other Biological Survey officials, who quickly became defensive of their well-funded program. Anthony had to tone down the accusation of such individuals as society secretary A. Brazier Howell, a zoologist at Johns Hopkins University, who was not appointed to the special committee.

Howell worked tirelessly to keep the debate at the forefront of conservation concerns within the society, in the Biological Survey, and in the U.S. Congress. He wrote at least two letters per day to mammalogists across the country, government officials, and members of Congress. The society secretary organized petitions that were signed by notable biologists from major institutions and forwarded them to the national press and people in places of power.[2] His hope was that scientists could end the Biological Survey's poison campaign by illustrating the inefficiency of its administration. Federal funding for such an inefficient and ill-conceived program, Howell and others hoped, would soon be cut.

Redington regularly responded to Howell's complaints about the Biological Survey, typically calling for cooperation and insisting that a solution to the conflict would be based on ongoing study. Many mammalogists, including Anthony, Lee Dice in Michigan, and Joseph Dixon in Berkeley, agreed with Redington on these points and asked him to initiate "absolutely impartial" investigations of the poison program. Howell and others were dissatisfied with any studies that took place while poisoning continued. At one extreme, Howell wanted to halt poisoning until new research could be conducted. Poison destroyed scientific evidence of the role of predators. At the other extreme stood Edward Goldman, once again stating that even the current investigations were a waste of time. Goldman claimed that he and other experienced field biologists already knew that poison was the only way to control coyotes and other predators, which he considered purely destructive. Those who took the more moderate and cooperative line—such as Dixon and his colleague at Berkeley, Tracy Storer—were sometimes considered weak by their more vocal colleagues.[3]

At the 1930 annual meeting of the American Society of Mammalogists, discussion of the national predatory animal control program included several members of the ever-expanding circle of scientists familiar with research on the Kaibab. Although some participants would later recall this meeting as a turning point in scientific attitudes toward predators, it was more an opportunity to question the degree to which the Biological

Survey's policies were effective in protecting domestic livestock from wild enemies. Since the Kaibab situation was one of the few examples where questions of game protection and predation had even been raised, and since there was widespread familiarity with the case, it was used repeatedly in making a variety of points. The question of game was nevertheless overshadowed by livestock concerns, both among opponents and proponents of predatory animal control. Whatever its intended mission or later meaning, the meeting did serve as an important forum for discussion of the potential value of predators.[4]

Edward Goldman opened the meeting with a description of the coyote as the "archpredator." He contrasted the current situation in America with a time before the arrival of Europeans, when abundant large game animals provided food for large predatory animals. He again insisted that "balance" formerly existed. With the expansion of agriculture, that balance had been destroyed. In the absence of abundant game, large predatory animals depended upon valuable livestock for food. Coyotes in particular had proven extremely adaptable, both in expanding their range and in utilizing domestic food sources. These were liabilities to range managers and government biologists. Goldman concluded, "Civilized man has hopelessly overthrown the semblance of a balance that once existed, by transforming the landscape or creating other artificial conditions nearly everywhere; and the balance can never be reestablished." In the artificial world that humans had created, predatory animals would have to be controlled as completely as rodents. The Biological Survey veteran wrote, "No half-way measures will serve the purpose." Poison, while not the perfect means to achieving this end, was by far the cheapest and most efficient. Goldman's experience as a naturalist and poison "expert" suggested to him that the case could be considered closed. He believed further studies would be a waste of time and money, both of which could be better spent on actual control work. His work throughout the country convinced him that "it is inconceivable that any investigations could alter the decision as to the necessity for . . . extensive repression [of predatory animals]." This specific opposition to further investigations was perhaps the most troubling comment for most members of the American Society of Mammalogists, who may have agreed with Goldman's assessment of predators' destructiveness but hoped for a better understanding of the means to control that destructiveness.[5]

The Biological Survey program, according to its senior administrators, served the purpose of providing expert and carefully documented control of predatory animals through the use of poison. They argued that the program should thus be preferred to handing out poison to ranchers. W. C. Henderson, associate chief of the Biological Survey, spoke on the value of having well-paid and fully trained federal employees conducting the necessary poisoning, rather than leaving it to "indiscriminate" ranchers. Henderson, on behalf of Chief Redington, insisted that Goldman, Vernon Bailey, Edward Nelson, and A. K. Fisher had consistently shown through their extensive field studies that the benefits of the poison program far outweighed its handicaps. The associate chief described investigations that repeatedly suggested the danger predatory animals posed to livestock, spending considerable time citing Joseph Dixon's studies of "food predilections." Interestingly, Dixon had concluded that coyotes in particular ate more rodents than livestock or desirable game, and much of what he had found in the stomachs of coyotes suggested that scavenging provided as much to their diets as predation. Henderson, however, used Dixon's evidence to conclude that the Biological Survey poison program would continue to eliminate carnivores that ate domestic livestock.[6] The flexible meaning of this scientific evidence again illustrated the complex role of science within controversy. That complexity did not go unnoticed at this symposium.

At the conclusion of this presentation, an astonished E. Raymond Hall commented, "Mr. Henderson's paper contains so many mistakes that I know not where to begin." He listed a series of errors and misrepresentations, emphasizing that Dixon's study had been "far from agreeing" with the conclusions Henderson reached. As for the supposed superiority of having Biological Survey trappers handle control activities rather than indiscriminate ranchers, Hall related his own experience with a number of Biological Survey employees in Nevada and California. These workers executed their duties in a most inefficient and self-serving way, sometimes trapping furbearing animals for valuable pelts rather than concentrating on the predatory animal species to which they were assigned. Other times, they placed poison in areas where there were no sheep or cattle to protect. Hall argued that these wasteful practices so far had only drawn the attention of local critics, but such systematic departures from policy resulted from poor administration at the highest levels within the Biological Survey. The trappers were never censured, as the survey turned a blind eye to their activities.

More importantly, Hall called for a reduction in predatory animal control and an elimination of poison use "until the long hoped for laboratory studies by trained stomach-analysts and field studies by competent, impartial, vertebrate biologists shall have been made to determine where killing is required and in what amounts." These studies, he believed, would be forthcoming if the Biological Survey's ten-year funding proposal was approved by Congress and contained sufficient direction on how the money should be spent. He feared that virtually all of the appropriation would be spent on poison to serve livestock owners in the West. Investigations, rather than destruction, deserved funding for "the greatest good to the greatest number of people," Hall concluded. His implication that the Biological Survey catered to special interests was thinly veiled and not appreciated by Henderson and Goldman.[7] Hall and other mammalogists challenged the Biological Survey to continue its investigations of predatory animals rather than rely on past policy in administering its program in the future.

Charles C. Adams pressed the point about implementation of control versus studies of predatory animals. He noted that the subject had, over the previous five years, "produced much heat but a comparatively small amount of light." With hundreds of thousands of dollars spent on predatory animal destruction and only a few thousand dollars spent on "scientific studies," Adams believed it was time for the Biological Survey to get into the business of "rational predatory animal control." He made this point by repeatedly emphasizing that Biological Survey policies directed trappers toward "exterminating" predatory animals from every corner of the country. Even on the Kaibab, where Adams believed mountain lions might be left alone for scientific study, they had been killed without any clear knowledge of the extent to which they preyed upon deer. Adams purposely stopped short of calling for an end to all predatory animal control, but he received applause for his several jibes at what he considered to be irrational policies.[8]

In the discussion that followed, Adams reiterated his point that "intelligent control" should take the place of current policy. A. K. Fisher, however, defended the Biological Survey's policies by pointing out that there was no safe place anywhere in America to leave wolves or mountain lions. In fact, the Kaibab would be just such a place. University of Arizona professor Charles T. Vorhies spoke up in agreement—that the Grand Canyon area was well suited to mountain lions, that they currently did exist there, and that they could be kept there. He added that in light of the destruction done to the range in recent years and his own prediction that at the present rate the deer might not be sufficiently reduced for another twenty-five years, the Kaibab needed the mountain lions. Somewhat surprisingly, Goldman spoke up in agreement. He said, "On the Kaibab it is true that the mountain lions were probably reduced too far in the past." The Kaibab, he continued, was a place with "peculiar conditions," but he was not prepared to see his agency's policy changed based on this exceptional case.

This hotly contested debate illustrated the state of mind of many professional mammalogists who opposed widespread use of poison against predators. Poison was indiscriminate and wasteful of animal resources. Defenders of the Biological Survey's policies, however, claimed it was preferable to costly and ineffective trapping methods. Throughout these proceedings, the Kaibab case lingered in the background. Several people questioned what role predators might play in the proper management of the game preserve, but no one was particularly certain of the actual numbers of mountain lions or coyotes that had been killed there. There existed no record of poison being used on the Kaibab, so it seemed somewhat beside the point. Yet if poison use did end, the future of predator control and its consequent effects on livestock and game had to be considered. Goldman and Bailey, thinking specifically of the Kaibab, showed signs of a curious desire to see what would happen on such a game preserve. In order to resolve the larger issue of poisoning methods, however, the Biological Survey and Society of Mammalogists planned a national joint investigation.

Goldman and Bailey publicly defended the Biological Survey's poison program over the protests of mammalogists and before a Senate committee considering the bureau's ten-year funding plan. Privately, however, the two sometimes admitted that predatory animal control and poison use did cause concern in certain places. Outside his official capacity, Bailey told Hall that poison use should be limited. He said he hoped to end poison use even as he defended the Biological Survey's larger mission, which was an unusual position for a survey man. In a report of his experiences on the Kaibab, Bailey adopted a complicated stance on the poison issue. The Biological Survey would need to deal with predatory animals on a case-by-case basis. The Kaibab, of course, was a special case. In the report, he aimed to put past studies into a plan of game management. Bailey saw mountain lions and coyotes as a threat primarily to human control of the deer and habitat, not simply as a threat to the deer. He hoped to clarify the situation by presenting "only the simple facts." He recounted some of the information that was by then familiar to regular observers. He noted that the present herd of thirty thousand deer was too large for the preserve. This had led to the starvation of small and weak deer every winter. Heavy browsing during the summer months caused damage to young trees, which prevented reforestation and destroyed the future food supply for the deer. Finally, if these conditions were allowed to persist, the deer would destroy the range and themselves.[9]

Bailey's emerging concern was for management that placed humans in control of habitat, deer, and predatory animals. Allowing one of these factors to take a natural course would pose a threat to the entire preserve. The range and the deer might recover and further destruction of these resources would not occur "under present management and control through cooperation of the National Parks, the National Forest, the Biological Survey, and the Arizona Game Commission," he continued, emphasizing the strides that these agencies had made. Bailey praised recent developments, stating that "there is no danger to the deer herd and the most intelligent example of game management ever attempted in this country is being developed, founded on a full knowledge of habits, requirements, and animal psychology of these beautiful animals." Bailey's extension of this plan of management and control included monitoring the range to ensure that recovery could begin. He also hoped to introduce new plant species that could be utilized as food by the deer. In this way, they might "double the carrying power of the range." Bailey explicitly suggested a plan that resembled range management as applied to domestic livestock, where the grazing animals would be reduced to allow the range to recover, then gradually increased again to the maximum carrying capacity. He also suggested some adjustment of the boundary between park and forest to simplify administration of the preserve.[10]

At the same time that Bailey advocated a reduction in deer, he continued to support the elimination of mountain lions—the most serious enemies of the Kaibab deer. He recognized the relationship between deer and those species that preyed upon them, but he downplayed the significance of predatory animals in the rapid increase in deer numbers. This strengthened his argument for management and control of the deer. Bailey was particularly fearful that mountain lions—not humans—would kill the surplus deer without the opportunity for human control. This would lead to a loss of mastery of the deer, coupled with a more serious loss of dominion over livestock herds. He warned that allowing mountain lions to increase might lead to "a lot of lions left over to make trouble for the live stock of surrounding areas." It seemed senseless to him, after all these years of predatory animal control, to begin a new policy of letting those animals increase. Allowing mountain lions to increase opposed human control and management of the preserve. He rhetorically asked: "But why raise these great cats that no one ever sees to go out at night and kill, tear to pieces and devour the gentlest, most timid and beautiful animals of the game refuge and National Park? If we have not sufficient intelligence to protect and control our native wild life we had better give up national parks, national forests, and game refuges and raise only Old World forms of domestic stock, handed on to us by our ancestors."[11] Bailey saw game management as a good way to promote successful hunting and perhaps more importantly as a good way to control all the major mammal species of an area, not just the tame deer.

THE NATIONAL PARK SERVICE PLANS A TAKEOVER

Evidence emerged slowly that the Park Service, in early 1930, was mounting a serious campaign to have its boundary on the Kaibab Plateau extended north to include VT Park. A rumor of the proposed change in administration appeared in a news brief published in Arizona. The newspaper stated that the change would be "nothing to get excited about." Both the Forest Service and the Park Service were referred to as equally troublesome federal agencies, but the news brief concluded with a comment that favored a change. Park Service policies prohibited slaughter of wildlife and attracted tourists, or as the article described it: "This much can be said for the park service: They have controlled adjoining areas in the Kaibab to the forest service lands. And the park service has never yet found it necessary to conserve the forest or the deer by staging an annual slaughter of the animals. They feed 'em and draw tens of thousands of dollars of tourist money into Arizona."[12]

No one was sure of the source of this information, and not everyone was prepared to applaud the change.[13] On May 16, 1930, A. E. Demaray wrote on behalf of the Park Service to Senator Henry F. Ashurst of Arizona regarding the proposed boundary extension to clarify rumors and protests that had already reached the senator. The assistant parks director explained that there was "a movement on foot" to extend the park both on the north and the south sides of the canyon. Because the Park Service faced accusations of making a power grab, Demaray explained from the outset that his agency was merely responding to scientific studies. He wrote, "The desirability and necessity for this extension is based almost wholly on biological reasons." His information came from studies conducted jointly by the Biological Survey, Forest Service, Park Service, and the Carnegie Institution. Demaray assured Ashurst that there was no reason to worry about current protests, since there would be an opportunity for any state or local group to present their views before action was taken.[14]

At the same time, Demaray sent a similar letter to Edmund Seymour, a national conservation leader and president of the American Bison Society. Seymour was planning a trip to the Kaibab to investigate the establishment of a game refuge in nearby House Rock Valley, where bison still grazed twenty years after Buffalo Jones gave up his attempt to create a hybrid domestic herd. Demaray hoped to bring Seymour up to date on Park Service goals for the plateau. The assistant director explained that Vernon Bailey's recent studies of the area had called for an extension of park boundaries. Demaray included a map, on which the hoped-for extensions had already been drawn. He noted that this was a "tentative proposition and not one agreed upon by the various Federal agencies involved," so Seymour would have to keep both the enclosed copy of Bailey's report and the map confidential. In fact, no one at the Forest Service had heard anything about the boundary change. Park Service officials justified these plans on the conviction that they could improve conditions on the plateau and make the area even more attractive to visitors. Demaray plainly stated that "it would not be the intention of the Park Service to interfere in the proper regulation of the Kaibab deer herds and would have no objection to the hunting of the deer in that area," if conditions continued to warrant hunting. However, he hoped that by planting additional forage and increasing deer transportation to other areas, the situation might be "bettered." For closer examination of these issues, Demaray expected Seymour to meet with Park Superintendent Tillotson in Arizona. When the Forest Service and Arizona officials learned of Seymour's visit, they made other plans.[15]

When Seymour reached Flagstaff a few weeks later, he was met by the chair of the new State Game Commission, Tom E. McCullough, and Game Warden R. Lee Bayless. The state officials had wired Forest Supervisor Walter Mann, asking him to meet them at VT Park and telling him that "Tillotson could have Mr. Seymour after we got through with him." The four men spent an entire day together driving around the various ranges of the Kaibab. Although McCullough had not previously visited the plateau himself, he put great energy into explaining the "serious condition of the winter range." At the end of the day, Seymour sat down with the local officials and shared the letter and the map from Demaray. He apparently did this, at least initially, without thinking that details of the Park Service's plans were for his eyes only. Mann inferred that the plans were intended to be kept from the Forest Service, and it must have occurred to Seymour too, since Mann later complained that he had not been allowed to take notes on the details of the plans. Mann nevertheless committed most of the contents of the letter and map to memory. Mann, McCullough, and Bayless provided greater detail of official Forest Service and state policies for Seymour's benefit. They explained how their own agency had come a long way toward proper management of the deer and range in recent years. The Park Service, they argued, deserved little credit for improvements. They refuted allegations and omissions in Demaray's letter, point for point. In the end, Seymour's allegiance had shifted. He confided to Mann that the deer herd should remain under Forest Service control, since he had the impression now that only the Forest Service was capable of proper management. Seymour promised to talk to Albright about dropping the proposed extensions. After the meeting, Mann reconstructed the plans laid out in Demaray's letter and sketched the approximate boundary extensions indicated on the map. He promptly sent these to the regional forester, explaining how their agency had not even received mention in Demaray's discussion of ongoing need for improvements in deer management. The regional forester in turn immediately forwarded Mann's documents to the chief forester in Washington.[16]

Two weeks later, Chief Forester Stuart and Parks Director Albright met face to face in Arizona—on the Kaibab—to examine conditions firsthand and discuss the boundary issue. Albright wrote a memo from Grand Canyon Village relating details of this meeting and indicating that both he and Tillotson would prepare full reports of the trip with Stuart. They would lay out plans for cooperation between the Park Service and Forest Service. These reports, if they were ever written, never made it into the files.[17]

Any boundary changes would have a significant impact on tourism in the area. For this reason, Stuart reported on their discussions to a Union Pacific Railroad agent, who was especially concerned that continued hunting would diminish the herd to a point where they would have to stop advertising it as a tourist attraction along their passenger line. Stuart wrote that the future of tourism was an important concern and that the Forest Service and Park Service would cooperate to ensure sound

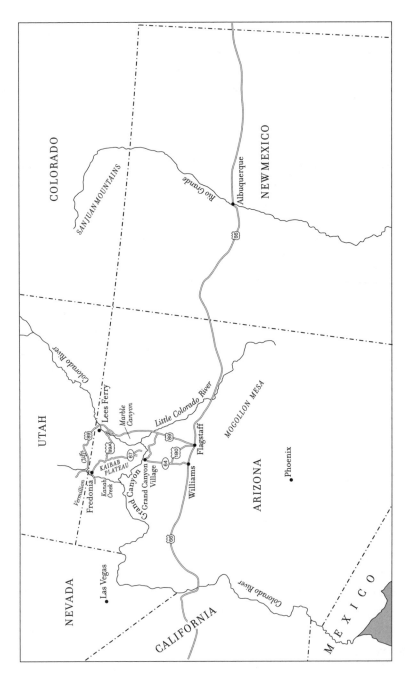

Locations on the Kaibab Plateau

decisions. Cooperation would begin with the assignment of park ranger James P. Brooks and Walter Mann "making periodic observations and studies, including counts of deer and a close check on the range." The tourism industry generally looked to the Park Service to maintain the attraction of the Kaibab, while the Forest Service, the state game department, and the Arizona Game Protective Association were promoting hunting. Compared with tourism at large, hunting brought fewer visitors, but did make more room for livestock grazing and did bring in revenue from licenses.[18]

Edmund Seymour made good on his promise to defend the Forest Service in a letter to Albright, observing that the "Kaibab Forest should be handled by one head as a whole proposition." Seymour was convinced that the Forest Service working with the state of Arizona had already proven to be the most harmonious means of administration, and it worked "to the best advantage of everybody concerned." After his experience with the Forest Service men on the Kaibab, Seymour seemed prepared to give them complete control, especially if they could continue to work cooperatively. The Park Service proposals for boundary extensions threatened that harmony. "I should be sorry to have this status disturbed," he wrote, "much as I admire the management of the Park Department, in praise of which too much can not be said, but as long as the Kaibab Forest is opened to tourist visitors and especially the VT Valley, which is the summer range of the deer and where no hunting is permitted, it seems to me the Park Department is getting about all that matters on the North side." The Park Service would be better off just letting the other agencies take over completely, with the assurance that tourists could continue to visit the relatively tame deer in the meadows on top of the plateau.[19]

Public perceptions of the situation, often fueled by Park Service rhetoric, made implementing cooperative efforts difficult, to say the least. Albright and Tillotson often made matters worse by continuing to hint at the need for boundary extensions and leaving room for interpretation in their public statements. The Forest Service, on the other hand, made significant strides in establishing its authority over the deer through a series of systematic studies.[20]

ANNUAL WINTER COUNTS

Forest Supervisor Walter Mann initiated an effort to "count and estimate" the deer in February 1930. He enlisted the help of Karl Pierson from the

Arizona Game and Fish Department and brought fellow foresters Robert H. Park and Q. David Hansen along to assist. The four men spent ten days traveling around the plateau on the winter range, counting what deer they could find and noting the number of deer tracks in the snow. Experience as foresters made this work familiar. They were comfortable "cruising" the terrain, making estimates of timber and acreage. The ability to calculate the amount of lumber in a forest without measuring every tree contributed to the sense that they could estimate the population of deer without counting every animal.

They began on the east side. After seeing seventy-five deer, and considering that severe weather had driven the deer into steep ravines over a wide area, they concluded there were approximately five thousand head on the east winter range. On the west side, Mann and his colleagues drove to Sowats Point, where again wind and snow "caused the deer to hold up down in the deep hollows and in the thick cedars." In this weather, they supposed fewer deer could be seen, whatever the actual numbers. They tried to startle some deer into view. When Mann stopped along the road, "the men got out of the car, went to the edge of the canyon nearby, watched and hallowed [sic], and at each stop would jump out a bunch of deer." They attempted to compare deer numbers from one area to another and estimate the number of deer seen with the total number believed to be present. They used percentages, like timber cruisers estimating lumber. Judging also from the tracks and browse conditions, Mann concluded that the deer were as numerous in the Sowats area as in the Slide and Jumpup areas. In the latter sections, the men figured they counted nearly 10 percent of the deer. From these comparisons and estimates, they concluded that there must be twenty-five thousand deer on the west side. New growth on the browse plants appeared to be 100 percent eaten. Under these conditions, a mild spring might still prevent serious damage since the deer could move quickly off of the rapidly diminishing winter range. The forest supervisor made plans to repeat the winter count every year.[21]

In anticipation of ongoing research on the Kaibab National Forest, Mann prepared a new plan for the Kaibab. One of his first initiatives was the need to make a determination of the "influence of deer grazing on the vegetative cover" through systematic measurement of plants on various plots and quadrats. In order to address the quantification of carrying capacity, observations would be recorded to determine which key plants could serve as indicators of carrying capacity. The forest supervisor recognized that each species could be utilized to a different degree by deer, and researchers would need to ascertain the "proper degree" for each important species. They would have to compare the palatability of plants during different seasons, recognizing the changing importance of different plants at different times of the year. They would consider the importance of mushrooms and grass in nonforested areas. Studies of the present carrying capacity would be compared with estimates of the "normal carrying capacity after recovery of the range." In this statement, Mann hoped that carrying capacity could be altered and increased with improvements in management. Research would have to compare the food needs of deer with those of sheep and cattle. Mann outlined his plan to determine the annual increase as well as the causes of losses to the herds. Losses would likely be due to disease, predatory animals, starvation, and hunting. The relationship between predatory animals and game in particular deserved further study, as predators might hold value for human interest and might even be used in limiting the deer population.[22]

Mann returned for a similar survey for six days in May with a committee consisting of Homer L. Shantz, president of the University of Arizona, W. G. McGinnies, professor of range ecology, Arizona Game Warden R. Lee Bayless, and forester M. E. Musgrave. On the east side, they noted slow recovery of the vegetation, but cautioned that a dry year "would result in great permanent damage." On the west side, they reported that the range was producing one-tenth of "the normal amount of browse." Again, favorable growing conditions had maintained the deer, but a dry year would "almost destroy all the palatable browse within reach of the deer." This led the committee to conclude: "A further reduction in the breeding herd must be made at once, if the winter range is to be brought back and maintained at its normal capacity." On a positive note, the committee observed that weather conditions had kept the deer on the summer range longer than usual the previous year, and an early storm had forced them onto the winter range soon thereafter. This short tenure on the intermediate range along the sides of the plateau in the fall had allowed some recovery there. Overall, however, the range could now support only a fraction of what it could have maintained "with proper management." The committee blamed the situation on the "misguided public sentiment" that had determined the course of management in previous years. As evidence of this misguided management and, in addition to the damaged range, dead deer were found in the open areas and in greater numbers near water holes. This suggested that the deer found insufficient food especially where they congregated near water. Based on this report, the state planned to allow hunters to take as many as three deer (one buck and two does), rather than the two deer allowed the previous year.[23]

Walter Mann was particularly proud of these recent efforts to identify the conditions of the deer and the preserve with cooperative assistance from the state. He wrote to a Michigan game official, describing the plan: "The State Game Department of Arizona now has a good game code with which to work and the Forest Service and the Game Department are in close cooperation in all phases of game management. And public opinion generally, all over the country, has changed and now is beginning to understand that real *management* must be applied to a deer herd and not *protection* only." The plans being laid in 1930, the forest supervisor hoped, would allow more effective reduction of the deer than trapping and transporting deer, and it was more acceptable than killing by salaried government hunters.[24]

As Mann continued to explain for various correspondents the Forest Service's management plan, he became increasingly explicit about the difference between human, rational management and uncontrolled events that amounted to nature taking its course. He clearly preferred the former approach. Managing a deer herd was, for Mann, similar to managing a cattle herd, a suggestion that was new to the public at large. The idea had led to a change in public opinion, and he added that "game *management* has become the ideal in various states, and attempts are being made to maintain a balance between the forage available and the numbers of deer. If nature is left alone it will maintain a balance." That balance, according to Mann, could be "a ruthless thing" since increases in deer would be followed by increases in mountain lions and coyotes, leading to a loss of deer and consequent drops in predator populations. These swings would take place every several years. Mann noted that public demands on the deer as a tourist attraction and for sport made such uneven swings unacceptable. With this in mind, he reported that officials of the Forest Service and Arizona Game and Fish Department believed that "man's management of deer can improve on the balance of nature and keep an even number which will be a tourist attraction and at the same time prevent economical waste of materials of food value." The forest supervisor concluded that the factors preventing such management in the past were largely the result of public opinion based on ignorance of these principles and enforced by well-meaning officials.[25]

Mann's duties as forest supervisor increasingly included efforts directed at improving public relations. He took this work seriously and responded conscientiously to inquiries from across the country, from private citizens, public officials, academic scientists, and members of conservation organizations. The best way to respond to these requests for information, he believed, was by compiling and providing as much data as possible related to the number of deer and conditions on the range. Mann also provided this information to his superiors within the Forest Service on a regular basis. A five-day survey of the range in August with park ranger James P. Brooks, Hugh Anderson from the state game department, and foresters Robert H. Park and W. W. Blakeslee resulted in a memorandum on the growth of forage plants on seventeen of the established study plots. Many of these plots included both fenced and open areas. All open plots had tagged plants that were measured for direct comparison in subsequent years. Some could be compared to data collected as early as 1926, although most plots were established after 1928. Mann noted that growth in the fenced plots did not far exceed growth in open areas, leading him to suggest a significant point: "Looks like it [a plant] needs a little browsing to stimulate growth." This suggestion led to an expansion of studies that included systematic clipping of browse plants in order to test the hypothesis.[26]

Mann also favored cooperative work with the state game department and the more recent contributions of Ranger Brooks. He reported on the immediate success of this work to Edmund Seymour, who had forced the issue of cooperative administration by exposing Park Service plans. Mann wrote, "I believe this present arrangement will iron out any differences of opinion between the two departments and I hope that harmony may exist among all those who have an interest in the management of Kaibab deer. It is a big problem and the first principle is to keep as big a herd of deer as possible as a tourist attraction, but the number of deer that can be maintained in VT Valley depends upon forage conditions back in the woods."[27] So while disagreement over the deer continued, mostly as a result of conflicting goals and differing personal perceptions of conditions, Mann's information began to serve as a relatively consistent point of reference.

Ecologist D. I. Rasmussen

The many calls for additional study on the Kaibab had not escaped the notice of academic scientists like Joseph Grinnell and Victor Shelford.

Shelford was at the peak of his career as a researcher and a teacher. Shelford advised several graduate students simultaneously during this period, urging them to take on studies of biotic communities throughout North America. In some cases, students did their research near their hometowns. Shelford valued the familiarity students would have with the local areas and saw it as a practical means to have his students spread out across the continent.[28]

Shelford and his doctoral student, D. Irvin Rasmussen, visited the Kaibab together in 1929, and Rasmussen conducted the bulk of his dissertation research there during the following two years. Rasmussen grew up in Mount Pleasant, Utah, about two hundred miles north of the Kaibab Plateau. He had attended Brigham Young University, earning a Bachelor of Science degree in zoology in 1928, and went on to complete his Master of Science degree in zoology and ecology at Illinois in 1930. In addition to this academic training, Rasmussen was an experienced naturalist, noted for his ability to locate cryptic wildlife in fading light. He could scan a patch of forest without looking for anything in particular, which would lead him to pick out patches of color or texture that seemed out of place. In those patches, he would then concentrate his gaze to see a quail standing in the shadows or a deer resting among pine needles. Rasmussen's doctoral project fit the Forest Service's needs at the time, and he served as a "forest guard" during the summers. Officials in Washington had asked the regional forester to assign a trained biologist to continue and extend studies on vegetation and carrying capacity initiated by local foresters. Rasmussen never formally served in such a position, but he did interact regularly with foresters and other local officials during his three-year tenure there.[29]

Rasmussen first reported on his dissertation research during the summer of 1930. During that year the deer appeared to be in better condition and seemed just as numerous as the previous year. He speculated that this improvement might have exerted a further cost on the vegetation. In June, deer numbers appeared consistent with previous observations, as large groups could be seen in the evenings at VT Park. The graduate student paid careful attention to the food eaten by those deer in the meadows, noting the preference for small mountain clover early in the summer and mushroom tops after long periods of rain. Notable changes in vegetation included the most desirable plants being "severely damaged." While in a few areas deer browsed relatively lightly, the general trend showed damage almost everywhere. Rasmussen wrote, "An examination of practically the whole top of Kaibab plateau shows the overgrazing by deer." Despite the ample rainfall of the past two summers, continuing damage to the plateau's vegetation left the range unable to recover even with favorable weather.[30]

As deer conditions improved, one result would prove especially ironic: healthier does reared more fawns. This could again lead to an increasing deer population. To check this increase, Rasmussen noted that coyotes sometimes threatened the fawns, but few actual kills could be verified. Mountain lions killed only two deer that year, according to his observations. While the lions were once considered the "worst enemies of deer," this was no longer the case since evidence of mountain lion activity was rare on the plateau. Coyotes were seldom seen. Highlighting the difficulty of matching observations with the actual situation within the preserve, Rasmussen had heard reliable accounts of coyotes killing "full grown healthy deer as well as fawns." Although apparently uncertain about the role of such predatory animals, Rasmussen mentioned them prominently in his brief report, and he would draw deeper conclusions about predators in later work.

Carrying Capacity

As Rasmussen continued his research, Aldo Leopold, who had worked for the Forest Service in New Mexico and was in the midst of preparing a report on game conditions in the Upper Midwest, looked at the ongoing studies on the Kaibab as a source of important information. Leopold was looking for a way of determining game conditions across different habitats. He wrote to E. Raymond Hall asking about water requirements of deer on the Kaibab. Leopold proposed that water use might be used in a scheme of classifying deer conditions. S. B. Locke, who also reviewed some of Leopold's information on the Kaibab, examined game management ideas at a symposium on range ecology sponsored by the Ecological Society of America. Locke referred specifically to the research underway on the Kaibab Plateau. His training in forestry, like Leopold's, influenced his thinking about game management. He noted the importance of understanding the relationship between game and its available food. This relationship could be expressed in terms of the carrying capacity of the range. This was particularly useful in areas where managers encountered difficulty counting the game directly. Locke wrote that "a careful study of the intensity of use on an area where numbers may readily be ascertained, gives information which may serve as a possible index of the game population on other areas where more reliable census information is lacking or difficult to obtain."[31]

The next year, Locke admitted that the idea of "wild life" management did not have the same familiar ring as "game laws or fish and game protection." As Mann had indicated previously, Locke noted that those ideas had failed—and specifically on the Kaibab they had failed miserably—because federal and state game administrators did not take actions they feared would be unpopular with the public. With administration of the preserve stabilized for the moment, the Kaibab could begin to serve as the outstanding example of how research was beginning to make a difference for management elsewhere. Locke went so far as to insist that Forest Service and Biological Survey officials fully understood the true conditions of the Kaibab early on, but they had been unable to take appropriate actions due to political pressure.[32]

Around this time, the term "carrying capacity" began to appear with greater regularity in management plans and official correspondence related to administration of the preserve. No widely accepted definition of this term existed, either among range managers or ecologists, and applications in game management were particularly imprecise. Forest Service and National Park Service officials increasingly used the term, but in ways that uniquely justified their respective management goals. For instance, the Forest Service continued to promote hunting on the grounds that deer still exceeded the carrying capacity of the range, despite criticism from certain sectors of the public where killing deer was considered immoral, cruel, or wasteful.[33] The National Park Service expected that the plateau, filled to its carrying capacity with deer, would provide a tremendous natural display for tourists. Discussion of carrying capacity did not necessarily coincide with an increased understanding of the actual number of deer on the plateau, their condition, or the number of deer that could be fed by existing vegetation. As more people became aware of the need to manage the deer in accordance with the carrying capacity, scientists became less sure of just what that meant. In response, officials from all agencies recommended more studies using new methods and materials in an attempt to generate solid data.

MR. TILLOTSON'S ADMISSIONS

As the differing goals of the Park Service, Forest Service, state game department, and the various constituencies of these agencies became explicit, each side believed that its position could be legitimated by scientific data. Agencies made the standoff more complex by keeping their separate goals secret in order to avoid criticism from the others and the public at large. This left ample space for speculation, which often led to accusations. The Forest Service feared the Park Service would make a land grab, while the Park Service suspected that the Forest Service hoped to remove deer in order to increase the federal lands available for domestic grazing. With grains of truth supporting suspicions on both sides, accusations became uncomfortably common.

Beneath these clouds of controversy, the Forest Service was best positioned to conduct further studies on the preserve. With a broader administrative mandate, larger technical staff, and a growing core of annual data for comparison, Forest Supervisor Walter Mann achieved increasing authority for Forest Service policies. Meanwhile, the Park Service enjoyed a greater role in increasing public knowledge of the deer herd. Park Supervisor M. R. Tillotson used Grand Canyon National Park's great national visibility to highlight the plight of park wildlife.

During the fall 1930 hunt, 2,074 hunters killed 5,033 deer on the Kaibab National Forest. Two-thirds of the hunters came from Arizona, and the majority of the rest came from California. This was by far the largest single-year kill on the Kaibab. In addition to the hunt, efforts to trap and transport deer had begun to show promise. Forest Service employees captured bucks, does, and fawns with very low mortality by trapping them in areas where they congregated regularly—they had abandoned attempts to capture individual deer in oversized box traps. In October and November they trapped sixty-six deer, including twelve bucks, thirty-five does, and nineteen fawns. Of these, the Arizona Game and Fish Department shipped sixty-one deer to sites around the state. Walter Mann also supervised a report on a new Forest Service program that offered permits to individuals interested in trapping fawns for delivery to private parks across the country. Of 371 fawns caught, 130 were delivered; the balance of the deer were held for later delivery.[34]

In the midst of the hunting season, M. R. Tillotson had visited Tucson. While there, he agreed to an interview with the *Tucson Daily Citizen*. In the resulting article, Tillotson was quoted as accusing the Forest Service of conspiring with ranchers in northern Arizona to reduce the deer on the Kaibab in order to open up more opportunities to graze cattle on forestlands. A similar article in the *Arizona Daily Star* quoted Tillotson as saying that deer hunting was a "scheme" designed to open up "the fine grazing range" on the Kaibab. With "plenty of water" and vegetation "always in fine shape," thinning out the deer might lead someone to see the range merely as government land on which to run their cattle. The *Daily Citizen*

published an editorial the next week that used Tillotson's claims to condemn the Forest Service and others who seemed to use the "scripture of
conservation" as a means to the greedy ends of cattlemen.[35]

Local Forest Service officials were outraged by Tillotson's reported
accusations. Chief Forester R. Y. Stuart in Washington DC received a letter from a forester on the Kaibab who wondered whether Tillotson had
evidence to support his statements. Stuart immediately forwarded the
letter across town to Park Service Director Horace Albright, with a request for clarification. Albright responded to Stuart before even checking out the situation with Tillotson. Albright assured Stuart that Tillotson
would never intentionally reflect negatively on the Forest Service, since
the superintendent was himself "an old Forest Service man."[36]

By the end of December, Tillotson finally explained that he had simply been misquoted. The newspaper reporter had taken the park
superintendent's explanation of state hunting regulations in an entirely
unrelated matter as the policy of the Park Service on the Kaibab.[37] The
park superintendent had recognized the misquoting immediately, but
had hesitated to correct it for fear that denial would have stirred up more
confusion. The *Daily Citizen* had published a retraction of sorts only a few
days after the editorial appeared, clarifying that Tillotson had previously
gone on record himself in favor of reducing the deer. That correction,
however, had come too late to stop the runaway accusations and
counteraccusations that began when local foresters saw the original article. Tillotson explained later that he was especially reluctant to make
more of the comments when they first appeared because he had just met
with state game officials, and they were closer than ever to an agreement.
He asked that Albright apologize to Stuart for the misunderstanding,
"even though I did nothing wrong."[38]

Albright's apology to Stuart rectified the situation for the moment.
They exchanged appreciative words and concluded that cooperative efforts were at an all-time high. Stuart then forwarded Tillotson's explanation to the local foresters, who had initiated the complaint. The exercise
took over a month and clearly demonstrated that while good will and cooperation may have been foremost in the minds of the leaders of federal
agencies, local officials who worked only miles from one another would
not even ask for clarification on public statements of their differing positions.

Disagreements shifted along the spectrum from the local to the national level, stabilized on one end by cooperative local fieldwork and on

the other end by national political agendas, only to be upset by misunderstandings as it crossed between these contexts. This skirmish over
Tillotson's comments in the local newspapers might have been smoothed
over if news of the articles had remained within the local context. At the
same time, the episode was more easily sanitized at the national level
because his comments about the greed of ranchers who only wanted deer
off their rangelands did not resonate with Washington bureaucrats. State
game officials and local foresters, however, felt the wrath of the ranchers
acutely. These included individuals who had worked together with ranchers for years, preparing grazing permits and discussing range conditions.
Arizona game commissioners were also under tremendous pressure from
the recently reelected Governor Hunt, who wanted to make more deer
available both for tourists and hunters. In fact, the on-again, off-again
governor hoped to reverse the efforts of Governor John Phillips, who had
succeeded and preceded him. Hunt wanted to dissolve the state game
commission and appoint a warden.

Forest Service Studies

Local, state, and federal agendas could not be disentangled, and to his
credit, Walter Mann pressed on with his work. As February approached,
the forest supervisor prepared for upcoming visits of state and federal
officials to the ranges of the Kaibab. Although he feared that unfavorable
weather conditions might force a change in plans, the objectives of the
trip were clear. He and his invited team would count deer, observe their
concentration and losses that winter, examine the amount of food available, and record the stomach contents of dead deer. They would count the
number of cattle and "watch for instances where it is plain that feeding
habits are in competition with deer." The first trip that winter would last
about twelve days and take observers to several points around the plateau
within the winter range. Mann wrote plainly: "What we want on this trip
is facts. The Forest Service has no preconceived ideas that we want to
prove; we want to know the actual conditions as they exist today and the
best methods of meeting those conditions."[39]

An inspection party traveled around the winter deer ranges from February 20 through March 1, 1931. It consisted of Mann and Robert Park
from the Forest Service, James P. Brooks and Art Brown from Park Service, K. C. Kartchner and W. D. Judd from the Arizona Game and Fish
Department, and D. I. Rasmussen, who had just returned to the Kaibab
after two months with Victor Shelford at the marine station in Friday

Harbor, Washington. The group used horses to cover the rough range on the west side of the plateau. On the east side, they used cars and stayed near the roadways. Much of the snow had already melted and the deer were scattered on the intermediate range, making it difficult to get a good count. Mann tallied the number of deer seen by all members of the party and found the total to be 2,752. From this, he estimated there were thirty thousand deer on the plateau. Other members of the party reached different conclusions due to what Mann described as "differences of opinion in the party as to what percentage we could actually count." Kartchner estimated there were twenty-five thousand deer and Brooks thought twenty thousand. Junior members of the party did not publish separate estimates.[40]

Mann suggested that the present herd was about one-fourth of its 1924 size, when he estimated that there were over one hundred thousand deer. He saw little evidence of predatory animal kills and no sign of coyotes on the east side. He noted again the trend for better condition of both vegetation and deer on the east side, but actually saw very few deer. This led him to conclude, "Because of the deer being widely scattered here the estimate of numbers is just a guess with very little facts for the guess." Most notable, Mann stated repeatedly, was the relatively large number of cattle on the west side and the complete lack of grass there.[41]

A day after completing this inspection trip, Mann, Park, Brooks, and Brown set out with Ed Laws, a park ranger, on another trip. They made this trip entirely on horseback and covered especially the southwest part of the range, including Dry Park, Indian Hollow, Big Saddle, and Swamp Point. They saw few cattle and even fewer deer, but grass had been grazed heavily and widely trampled—signs of heavy cattle use. During this time of year, Mann traveled around the plateau almost constantly. He seemed determined to gather as much evidence of the conditions on different parts of the range as possible. He quantified this evidence in the form of tables emphasizing the numerical content of his data, but descriptions of his rides showed how little he actually saw of the deer, cattle, predators, and vegetation. Mann's reports contained more numerical data each year, which aided in quantifying comparisons. At the same time, his discussions of the numbers revealed that in many ways his uncertainty remained the same.[42]

Mann's objectives for these visits demonstrated his particular insistence on repeatedly observing conditions on the Kaibab in hope of finding new answers to questions that some had abandoned and others thought had already been answered. S. B. Locke, who collaborated with

Mann on a comprehensive history of the deer situation, was one who felt many questions had long since been settled. Locke believed that it was time for the public to acknowledge the plight of the deer and to accept the reality that deer would either be hunted or starve. Recent Forest Service plans on the Kaibab, including the previous year's hunt that removed over five thousand deer, demonstrated the promise of wildlife management. Locke argued that more discussion would not solve ongoing problems. The question that required more study, he suggested, was the relationship between game and livestock on the range, and opportunities to search for answers expanded as cooperation increased.[43]

On the local level, at least, signs of cooperation between the Forest and Park Services made Mann very optimistic. James Brooks, chief ranger in the Grand Canyon National Park, wrote to Tillotson describing a recent inspection where Brooks and an assistant ranger joined Mann and Kartchner for about ten days. They agreed on most matters, according to Brooks, who also listed the points where his own opinion seemed in conflict with that of the foresters and state game warden. For example, rather than the dramatic killing seen in 1930, he suggested that future reductions of the herd be very gradual, allowing hunters to take only one deer each year. He reported to Tillotson, "I gave as my opinion that another year or so of intensive hunting would reduce the herd to a state where there would not be any large bands of deer on the summer range."[44]

Brooks also raised the issues of predatory animals and livestock grazing, noting that opinions differed most markedly on these points. Predatory animals, according to Brooks, would always cause losses on game ranges, but these would offset winter starvation. With regard to livestock, the Kaibab ranges were not suited for domestic grazing since they were naturally short on grasses and grazing vegetation. He concluded, "I consider the Kaibab as a whole more adapted to a browsing range for deer than a grazing range for domestic stock." His comments fit the larger Park Service plan for leaving predatory animals in place and removing virtually all livestock from the preserve. These goals could not be accomplished, however, without the Forest Service's full agreement.

While Brooks perceived differences of opinion between himself and his colleagues in the Forest Service and state game department, he reported that a "fine cooperative spirit" existed among the men. That spirit may have resulted from the pleasant setting of their common experience. Points of disagreement that were amplified during the day became muted around an evening campfire, below the snow-covered plateau.

Just as Tillotson's statements in the popular press had created a controversy by alerting the Forest Service to the question of sharing resources between deer and cattle, so too did studies of the deer question by Mann and others increasingly focus on the proper balance between wildlife and livestock interests. The predator question faded into the background, as indeed it seemed that the predators themselves were gone. On the face of things, then, the Forest Service might have concerned itself mostly with grazing permits, as it had twenty years earlier. The controversy over protecting wildlife, including deer and predators, remained very near the surface, particularly where Park Service interests were concerned. For both questions, the Kaibab remained the central example for all interested parties, particularly since everyone could make their separate (and sometimes conflicting) cases based on some evidence gathered there in the previous decade.

7

Big Game Management Plans on the Kaibab

At the end of January 1931, Assistant Forester Chris Rachford initiated plans for an investigation of the Kaibab that would resemble the 1924 Investigating Committee. He wrote to Regional Forester R. H. Rutledge stating, "I feel sure a committee composed of such representative men as we could secure from the different interested organizations would aid administration, clarify the present situation, and create an enlightened public sentiment." Rachford wanted to know when the trip should take place and who should be included. H e attached a diverse list of organizations that might be represented, which included the Forest Service, the Park Service, the Biological Survey, the American Game Protective Association, the Audubon Society, the Camp Fire Club of America, the American Bison Society, the Izaak Walton League, the Arizona Game and Fish Commission, and the University of Arizona. The direct involvement of conservation groups like the American Game Protective Association and the Izaak Walton League increased the public visibility of the committee, especially because they reported on its progress in their popular nature magazines.[1] This list evolved over the next few months as more groups insisted on being included and others found they could not afford the expense of sending a representative.

Rachford also compiled a massive set of documents and official correspondence relating to the history of the Kaibab deer. This collection quickly became the standard source of information on the efforts to protect the deer, although it provided a fairly one-sided account that mostly favored the Forest Service's activities. The assistant forester did not attempt to cast a shadow over the Park Service or the state of Arizona, but he was selective in including those materials that illustrated his own agency's most successful work. The reason later accounts of the Kaibab deer referred explicitly to the many warnings of local foresters resulted from documents Rachford assembled in his report.[2]

Whatever the historical failings of Rachford's collection, it served a very important need at the time. Demands for information on the deer continued to arrive from around the country, and the Forest Service responded by offering Rachford's collection. For example, Karl T. Frederick used those documents, combined with his own observations to write a summary of the Kaibab situation for the Camp Fire Club. Frederick concluded that the deer herd should be reduced by killing eight thousand to ten thousand deer. In addition, he advised that all the cattle and sheep be removed from the plateau. This would allow the administrators of the preserve to "start over again" with their attempts to protect the deer. When he learned of the proposed summer investigation, Frederick hoped that he could represent the Camp Fire Club himself.[3]

Another request for information came from Edmund Seymour, president of the American Bison Society. Seymour continued to hope that the herd of bison in House Rock Valley, adjacent to the Kaibab Plateau, might benefit from further improvements in management on the deer preserve. When the Bison Society appeared on the initial list of potential participants for the summer investigation of the Kaibab, Seymour asked the question on everyone's mind, "[H]ow many deer can subsist there?" He believed that the maximum number, whatever it was, should be the number maintained. A month later Seymour refined his question and asked, "[F]irst, how many deer are there in the Kaibab Forest? Second, how many deer will the Kaibab Forest support in an average season?" In this way, he went from suggesting a maximum number of deer to asking first about the number of deer, then acknowledging that this number might be too high or too low at present. This less certain stance was a step away from the position of those who hoped a final investigation would lead to decisive management guidelines.[4]

On April 2, 1931, the Forest Service compiled a list of organizations that it expected would be represented on the summer Kaibab investigation. The list, mailed to National Park Service Director Horace Albright, included the National Association of Audubon Societies, the Camp Fire Club of America, the Izaak Walton League, the American Bison Society, the American National Livestock Breeders Association, the American Game Protective Association, the Arizona Game and Fish Department, the Biological Survey, and the National Park Service, as well as the Forest Service. Albright updated the list with additions and deletions that came to his attention over the next few months. He added the American Forestry Association and the American Society of Mammalogists; he eventually deleted the Bison Society after they withdrew due to lack of funds.

Director Albright listed the other individuals he knew to be representing each organization. For example, T. Gilbert Pearson would represent the Audubon Society, Karl Frederick the Camp Fire Club, and John M. MacFarlane the Livestock Association. George Pratt would do double-duty, serving both the American Game Protective and the American Forestry Associations. The Biological Survey would have at least two representatives: Edward Goldman and Paul Redington. Arizona Game Warden K. C. Kartchner would represent the state game department. The Park Service representative, Joseph Dixon, was named by Albright in a letter to Chief Forester R. Y. Stuart confirming their participation in the investigation.[5]

The addition of a representative for the American Society of Mammalogists resulted from the protests of members who saw the omission of their society on the Kaibab investigation as an attempt by the Forest Service to keep them from raising questions about predators on that important range. The joint studies of predators conducted by mammalogists and government biologists had provided virtually no consensus on the matter. A. Brazier Howell, corresponding secretary for the society, had known of the planning for the upcoming Kaibab investigation since January and solicited Joseph Grinnell and other mammalogists to demand inclusion. In March, Howell wrote to Assistant Director of the Park Service Harold Bryant on behalf of the mammalogists. Since Bryant was a member of the society, Howell expected him to appeal to Albright and get a mammalogist on the list. Howell explicitly accused the Forest Service of intentionally excluding the American Society of Mammalogists. He wrote, "This is very likely an additional result of our criticism of federal poison policies, indirectly applied, which we must be prepared for." Howell eventually learned that the professional mammalogists' organization had been overlooked because they were a "technical society not much concerned with conservation." Howell suggested that the investigation could not be "authoritative" without a society representative and continued to press for a spot on the list.[6]

By the middle of April, Howell reported to Chief Forester Stuart that he had received "so many letters of protest from our members that I now have no choice but to write you about it." No doubt Howell himself had stirred up the membership, but he now felt justified in demanding an explanation from the Forest Service. He applauded his own diplomacy: "I have written our interested members that the omission of the Society's name from the investigation was doubtless an oversight, but they are not inclined to think that the oversight of an organization of this size was likely." Pressing harder, Howell added, "At any rate I wish you would be good enough to clear up the matter, one way or the other, for me before our annual meeting the first part of next month, when the matter will be brought up for discussion and action."[7] Stuart did the only thing he could have done, and the American Society of Mammalogists was added to the delegation. At the society's annual meeting E. Raymond Hall was selected to join the investigation. Some members had been particularly angered by Goldman's last-minute attempt to keep Hall out by volunteering to save the society money by representing both the mammalogists and the Biological Survey himself. Harold Anthony, chair of the American Society of Mammalogists' Special Committee on Problems of Predatory Mammal Control, later noted that this would have been a travesty of the society's goals. The proposal was quickly shot down. Yet, getting Hall on the committee seemed like a minor victory for the mammalogists in light of the Biological Survey's recent success in having its ten-year funding bill pass through Congress with no significant revision of its poison program. Howell and Anthony would continue to push for reform of the program through further investigation of sites like the Kaibab.[8]

Joseph Dixon, who opposed indiscriminate predatory animal control, had begun working for the Park Service in 1930. He was chosen to join the Kaibab committee, and Bryant briefed him on Park Superintendent M. R. Tillotson's perspective of the situation. Tillotson believed that "commercial" interests should be kept out of the northern section of the park in particular. In forwarding one summary from the park superintendent, Bryant noted that hunting had added "a commercial aspect" to the deer situation. The state of Arizona took in about twenty thousand dollars per year from hunting license revenue. The Forest Service also made "a considerable sum as a result of the hunting." This fact, along with the greatly reduced display of deer around VT Park, created a serious concern for Park Service administrators. The decline of the deer population, whether by starvation or predation was now substantially accelerated by hunting. Bryant and Tillotson were not alone in thinking that the trend would continue, motivated by demand for hunting revenue and pressure from livestock owners. Park Service officials' enthusiasm for a thorough investigation was founded on the hope that reduced deer numbers would serve as evidence to reverse the hunting policy.

In order to address the grazing issue from the ranchers' perspective, the American National Livestock Breeders Association desperately hoped to send a vocal representative to the Kaibab in June. In a letter to the Forest Service, the livestock association's secretary argued that protected game throughout the West was "crowding livestock off the forests." To make matters worse, articles in outdoor magazines were "making all kinds of abusive statements regarding stockmen and their attitude toward game, which can have only the effect of stirring up a reaction against all hunters, good or bad." Tillotson's opposition to hunting was only the tip of an iceberg of public opinion among game enthusiasts.[9]

As the 1931 Kaibab investigating trip approached, the Forest Service made final arrangements to have all members of the committee present on the Kaibab. The Park Service made arrangements of its own. Undoubtedly remembering how the Forest Service had scooped them previously, Albright wrote to Tillotson insisting that the superintendent and Brooks remain with the group "from the time they land on the Kaibab until they leave." The director wanted his local team prepared to express the Park Service position early and often. Albright wrote: "It should be brought out in the very beginning that one of the essential elements of difference between the Forest Service and the Park Service viewpoint is the matter of the number of deer. Also, you should make clear our great concern about the disappearance of deer on the VT and other parks during the summer months." The disagreement between the Forest and Park Service views, however, was a delicate matter, and Albright asked that Tillotson express their view "modestly and with the utmost fairness toward the Forest Service and the Bureau of the Biological Survey." At no time, however, should they consider agreeing with other representatives only to appear cooperative. Albright advised Tillotson to make the most of the experience he had gained as "a Forest Service man." Albright also counted George Pratt as an ally and recommended that the Park Service representatives stay close to him.[10]

In fact, Pratt was considered a pivotal member of the committee. If the Park Service counted on him to take their view of things, the Forest Service was looking for ways to win Pratt over, or at least neutralize him. In a letter marked "confidential," Assistant Forester Chris Rachford asked that foresters on the Kaibab "make a special effort in explaining the situation to Mr. Pratt and showing him that all our cards are on the table and

that we are seeking the best advice and help it is possible to obtain."
Rachford had expected to join the investigation himself, but a minor sur-
gery forced him to change his plans. He asked Rutledge, therefore, to take
the lead in conveying the Forest Service's desire to remain impartial in
the proceedings of the committee.[11]

The main issues for consideration, according to Rachford, included
the further control of predatory animals, the extent of interference between livestock and game, the need for close cooperation, and of course,
the condition of the range. This last point included related questions of
food for game, need for further hunting of deer, and the possibility of
improving the food supply by reseeding and artificial winter feeding.
Regional Forester R. H. Rutledge replied from Ogden, Utah, with a request that some other representative of the Washington office be sent in
Rachford's place. The regional forester was especially concerned about
dealing with Pratt, who he described as "opinionated, conceited, and he
takes a broad shot at questions and believes he knows all about them."
Worst of all, Rutledge described how in his personal experience Pratt gave
no weight to the opinions of forest officers. The forester in Ogden feared
that with high-ranking Park Service officials on hand, a move toward
adjusting the boundaries of the park on the plateau would be inevitable.
He did not want his own agency disadvantaged by discussions of boundary changes. Because no one was available to come from Washington,
Rachford suggested that local Forest Service men work with Biological
Survey Chief Paul Redington to defend the status quo.[12]

The national conservation groups also struggled to identify appropriate representatives to protect their interests. Although they generally opposed hunting, they also hoped to prevent starvation of the
deer. The Izaak Walton League delayed in selecting a representative.
At the end of May, still undecided, the league asked what other men
would be joining the investigation. The conservation group hoped to
send an appropriate complement to the government officials and
other representatives already named. The chair of the league's Committee on Conservation wrote, "We are particularly anxious to give the
utmost support to government bureaus that are trying to solve difficult problems [and] are seriously hampered by persons of violent
opinion and local prejudice." These fears seemed justified in light of
the seemingly endless and sometimes bitter disagreements that had
surrounded the Kaibab deer. The league hoped to provide a produc-
tive representative. Mark Anderson from Provo, Utah, represented

the Izaak Walton League. The president of the Arizona Game Protective Association selected as its delegate A. A. Nichol, a professor at the University of Arizona. Nichol was already slated to participate on behalf of the state game department, but rumors that Governor Hunt might dismantle the department at any moment threatened to drop Nichol from the committee. Serving the state's unofficial game organization would retain him. Game Warden K. C. Kartchner would also remain a member of the delegation and could report to what remained of the official game administration of the state.[13]

T. Gilbert Pearson was named chair of the committee, and George Pratt served as vice chair. A total of twenty-eight men participated in the investigation—nine from the conservation and livestock organizations, eight from the Forest Service, three more from the Park Service, three identified as sheep or cattle ranchers, two from the University of Arizona, and a number of others from Washington DC or Phoenix who did not list affiliations.

Members of the investigating committee looking out over the canyon. Photo courtesy of Kaibab National Forest.

Kaibab investigators, seen here gathered around a sapling, inspected the vegetation of the forest. Photo courtesy of Kaibab National Forest.

The group traveled around the Kaibab Plateau from their base camp in VT Park, covering approximately 650 miles in eight days. They spent part of one day on horseback between Swamp Point and Powell Plateau. Travel by automobile allowed them to observe "practically every forest type and condition within the Kaibab area." Photographs of the investigators show them driving across the open desert north of the plateau, gathering around small trees to examine the toll taken by browsing deer, looking out over the canyon from rocky crags, and waiting by their cars to be taken to the next point of interest.[14]

Little record of the individual reactions of participants has survived. Tillotson kept notes on each member's comments at their general meeting, held at VT Park on the morning of June 13, near the end of their investigation. These notes, summarized in a letter to Director Albright, served as a second-hand record. Rutledge reportedly stated that the Forest Service did not want to kill more deer than was absolutely necessary. He also suggested that the Forest Service should probably reduce the number of cattle. Mann agreed, noting that drastic reductions in the deer herd since 1924 came mostly as a result of starvation, which he hoped would not be repeated as the range improved. Homer Shantz, a botanist and president of the University of Arizona, was particularly concerned with making clear the political situation in the state, where Governor Hunt had abruptly removed the game commission, despite legal suits to stop this action. Kartchner, unsure of his own position as game warden, promised to cooperate in every way possible, if he managed to survive the personnel changes in the state department. A number of the participants noted the need for further research and hoped for continued cooperative efforts.

Livestock representative John MacFarlane took the opportunity to describe the contributions of ranchers on the Kaibab over the previous fifty or more years. He went on at length about the history of the early cattle business on the Kaibab, according to Tillotson, "eulogizing the cattle men as pioneers and for the part they played settling up the country." This contribution, MacFarlane believed, earned livestock owners the right to continue on the range surrounding the plateau, especially given the drastic reductions they had already accepted. He asked that the land not be given over entirely to "recreational purposes."[15]

Tillotson himself, serving as chair of the meeting, did not say much. Instead, he collected his comments into a kind of closing statement. There he emphasized several points that Albright and other Park Service officials had hoped would influence the committee. The park supervisor explained that his agency's primary purpose was to provide a "scenic spectacle" for the public. He quickly added, "Somewhat secondary to this, but of almost equal importance is the scientific side, so that a National Park may be as it should be—a great outdoor laboratory for the study of wild life, as well as for the study of all other natural features." In order to accomplish both goals, Tillotson insisted that a large number of deer—two or three hundred—should be visible to summer visitors in the open meadows.

Following Albright's advice, Tillotson reminded the committee of his tenure as a Forest Service employee and proceeded to agree cautiously with the current Forest Service plan to continue hunting. He noted that because of serious damage done to the range in previous years, hunting of the deer must continue. He made a stronger point about the need to reduce livestock, arguing that it would be difficult to explain to the "man on the street" that hunting of deer continued without further reductions in cattle. Tillotson then suggested that predatory animal control be halted entirely. He said, "I am convinced that within the Park we have gone far enough along this line, or perhaps even too far. On the theory that a National Park is an area in which natural conditions should prevail, further extermination of predatory animals within the Park has been definitely discontinued." With these points of emphasis, the park supervisor concluded that he was anxious to assist and cooperate in whatever way possible.[16]

Before even leaving VT Park, E. Raymond Hall related to colleagues at Berkeley, including Joseph Grinnell, the difficulty of working through the many issues relating to the Kaibab with the committee. He wrote, "I feel as though I had done double duty at some hard job of physical labor." Hall received direct praise for his participation on the Kaibab from the American Society of Mammalogists, particularly Harold Anthony, who congratulated Hall for his "manifestation of backbone in standing up for the vital principles of true conservation." Anthony was especially pleased because getting a representative on the investigation at all had been such a struggle. He stated, in fact, his certainty "that there has been a conscious effort to keep a Society representative off of such committees." By that time it was water under the bridge for most members, but Anthony remained vigilant. Park Service administrators also praised Hall's performance on the Kaibab for what they saw as a defense of their own policies.[17]

Hall was not entirely satisfied with his accomplishment in persuading other members of the importance of certain points from his perspective as a mammalogist. He wrote to Grinnell: "Pearson, Redington and Mr. McFarlane [sic], the latter an astute 'Livestock Association' representative constitute a trio of no mean ability and one against which no small amount of mental maneuvering is required to gain, within the main body of the report, the acceptance of what I regard as sound biological principles. Perhaps I again stand out as 'stubborn' and perhaps I did not gain acceptance of every point that a more experienced person would have, but, be that as it may, I think I beat Pearson and at least played to a tie with Redington and McFarlane [sic]."[18] Hall hoped his struggle to sway these three in particular would pay off in the larger debate over predators and poison use. He commented that Redington seemed, in the end, a fine fellow, but the Biological Survey chief could often be played to conform to any number of political convictions. Hall noted, "His poorly disguised efforts to gain the favor of the Livestock representative here was generally amusing but sometimes pitiful."

Given Redington's wavering leadership, Hall predicted that Grinnell might win him over to their side when he visited Berkeley that summer. If the two mammalogists would stand firm, Hall believed Redington would be forced to back down on poison use. The mammalogist had seen firsthand how faithfully Redington played the part of a politician. He wrote, "I am more than ever impressed with the fact that his desire is to anticipate, and then conform to, legislatively powerful public opinion on biological questions rather than to mold public opinion by championing sound biological principles." Recognizing this tendency would be useful to Grinnell. The mammalogists would have to convince Redington that changing federal policy on predator control would be in the public's best interest, whatever the biological evidence might suggest. Hall believed Redington would undoubtedly need the American Society of Mammalogists' support on future issues. At the same time, the battle over the poison use and the role of predators seemed far from complete, and the Kaibab Investigating Committee's report made this point painfully clear.

AN UNSETTLING REPORT

The report of the 1931 Kaibab Investigative Committee did not necessarily represent a landmark in scientific understanding of deer management, wildlife biology, or conservation on the Kaibab, or anywhere else for that matter. It did, however, establish the Kaibab as a hallmark for game management and conservation. The 1931 committee had convened with a different mandate than the 1924 committee. While the public had less interest now that the courts had settled the decision to allow hunting and deer did not seem on the brink of starvation, the intense debates within the biological community kept questions about the future of the Kaibab deer in the news.

The committee summarized its conclusions in a report prepared for release on June 25, 1931. The report offered several valuable observations, summarized as two major points. The first was to clarify the reasons for ongoing disagreement over proper protection and management methods. The second was to take a broader view of the significance of the Kaibab situation in American wildlife attitudes. Members of the committee agreed not to discuss their findings publicly apart from their joint report. For example, John MacFarlane, the Livestock Association representative, returned to Utah and told the *Salt Lake City Tribune* only that they had spent eight days on the plateau and had seen impressive views of the Grand Canyon from Dutton Point.[19]

On the first point—the reasons for ongoing disagreement—the committee noted that in certain parts of the preserve, good forage still existed. The key to understanding conditions on the Kaibab, the report stated, was an extensive survey of the area: "The casual visitor, therefore, may readily get the erroneous idea that there is still much forage for deer in the entire region and that all is well with the deer. This idea is further accentuated when the large number of deer are observed feeding in the meadows of VT and Little Parks." This observation accounted for both the Park Service reports of a large but declining herd along the highway and the Forest Service position that too many deer remained in the preserve. The critical illustration of damaged vegetation and the need for recovery came in the fenced experimental plots set up by the Forest Service. These showed that "the Kaibab area is not now producing more than 10 percent of the available and nutritious forage that this range once produced." The solution, at least in the short term, was continued, supervised hunting. Hunting, they recommended, should continue in the fall at the same level as in the previous year. This meant that the committee expected the Forest Service to supervise a hunt of approximately five thousand deer, which in 1930 had been accomplished by just over two thousand hunters who took on average more than two deer apiece.

The committee addressed the main issue they believed had contributed to ongoing disagreement: the conflict between deer and livestock. Members of the committee recognized that deer prefer browse plants and cattle prefer grass. Ranchers and livestock industry experts cited this difference to argue for maintaining cattle on game ranges. Despite these different preferences, the situation on the Kaibab required further consideration. The report stated, "There is, however, conflict in the use of forage as between cattle and deer when utilization is carried to the extreme." The cause of depletion on the Kaibab was a combination of both.[20] Since livestock owners had removed most of their cattle and sheep from the plateau in recent years, and the Forest Service permitted a relatively small number to local ranchers, the committee concluded that removing "unauthorized cattle" was a necessary step but not a sufficient solution. Deer reduction remained the only workable solution to the conflict.

The committee described the place of predatory animals on the Kaibab as the final issue that contributed to disagreement about protection and management of the deer. The Park Service favored an end to predator control as a possible solution to the deer problems; the opposite argument had long been the standard in game protection and most members of the Kaibab committee were unprepared to decide the matter. They recognized the problem created by unrestricted growth of the deer and concluded discussion of the matter without making any practical recommendation. The report stated, "There is, of course, a theory that if the coyotes and cougars within the Park area are not hunted or trapped that eventually these predators will reduce the deer to the grazing capacity of the range and that serious injury to forest and forage species will then cease." Calling this sequence of events a "theory," along with the fact that the committee reported nothing more on the subject, suggested that members were unprepared to commit themselves further. During the remainder of the summer of 1931, individual mammalogists distilled evidence from the Kaibab and less-publicized studies of the Biological Survey's predator programs into a series of articles that appeared to escalate the debate over the value of varmints.[21]

On the committee's second major point—the significance of the Kaibab for wildlife attitudes—the group took the opportunity to look to the future, stating, "It is believed that the Kaibab study and demonstration should mark the beginning of a new era in big game management in the Western United States." This led to a review of administrative problems that plagued the Kaibab deer: the forest plan did not include a game plan; use by livestock had set the stage for overuse by deer; game belonged to the state, and rangeland belonged to the federal government. This situation was not unique to the Kaibab, but the committee intended to point out that these problems could be avoided elsewhere if administrators were mindful of the Kaibab example. The case was strengthened by the recent advances made in cooperative administration. Describing efforts in the past two years, the committee wrote, "The handling of the Kaibab situation by the Arizona Game Commission and the U.S. Forest Service offers a splendid example of the efficiency of closely supervised hunting to remove both male and female deer from overstocked areas."

Crucial to continued management success, the committee noted, was "cooperation and research." On the Kaibab and elsewhere, members suggested: "There should be more coordination and cooperation among Federal Departments concerned with the solution of biological and economic problems as affecting the management of Federal lands and the plant and animal life produced thereon. The committee urges the extension of the research activities of the U.S. Biological Survey, in order that this scientific Bureau may lend greater assistance to the Forest Service, the Park Service, and all other Government agencies confronted with perplexing biological problems." In order to add substantially to those efforts, the committee recommended better coordination between government and academic research on the Kaibab. Since a number of representatives from the University of Arizona joined the committee, their participation could serve as a model. Such collaboration was particularly pertinent in Arizona at that very moment, given Governor Hunt's ongoing efforts to control game management directly from his office. The report stated, "Scientific men connected with State universities and colleges should serve as helpful sources of impartial information and render exceedingly important service to State Game Departments in the development of game management plans." These efforts so far had only scratched the surface, and many observers hoped that "much additional exact information" would lead to more exact solutions to the problem, such as valuable comparative data from the fenced experimental plots.

In the end, the investigators demanded further reductions in the deer population and no increases in livestock numbers on the plateau and surrounding lands. These recommendations did not differ substantially from what participants like Tillotson and Mann, for different reasons, had advocated earlier. This may have disappointed those who hoped for dramatic changes to correct the situation, but the committee accomplished something more significant than any specific suggestions. It broadened the appeal of these recommendations by articulating them from a wider constituency. Proposals from a park superintendent or forest supervisor lacked the mandate of a diverse, cooperative investigating committee. Even where the committee disagreed about conditions, their recommendations appeared unanimous in the report. Perhaps because the report did not authoritatively answer the quantitative questions asked by Edmund Seymour, the national conservation leader reacted with disappointment. The Bison Society had not sent a representative, so the committee mailed an advance copy of the report to Seymour. He wrote, "Like all these Committee reports it doesn't say anything very much. It gives no figures." Seymour had hoped that the investigation would finally discover the exact number of deer and how many the range could support. Instead, to him the report merely provided an update on the kind of information that had circulated since 1924.[22] For the Forest Service, the report at least offered a mandate to restrict grazing and remove deer.

Hall wrote a few shorter accounts of the investigation focusing primarily on his dealings with Goldman. Because of their differing opinions on predators and particularly on the Biological Survey's poisoning program, Hall and Goldman had occasion to square off on the Kaibab. Hall reported, "Goldman and I had one good fight, and were the best of friends the rest of the time. I don't believe Goldman really dislikes me, but rather thinks I am a misguided youth who may see the folly of his ways. Since the Kaibab conference, I am afraid he has given up hopes in that direction too." Hall also described his attempts to promote the idea that grazing should be the last of all uses of the natural resources on public lands: "I was so bold as to state that those seeking grazing privileges should recognize that grazing could be permitted only when it in no way interfered with those other functions of the Forest Service. Of course, the idea did not get anywhere so far as actual expression of it in the report was concerned, but some of the forestry people seemed to take to it kindly, and one even said that he would welcome the day when no grazing was allowed, at least on the Kaibab." Opposition to grazing on public lands was gaining momentum partly because of the Kaibab situation and the Park Service's attempts to define policies of preserving natural conditions.[23]

Shortly after the committee disbanded, Hall corresponded with Aldo Leopold. With the question of predatory animal control still unanswered and the experience of the Kaibab fresh in his mind, Hall, who knew the former forester was working on a book on game management, asked Leopold to write frankly about "facts relative to the over control of predatory animals, in so far as it bears directly on game management." Leopold declined to take a position, but stated that he was looking forward to reading the "new Kaibab report." His view was that neither the Biological Survey nor its critics were as yet "at the bottom of the question." Leopold promised to explain his views in "the book."[24]

Despite growing interest in preserving predators, some conservation organizations continued to lobby for the complete elimination of predators. For example, D. L. Vasbinder, president of the Southern California Council of the Izaak Walton League, questioned why predatory animals were to be left alone at a time when hunting could do the job of reducing the deer, if only hunters were given more of an opportunity. He asked, "Rather than cease all predatory control, would it not be better to allow the present surplus of deer be utilized by man rather than lions, etc.?" This familiar argument for efficient use would save valuable deer from becoming "lion feed." Vasbinder noted that he had already discussed this approach with Game Warden Lee Bayless. Local officials not surprisingly agreed in principle, especially since Vasbinder was from California, meaning Arizona could charge him and all Californians additional licensing fees.[25]

Published responses to the report reflected the accomplishment of bringing potentially conflicting groups to a set of harmonious conclusions. An editorial in *American Game* praised the investigation's outcome: "The committee . . . has made an excellent report. It very wisely refrained from getting into the controversial subject of how many deer there are on the Kaibab. It found that the herds must be reduced and recommended remedies." The complete report was published in that issue, along with photographs of the fenced experimental plots and famous high-lined trees. An essay appeared in *Bird Lore* that gave a brief history of the deer and quoted extensively from the report. The quotes covered the topics of range depletion to ten percent of its previous production, overgrazing by both cattle and deer, and the need to reduce the deer. The essay concluded with a statement of just how important the Kaibab was in emphasizing changes in attitudes toward deer: "The Kaibab situation demonstrates that in some cases it is possible to have 'over conservation.' 'Game Management' is a phase that will probably soon come into daily use in describing the management of various big-game problems now developing in different parts of the country, if these are to be handled with wisdom."[26] Even with this insight, no one knew how many deer were on the Kaibab Plateau, nor did anyone know how many deer the preserve could support.

Improving Vegetation

Favorable conditions for plant growth in northern Arizona during 1931 meant that the deer would suffer less in the coming winter than in previous years. Chief Forester R. Y. Stuart visited the plateau on a tour of the region with Secretary of Agriculture Arthur M. Hyde. Superintendent Tillotson had the opportunity to meet Stuart, and described him as "most open minded" even in discussing the possibility of enlarging Grand Canyon National Park on the Kaibab Plateau. Tillotson also met Governor Hunt on at least one of the governor's four trips to the Kaibab that summer. Despite the gains made in cooperation by the committee, Hunt had plans of his own to get control of the Kaibab deer and make changes in their management. He proposed regulations that would restrict hunters to only one deer apiece.[27]

Recognizing a promising improvement in vegetation conditions, Walter Mann was not particularly concerned upon learning of the governor's proposed scheme. He submitted a federal hunting plan to the regional forester that differed from the recommendation of the Kaibab Investigative Committee. He explained that the state hunting regulations allowed one deer per hunter in the coming season, meaning that a much smaller number of deer would be killed. Since the range had improved, however, Mann was either unconcerned or oblivious to the ramifications as he made his plan public. He suggested that they go along with the new regulations and expect a smaller reduction than the committee had recommended. He was unaware of the uproar his proposal was about to cause.

Regional Forester Rutledge forwarded this news to Stuart, explaining that the state regulations and game personnel had changed. These changes put the chief forester in a bind because he felt a strong obligation to honor the results of the investigation he had commissioned. Now, he was forced either to defy the state and once again face the legal repercussions or to ignore the Kaibab committee and run roughshod over its carefully considered recommendations. He chose the latter, but opted to explain the necessity of the Forest Service's action. At the same time, he castigated Rutledge and Mann for going public with the plans and their apparent lack of foresight. Stuart thought it unfortunate that the local foresters had not considered the scope of these proposals. Stuart wrote that Mann had "failed to appreciate the Kaibab situation as a Service-wide problem and that courtesy demanded reference to the different members of the committee before public announcement." People throughout the Forest Service and across the country were keenly interested in the progress of the Kaibab deer situation, and this shift in policy would reflect poorly on his handling of the situation at a time when he had just started to hope it was under control.[28]

In a letter to members of the investigative committee, Stuart explained Mann's proposals as the result of new state game laws, which made the planned deer removal "problematical." One deer per hunter would be allowed, and they should expect a smaller number of hunters than the previous year due to the economic depression. The committee recommended removal of as many deer as the previous year. That goal seemed out of reach. An equal number of hunters would succeed in killing fewer than two thousand deer. Stuart relied on Mann's optimism to suggest that improvement of the range meant a smaller reduction might be acceptable. He assured committee members that the Forest Service would do its duty, removing a sufficient number of deer, even if it meant resorting to other measures. He asked for their frank comments.[29]

George Pratt responded first. He was sorry to hear of the change in state regulations and believed deer would soon be starving because of it. He called on Stuart to carry out the committee's recommendations, hinting that the forester need not publicly divulge any plans for actions that might violate the state regulations. Pratt doubted the reports of range improvement. He wanted to see hunters take the deer before starvation had its chance. Stuart received a similar reaction from John MacFarlane. The Livestock Association representative quoted directly from the committee report on the need for hunting to be continued with "a removal not less than last season . . . by licensed hunters or by other legal methods." MacFarlane went on to explain that the phrase "other legal methods" was a "mellowed down" version of the majority opinion of the committee, who agreed that Forest Service employees themselves should go in and reduce the deer by the prescribed number if game hunters did not accomplish the goal. Committee members had made their recommendation more subtly in July in order to avoid antagonizing Governor Hunt. MacFarlane concluded: "I am of the opinion that the only reduction in deer will be by starvation, unless the Forest Service takes action. You have asked for my frank opinion, so I am trying to give it." Joseph Dixon expressed a complete lack of surprise at the governor's action. He noted that, in fact, many members of the committee anticipated the change. Dixon sympathized with Stuart's position, but he expected the Forest Service to do everything possible to meet the committee's recommendations.[30]

With Mann's continued insistence that the range would support more deer, the Forest Service took no further action. The fall hunt complied with the new state regulations. Hunters killed 965 deer. With the smaller than suggested reduction, some might have hoped that predators would further decrease the deer population. The lack of predator control on the plateau provoked local ranchers and trappers to believe the Kaibab was becoming a breeding ground for predators. They had already petitioned their U.S. senators to change the federal policy and resume predator control. In the face of this pressure, Biological Survey Chief Paul Redington received a telegram from Regional Forester Rutledge and a letter from the chief forester's office asking that the survey not resume predator control activities. Rutledge noted what Redington must already have known about the deer, "Actual number uncertain but fact remains number dangerously near exceeding forage supply—stop."[31]

Rasmussen's Research

In the early 1930s, D. I. Rasmussen was a graduate student gathering data and practicing some modestly innovative quantitative methods. The most extraordinary aspects of this research were actually the least recognized by others on the Kaibab. His interest in the broader biotic communities on the plateau received little attention. His description of the deer herd's checkered past and the graph he included to illustrate that history became widely cited, but not until much later. It was in more subtle ways, then, that Rasmussen's contribution to understanding the Kaibab deer initiated changes in the conceptual approaches to wildlife study and the activities of wildlife biologists.

Rasmussen defended his dissertation in 1932, when he was not yet thirty years old. He did not publish it until almost a decade later, and in the meantime it was virtually unknown to ecologists other than his advisor, Victor Shelford. The dissertation contained a mixture of previously reported conditions and novel conclusions based on Rasmussen's exhaustive research. He relied on accounts provided by veteran foresters and local residents combined with his own observations and comparative field studies. Perhaps most significantly, this work marked the first time a nongovernmental researcher presented an examination of the Kaibab Plateau in the form of a scientific report. The table of contents listed sections on the "scope of work and methods" as well as separate studies of each of the major biotic communities of the plateau. Rasmussen's graphs, maps, plates, and bibliography were also unprecedented. This was more than mere form, however, as the text itself suggested.[32]

Shelford hoped to initiate studies of ecological communities across North America. He enlisted his graduate students at the University of Illinois to conduct such studies in a wide variety of locales, although most chose the nearby environs of Champaign and Urbana. Rasmussen fulfilled Shelford's ambitions for community studies admirably. While other Shelford students focused on insect communities and collected specimens from a relatively small site, the Utah native was increasingly aware of the need to include larger vertebrates in ecological studies through observation—the typical method of naturalists for decades. Rasmussen also used the method of reconnaissance developed by foresters, who commonly referred to their initial survey work as "cruising." They began by carefully mapping and surveying the land, as well as estimating the amount of standing timber. Rasmussen paid less attention to the timber, but made extensive maps of the diverse floral and faunal communities on the plateau. Other ecologists had primarily focused on study areas with rich invertebrate populations and limited small mammal and bird populations. They chose to study insects in order to make their fieldwork "more definite and exact," focusing on study areas with fewer and smaller species. They rarely encountered larger mammals and scarcely mentioned them in their regular studies if they did. In order to accomplish their narrower quantitative goals, they studied communities that lacked diversity of mammals and birds. These simplified communities were, after all, much more common in areas that surrounded human development.[33]

Referring to those studies, and with perhaps a smattering of one-upmanship, Rasmussen wrote, "None of the studies were concerned with the original fauna in its entirety—the location of study areas have precluded that." On the Kaibab, Rasmussen was explicitly interested in large mammals and keenly aware of the complications they would introduce to his research. At the same time, he was determined to satisfy Shelford's demands, including the need for quantitative data. He wrote: "The present paper deals with the results of a study of land communities and their habitats and the application of quantitative methods to the study of abundant and influent animals of the area. It is not only concerned with the smaller forms but an attempt is made to apply quantitative methods of study to a number of large and influent native species. These larger species are, at present, greatly restricted in numbers and range and only a few areas contain a complete representation of the original biota."

Rasmussen's interest in the influence of human activities on the Kaibab Plateau was unusual in ecology at the time, at least for an academic ecologist and particularly for a graduate student. He did not attempt to ignore or negate human influence, but saw it as a part of the task of understanding the biological communities there. He introduced the situation in general terms, only hinting at the years of upheaval. He wrote: "The area studied has been greatly advertised because of its native animals; man in his attempt to increase the numbers of certain species has seriously interfered in the relations of the major animal species, with the result that there has been a change in a number of features and conditions within the community. The study was undertaken because of interest in these variations."[34]

For collecting invertebrates, Rasmussen followed the same sweep-net protocol outlined by his graduate-student colleagues at Illinois. For vertebrates, the young ecologist expanded his methodology to include procedures reviewed recently by Biological Survey zoologist Walter Taylor.[35] These included different techniques for virtually every species encountered: trapping smaller nocturnal rodents, carnivores, and some diurnal rodents; staking and observing plots for other rodents; observing "sign" of wood rats; pellet counts for rabbits; area counts and cruising for squirrels; following local Forest Service observation protocols for deer; listening, tracking, and observing coyotes; observing "sign" of cougars; and listening for birds. When possible, he attempted to check one study method against another. Ultimately, Rasmussen expressed a bit of uncertainty both in his dissertation and in the later published report. He admitted, "Estimates and counts by present methods may be filled with error."[36] He

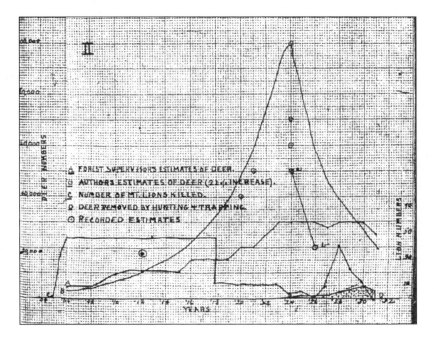

For his 1932 dissertation, D. I. Rasmussen assembled data from forest supervisors' reports, local estimates, and his own studies to construct this population graph.

attempted to absolve himself by referring to a comment that Shelford had recently published in *Ecology* that "the more strictly quantitative the work is, the better it is likely to be."[37]

Rasmussen also tended to qualitative elements. He provided the most complete description of the physical environment of the Kaibab Plateau and surrounding areas of any published work, down to the present. Along with detailed maps, he described the physical geography and climate of the area for the period of his study. Rasmussen's account of the history of the plateau and game preserve was also notable. He included not only the activities of the federal government beginning in the twentieth century, but he suggested a significant role for American Indians on the plateau

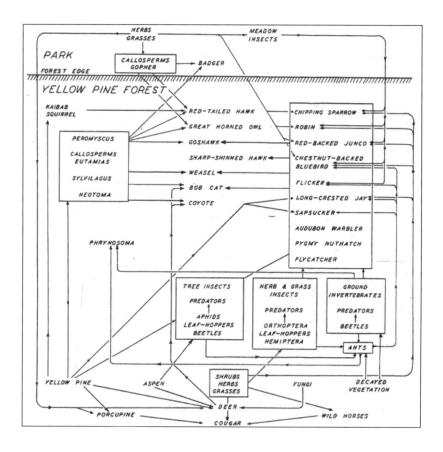

Rasmussen also created a diagram showing the food web of the biotic communities of the Kaibab. Reprinted with permission.

prior to the mid-nineteenth-century settlement of livestock owners. He considered Indians to be a potentially important limiting factor for the deer population.

In his history of the preserve, Rasmussen reduced the population changes of the deer and certain predatory animal species to a single graph. Parts of that graph suggested a rapid increase in the deer followed almost immediately by a crash in the population due to starvation. He described how the government prohibited killing deer and at the same time hired hunters to kill mountain lions, wolves, coyotes, and bobcats. The deer population increased "until the estimated 4,000 in 1906 had become an enormous herd of 100,000 in 1924. The peak was reached, the range depleted, the population started downhill. There were deaths by thousands from malnutrition and related causes." Between 1925 and 1930, due to starvation and hunting, the 100,000 deer fell to 20,000. "The range has been so severely damaged that 20,000 is now an excessive population from the standpoint of the forage species."[38]

Rasmussen suggested that a lack of knowledge was due to the "entirely new" situation that arose as a result of the creation of the preserve in 1906. The solution, first suggested by the Forest Service, was to limit the number of deer, but this met with a "storm of protest" based on prejudice and misunderstandings, according to Rasmussen. When committees examined the situation in 1924 and 1931, he reminded the reader, they were "definitely shown the seriousness of the situation and the depleted conditions of the range." The failure to prevent the disasters that reportedly occurred was caused, according to the graduate student, by the divided jurisdiction of the preserve. The one good result of those disasters, he suggested, was that scientists, the government, and the general public were more attuned to the challenges facing wildlife management.[39]

Rasmussen described each of the general communities of the plateau and relationships between them, then divided the remainder of his paper into sections detailing the vegetation, large and small mammals, birds, reptiles, and invertebrates in each community. For each community, he spent considerable effort describing the changes wrought by the rise and fall of the deer herd over the previous twenty-five years. He noted the influence of other plant and animal species on the deer and vice versa. For example, vegetation, if browsed lightly by deer, might actually grow more rapidly. Under conditions of severe overbrowsing, however, vegetative growth suffered and many plants died.[40]

The role of predators within the animal community was significant for Rasmussen. Mountain lions in particular were dependent upon deer for food. Rasmussen wrote, "The cougar seemingly has a very definite place in the biotic relations of the pinon-juniper community, if by its abundance and its pressure on deer, the deer population is controlled."[41] He estimated that fifty cougars lived on the plateau, mostly near the canyon, during the period of his study. Coyotes were far more numerous and had actually increased as the herd declined. These animals rarely killed deer, however, and Rasmussen explained that the coyote's primary food source was small rodents. He returned to the big cats repeatedly, however, stating, "The removal of eight hundred mountain lions from the area, from 1907 to 1930, appears to be the major cause of the great increase in numbers [of deer]."[42] Although the young ecologist did not refer to predator removal as the sole cause of the deer increase, subsequent reviewers focused on the lions.

Rasmussen reviewed the current literature on population cycles, diseases, and other factors that influenced animal numbers. He commented on virtually all of the major populations, from grouse to squirrels to mountain lions to porcupines and on to beetles and other invertebrates. He noted that the "balance in nature" did not exist as a static condition of equilibrium and that most species exhibited "normal" variations. The young ecologist wrote, perhaps to the dismay of Grand Canyon National Park officials who hoped for a constant supply of awe-inspiring wildlife, "The 'balance in nature', as near as one has ever existed, is a dynamic and fluctuating phenomenon, with abundance cycles and periods of scarcity." This observation correlated with the recent studies of lemmings by Charles Elton and observations of rabbits and hares by Aldo Leopold.[43] Rasmussen suggested that the cause of population changes in most cases depended upon fluctuations in other species.

This account of events between 1906 and 1931 marked a kind of watershed in the making of what later came to be known as the lesson of the Kaibab and after that the Kaibab myth. The straightforward suggestion that the population increased from just four thousand deer to one hundred thousand at an annual growth rate of about 20 percent became a common reference for maximum increase in deer. Rasmussen's emphasis on the mountain lion as the missing check against such rapid growth became generalized for predator-prey relationships in almost any other imaginable or observed situation.

When the graduate student left the Kaibab in November 1931, he planned to be back, to teach a field course on the Kaibab Plateau the following summer and hopefully work for the Forest Service as a permanent researcher. After Rasmussen defended his dissertation in Illinois in 1932, Shelford sent an inquiry to Charles Adams in search of "funds to keep Rasmussen working in the Kaibab." He hoped that the American Game Protective Association or the Roosevelt Wild Life Forest Experiment Station could provide a small stipend. Such a move, Shelford suggested, would have had "the advantage of giving the work continuity and be much cheaper than starting a man in anew." Adams knew of no institution that would provide such an unprecedented stipend. So instead of going west, Rasmussen remained in Illinois where he took a job as assistant aquatic biologist for the Illinois State Natural History Survey. After only a year, Rasmussen returned to his home state of Utah to work for the Forest Service, first as a forest guard in the Wasatch National Forest in the north-central part of the state, then as a range technician at the Intermountain Forest and Range Experiment Station in Ogden.[44]

In 1934 Rasmussen joined the faculty of the Utah State Agricultural College as an associate professor, and there he organized a Department of Wildlife Management and became head of the department. Because of his location in Utah, his experience on the Kaibab, and his increasing expertise in wildlife management issues, Rasmussen continued to work with Kaibab foresters but never resumed intensive research of the deer and related communities as he once hoped he might.

For the balance of the 1930s, studies on the Kaibab continued on a trajectory that was largely unchanged by Rasmussen's work. There was a growing local awareness of the need to understand the habitat and habits of the deer alongside other members of their ecological communities. To a certain extent, the young ecologist introduced a kind of ecological thinking that other investigators had not expressed or practiced. This ecological thinking, however, did not provide immediate answers to the timeworn questions about the deer and problems related to their management.

Public Relations Work

Forest Supervisor Walter Mann spent two weeks examining conditions on the Kaibab in January 1932, along with five men from the Arizona State Game Department, the Park Service, and the Forest Service. They encountered deep snow, more than any of them had seen "in a great many years." The snow rendered their three automobiles useless and eventually buried the cars until spring. However, fresh snow that fell during their inspection aided in estimating the number and distribution of the deer, and they could count and examine deer tracks, knowing precisely when the tracks were made. They counted 2,541 deer on the west side of the plateau and rated this count as twenty percent of the total, about 12,700. Due to the heavy snow, Mann was unable to get to the east side of the plateau until March. Assuming the 405 deer he saw there represented twenty-five percent of the total on that side, his grand total on the plateau that winter was 14,700. When this number was reported, it was compared immediately to the much rounder figures estimated in previous years: at least twenty thousand in 1931; between twenty thousand and thirty thousand in 1930. Mann went on to note that the extremely heavy snow was responsible for increasing competition between cattle and deer. Mann stated, "There is direct and acute competition between deer and cattle for feed at this time." Efforts of cowboys to move cattle into the canyon only intensified the damage already done there by livestock. The activities of the coyotes and mountain lions were also evident, but the inspectors could not determine whether the predators had killed deer or were merely eating carcasses of starved deer.[45]

During the following summer, with official estimates of deer numbers well below what they had been in recent years, visitors reported a notable scarcity of deer. This came as unsettling news to Park Service officials, who with the previous year's smaller hunt and success in public relations, hoped for gains in tourism on the North Rim. Superintendent Tillotson himself saw no groups of deer numbering larger than a dozen on VT Park, where sometimes several hundred browsed. Bill Rust, a seasonal resident and employee of the park had not seen more than twenty or twenty-five at a time. A similar report of even greater consequence came from F. W. Robinson, vice president of the Union Pacific Railroad. Robinson's employees along with regular travelers on his lines who visited the Kaibab each year commented on the diminution of the visible herd. A new road through VT Park offered the travelers a more pleasant trip, but they complained that there was less to see. No one connected the increased traffic on the road with the lower deer frequency in the area. They did, according to Robinson, note a rapidly increasing population of coyotes and cougars. The predators and annual deer hunt, the railroad executive suggested, had drastically reduced the deer spectacle.[46]

That same summer, Park Service Director Horace Albright received a passionate letter from a Maria Jackson of Portland, Oregon. On a recent visit to the national parks of the Southwest, she had found among the deer on the Kaibab no fawns at all. The reason for the scarcity of young deer was confirmed in her mind when she and her companions encountered a "wolf" in the road. Jackson explained to Albright that she feared for all of the animals, wild and domestic, that were threatened by "the terrible wolves." Since Jackson admitted in the letter that this was the first time she had seen a wolf in the wild, and since no wolves had been reported on the Kaibab in almost five years, local officials dismissed her report when she asked them to "go get the wolves." Jackson learned from those officials that predatory animals were protected in the park. She asked Albright to do something to change the minds of people in Washington who objected to killing "vicious, no account animals."

The National Park Service increasingly defended the protection of predators in the late 1920s and 1930s on its lands. Justification of this policy extended beyond the specific issues on the Kaibab, but studies there eventually played a significant role in popularizing these policies. For the immediate question raised by the Portland resident, Assistant Director Harold Bryant replied to Jackson, insisting that protection of predators in national parks was sound policy, but that the park owed reduced deer numbers to annual hunts on surrounding Forest Service lands.[47]

Upon receiving notice of the planned fall hunt for 1932, Tillotson took another trip to the Kaibab, this time measuring out a distance of eight miles on top of the plateau over which he saw a total of eight deer. He wrote to Albright again, reminding the director of the days when deer numbered over a thousand on the same stretch of land. Tillotson did not mention the fact that deer were most numerous around VT Park in June and July, and his recent survey took place in mid-September. Rather, he pointed to a more serious reason, "The answer simply is that large herds of deer are no longer a feature of the North Rim and of the Kaibab National Forest." Tillotson's solution was to add VT Park to National Park Service-administered lands.[48]

Harold Bryant also visited the Kaibab during the summer and reported to Albright that the deer were much scarcer than in previous years. The director wanted to avoid a direct confrontation with the Forest Service that might make the situation worse, so he wrote to his old ally, George

Pratt. He let Pratt know that the Park Service did not want to interfere in the arrangements worked out between the Forest Service and the state of Arizona. Albright did want Pratt to know about the reports of the deer situation, and he informed Park Service biologists Joseph Dixon and George Wright as well. If Dixon and Wright examined the Kaibab before the hunt, they could make comparisons with earlier observations.[49]

George Wright began wildlife work in the national parks in 1928. He initially funded the work himself, but around the time Dixon joined him in 1930, the National Park Service instituted Wright's work as their new Wild Life Division. In the early 1930s the Wild Life Division—consisting of Wright, Dixon, David Madsen, and Ben Thompson—became the source of wildlife studies in the national parks.[50]

Albright wanted to keep the Park Service out of a possible conflict with the Forest Service on the Kaibab, but writing to Pratt did not help him in this effort. Pratt showed the letter to Gilbert Pearson, and Pearson immediately wrote to Chief Forester R. Y. Stuart asking if there was any foundation to the "rumor" that the deer were nearly gone. Pearson also asked for an explanation of the planned hunting season. Chris Rachford responded on behalf of the Forest Service. He wrote flatly that the rumor was without basis. Rachford referred Pearson to the fifteen thousand deer estimated in Mann's winter surveys and offered the regional forester's opinion that at last they had "reached very close to a proper balance between the number of deer and the capacity of the range." Their current estimates suggested that hunting would remove approximately six hundred deer and would serve to maintain that balance. When Pearson forwarded a copy of Rachford's letter to the Park Service with an explanation of his involvement, Assistant Director Bryant let it drop. In a memo to Albright, Bryant simply wrote, "Thought best not to answer this for we do not want the Forest Service to think we are stirring up criticism against them."[51]

Albright's hope of getting Dixon and Wright to visit the Kaibab was lost because the two were already committed to other Park Service projects. In their place David Madsen, fellow Wild Life Division researcher, headed down to the Kaibab as soon as he learned of the need for additional observations of the deer and conditions. Madsen saw 70 deer around VT Park in early October and could find no one who had seen more than 120 in recent months. He examined the plateau with Odell Julander, the Forest Service's new range researcher on the Kaibab. Madsen considered the range to be in excellent condition. Most significantly, however, the fawn crop appeared extremely small. Madsen blamed coyotes for the shortage of fawns and predicted the herd would not increase at all in the coming year. In addition, he felt that Mann's estimate of over fourteen thousand deer was too high. Because he recognized that nothing could be done to stop the fall hunt at that late date, he proposed a solution of his own. Madsen, with credentials as a former state game commissioner and wildlife conservation director for the Park Service, released a statement to the Salt Lake City press. In it, he described the scarcity of deer on the Kaibab and the likelihood that hunters could find more deer in Utah than in northern Arizona. This news, he hoped, would reduce the size of the hunt and protect the remaining Park Service spectacle.[52]

The emphasis Madsen placed on the role of coyotes in reducing the fawn numbers led Assistant Park Service Director Arno Cammerer to support renewed predator control in the area. Bryant was quick to disagree.[53] The Park Service's broader policy protecting all wildlife including predatory species was relatively new, and Bryant did not want to start making exceptions, particularly in such a visible case. The evident reduction in current deer numbers provided the Park Service an opportunity to argue that hunting the deer had served its purpose and now should end. Predators could be protected in the park as part of the natural spectacle that had so enthralled Maria Jackson. Had the deer been more abundant, her complaints about the coyotes might have been transformed into amazement.

The Forest Service, on the other hand, seemed prepared to use the reduced deer population as a legitimization of the need to resume predator control, not to end deer hunting. At least, that was the "vague rumor" that reached E. Raymond Hall in Berkeley, where he was assistant director of the Museum of Vertebrate Zoology. Hall wrote to Walter Mann on the Kaibab asking about plans for predatory mammal control. Mann replied that while he had estimated over fourteen thousand deer that spring, a smaller-than-expected fawn crop raised questions about the future of the herd. He also reported seeing more coyotes than ever before on the Kaibab. This, according to Mann, was the cause of "very heavy losses in the fawn crop." Coyote control would be limited to the efforts of a few permitted trappers. The supervisor informed Hall that no poison or salaried trappers would be used. Mann went so far as to admit that hunting would probably not be necessary, but because of the depressed economy he expected few hunters to turn out anyway. Hall actually responded that he was delighted with Mann's plans and praised the forester's leadership. To him, the moderate coyote control marked a major improvement over past practice. Mann wrote back with the further information that the Biological Survey agreed with his plans to limit predator control to the few private trappers who could profit from the furs rather than send in federal trappers. He also indicated that very few mountain lions were to be found in the area and that two lion-hunting parties had recently gone home empty-handed. If Hall had been prompted by Park Service officials to check on the Forest Service, he seemed fully satisfied by Mann's "splendid 'management plan'" and said so.[54]

In a reversal of the attitude of most members of the previous summer's committee, virtually all observers began to agree that the herd was smaller than at any time in recent memory—perhaps smaller by half than just a few years earlier. As Rasmussen's studies revealed, however, the deer were part of a much larger array of biotic communities, and the extent to which those communities could be manipulated remained unknown. In order to most directly achieve their goals, the Forest Service and Park Service again embarked on efforts to increase the deer. A quarter century earlier, Theodore Roosevelt had established the preserve with this goal in mind, and in 1932, the easiest way to accomplish this goal still seemed to be by removing enemies of the deer. The Forest Service preferred a return to predator control, while the Park Service would rather eliminate hunting.

IMPLEMENTING A GAME PLAN

Data pertaining to the condition of the vegetation and the health of the deer herd accumulated steadily in the early 1930s. Scientific work could be based on a broader foundation and began to borrow from a wider range of methods. An increasingly clear picture of how the preserve had recovered suggested that administrators had more options available to them. With this information and greater familiarity, officials on the local and national levels made bold plans. These plans, however, rarely considered the diverse goals of all the groups that had struggled for protection of deer, hunting rights, and predator control on the plateau.

The Forest Service had taken the administrative lead in managing the Kaibab deer since the late 1920s, and that authority increased each year as Walter Mann organized and supervised the annual deer counts and the fall hunt. In order to counter the apparent trend of a dwindling deer herd, Mann and others stepped up arguments in favor of resuming predator control. They wanted to maintain regular hunting seasons on the plateau and enhance their command over the animal community by removing predators year-round. As officials considered this approach, support from a long-time predator control proponent, Edward Goldman, suddenly diminished. The Forest Service also found it more difficult than ever to convince peers in the Park Service of their management rationale, especially lacking conclusive evidence that predators were killing deer on the Kaibab.

In late 1932, Edward Goldman, the Biological Survey's staunchest defender of predator control up to that point, made a startling admission, which was paradoxically based on the Kaibab situation. In an address at the American Game Conference in New York City in late November, Goldman described the Kaibab as a situation that "afforded a striking illustration of the vital importance of disposing of the surplus [deer] when the forage-producing capacity of the game range is threatened." He noted how early preservation policies there had both ended hunting and led to reduced livestock grazing. Goldman counted the elimination of predatory animals as another aspect of preservation policy. In recounting his own examinations of the Kaibab in the early 1920s, the government biologist emphasized that recommendations to reduce the deer were ignored. Renewed hunting was deemed imprudent on such a fine game preserve. Without action, however, many deer, particularly the young, would not survive the harsh winters. Although Goldman had objected at the time, he now admitted that discontinuation of predator control by the Biological Survey had perhaps prevented even more widespread starvation of the deer.

In discussing the potentially valuable role for predatory animals on the Kaibab, Goldman's argument for destroying predators required modification. Instead of thinking only of his agency as a destroyer of livestock enemies, he acknowledged the threat of overabundant deer to forage and suggested that in areas where hunting did not effectively limit game numbers, "predatory-animal repression should be lightened as far as possible without serious injury to local economic interests." Goldman expressed this opinion more personally, showing how he had been recently convinced by evidence on the Kaibab: "Formerly I was of the opinion that with an increasing army of hunters and a diminishing supply of deer, animals as destructive as mountain lions should be eliminated, except in a few very remote places. The recent upward trend in numbers of our larger game has, however, materially altered my viewpoint. I now believe that a moderate number of these great cats may serve a useful purpose in checking undue increases of deer, especially in regions little grazed by domestic stock. Besides, the hunting of lions affords rare sport, and they can be controlled almost at will." In light of these avowals, Goldman was prepared to embark on a new system of management that would protect some predators as well as encourage forage studies and carefully regulated hunting. He noted, "Obviously predatory animals are an important part of the biological complex, requiring careful consideration, and control in places, if game resources are to be maintained." Goldman's comments did not constitute a complete reversal of his attitude toward predatory animals, nor did he espouse an enlightened ecological consciousness. His was an acknowledgment of the practical realities he faced in widely varying local contexts. In order to achieve this new system, professional wildlife administrators would have to combine, according to Goldman, "broad technical knowledge and the instincts of a naturalist with capacity for dealing with hard, factual realities."[55]

Walter Mann had begun to emerge as just this sort of administrator. His game plan for the forest included several range studies aimed at determining the recovery rate and carrying capacity of the forage for deer and livestock. He updated this plan regularly and shared it with the regional forester and Chris Rachford in Washington, reporting that 670 hunters took approximately 640 deer in the fall hunt—more than expected but not enough to seriously risk the health of the herd.[56]

As the 1932 hunt on the Kaibab was winding down, Director Horace Albright worked with the Wild Life Division and his staff in Washington to challenge future Forest Service hunts. David Madsen's observations had supported earlier reports of a dwindling herd, and Albright resolved to use this evidence to shift opinions and policies wherever possible. Before Albright sent his letter, George Wright emphasized for the director the unique importance of the Kaibab. The biologist stated, "My personal reaction from the first, and recent developments have served to strengthen the feeling, is that the policy of the Service should be a most moderate one as regards the Kaibab. This is the one place where other interests and agencies will be quickest to accuse us of being aggressive." This comment might have been enough to slow Albright down, but the biologist had more to say on the Park Service's goals with regard to the Kaibab deer. He continued: "One cannot help but doubt seriously that the great herds of deer seen a few years ago was a natural phenomenon. If the plan of having these abnormally large herds of deer is carried out, how can it be done except at the expense of the carnivors [sic], at the expense of the vegetation, and finally at the expense of the deer themselves?" In order to keep management of the deer from an escalating political debacle, Wright asked Albright to act as a moderate partner in administrative plans.[57]

Albright's assistants read Wright's letter and in a series of handwritten comments agreed that the biologist's opinion should not be ignored, but neither could it be effectively incorporated into Albright's already-drafted missive to the forester. They acknowledged Wright's concern about the unnatural condition of seeing hundreds of deer in VT Park and wondered if their proposed goal of seeing this return might be ill fated. The group, led by Bryant, was shocked to learn that Albright had already sent his letter to Chief Forester R. Y. Stuart with alterations apparently approved only by Tillotson.[58]

The letter to Stuart included long quotes from the earlier reports of Park Service men—Bryant, Tillotson, and Madsen—illustrating that "a dangerous situation is developing." Albright emphasized that Park Service accounts of the deer situation were unanimous and conflicted with Forest Service inventories. The director insisted that hunting be discontinued based on his staff's estimates. He ended by complimenting the Forest Service's "fine scientific data on carrying capacity" and range improvement plans. So while Albright managed to conclude with a congratulatory statement, he had demanded in an objectionable tone that hunting stop.[59]

Stuart replied promptly for the Forest Service. He was unwilling to argue about the deer situation, but he clearly doubted whether Tillotson and Madsen had "given due consideration to all available facts and problems involved." Aside from this, Stuart was particularly anxious to have the Park Service define its ambition to maintain a "spectacular deer show," as Bryant had recently put it. The forester asked, "Do you believe that numbers of deer along the highway should be sufficient to furnish the average traveler a view of one or two or three deer, or do you believe that the spectacle should consist of 'seventeen hundred' as Mr. Tillotson states he remembers counting in the area?" Such a spectacle, Stuart pointed out, would almost certainly require that most other areas of the forest contain failing food supplies, as most reports agreed was the case until recently on the Kaibab. The Forest Service would not willingly "sanction the destruction of forest resources elsewhere in order to provide a spectacle for the traveling public." Stuart hoped Albright would clarify Park Service goals, and he assured the director that the Forest Service stood ready to reduce or entirely eliminate hunting whenever ongoing investigations justified that action.[60]

Albright also heard back from his own staff. Assistant Director Arthur Demaray sent a memo acknowledging that George Wright's counsel had been flatly ignored in posting the letter to Stuart, and now the Park Service was on the defensive. Demaray suggested that the Forest Service and Biological Survey be allowed to continue their work, with the Park Service only interjecting its hope that the herd "be kept as large as possible." The main point for Demaray was to keep that number, however large, within the limit that could be "carried safely" on the range.[61]

The assistant's suggestion was mostly disregarded, as Albright and Bryant drafted a new letter to Stuart. They added a paragraph on the primary importance of considering the carrying capacity of the range. This standard, according to Bryant, indicated that present deer numbers were "subnormal" and improvements were needed, meaning that a larger number of deer would be more normal. Albright and Bryant both believed that paying attention to carrying capacity was the best way to bring the herd to its maximum number. This would allow the Kaibab to once again provide a "superlative deer show" as it had in the past, in their minds, without artificial destruction of forest resources. It would also correspond with the similar spectacles the Park Service was working to provide for the public, particularly at Yellowstone.[62]

Stuart recognized the continuing disagreement between the two agencies in their use of carrying capacity. To him, the improvements that were needed were with the food supply itself, not with the numbers of deer on the range. In order to accomplish this, he instructed his staff to keep the deer population low so that the range would fully recover, which would eventually allow a larger herd to exist naturally. If the Park Service insisted on an even larger display along the highway, it would have to be established by artificial means. Stuart would not allow other parts of the range to be destroyed in order to increase the "natural display." He carefully offered to cooperate in every way and insisted both to Albright and his staff that full agreement would be possible through obtaining "the best data on range and game conditions."[63]

At the same time, George Wright provided Albright with another assessment of the Kaibab situation, this one taking a slightly longer view of changes on the plateau. The biologist divided the current problems into a three-stage history, including a "primitive" period, a period "under white man's influence," and the "present" period. In the first era, according to his best reconstruction of the scant data available, Wright listed four statements:

1. The plateau supported a good stand of palatable forage.
2. Deer were abundant.
3. Predatory animals controlled the deer.
4. Indians hunted there extensively, further controlling the number of deer.

This was perhaps the most succinct prehistory of the area to date. Since the arrival of white settlers, the deer had been slaughtered, then protected from human hunters and animal predators, all the while competing with domestic livestock as food became scarce. Starvation along with hunting began to reduce the herd until the deer reached their present situation. Wright stated that currently the deer were, in fact, "greatly reduced in number." The range had begun to improve and predators were increasing.[64]

For the future, Wright noted that a management plan for the Kaibab would have different objectives for each of the different agencies administering it. He recognized the Park Service's goal of restoring the spectacle of deer along the highway, but he cautioned that the range would first require several years to reach its "full carrying capacity." Because predator control was already being suggested as a means of increasing the deer, Wright plainly stated that this, along with the abolition of hunting would allow the deer to multiply so rapidly that range improvement currently in the works would by nullified "in almost no time." He advised that the range must recover before increases in the deer could be seriously contemplated.

Albright replied to Wright, thanking him for the helpful comments on the situation. Since Albright had ignored Wright's input in November, it was ironic that the director wrote to Wright, "We only wish we had had [your comments] in hand before writing our letter of December 23 to the Forester."[65] If Albright had prematurely called the lack of deer to Stuart's attention, it may have been because he simply did not care to collect more facts. In a letter on this subject to Senator Frederic Walcott, long-time

Yale Forestry professor Herman H. Chapman called for accountability of
the Park Service director. Chapman accused Albright of "making inaccu-
rate or misleading statements not based on facts and refuted by facts
which were publicly available, and of doing this for the purpose of secur-
ing some public policy or specific act which was not in the true interests
of the general public." Such behavior, the professor added, "should not
be permitted in a government official and public servant." Chapman had
followed the Kaibab case closely for almost twenty years. The professor
testified that students in the Yale Forestry School—including Aldo
Leopold, R. Y. Stuart, and some eight hundred others over the years—
were of the highest caliber, and he could not tolerate Albright's "tactics"
on the Kaibab issue and elsewhere, which clearly flew in the face of the
facts as they were known to Forest Service officials.[66] Albright's tactics
may have been appalling to people outside the Park Service, but most of
his own employees were committed to finding some way of keeping the
Kaibab deer visible to park visitors.

Wright and Joseph Dixon, visited the Kaibab in February to make
further observations. From those, they put together a more comprehensive list of objectives for the Park Service. They wanted to see a
"long-term policy on the Kaibab deer management" that would stand
the test of time when minor fluctuations in the population size inevitably occurred. First, they wanted to be clear that an "adequate population" be maintained within the park boundaries. Second, the size of
the deer population would have to be sufficient to allow visitors a
chance to see deer along the roads and kept at a level "neither in excess
of nor too far below the carrying capacity of the winter and summer
ranges." The first objective would be attained ideally by adding land to
the park to give the service "365-day-out-of-the-year jurisdiction"
over the deer. Since boundary adjustments were unlikely, a number of
other steps would have to be taken to meet the objective of maintaining deer along the road. These included reducing livestock to the minimum possible, keeping the range at "full carrying capacity" and the
deer at a number "approximating but not exceeding the range capacity," controlling predators on Forest Service land, protecting deer at all
times in the open meadows along the roads, and the "adoption of any
measure calculated to attract deer to the roadside areas during the
travel season, such as salting, watering, etc." The biologists concluded
that forthcoming reports of the Forest Service's winter investigations
were expected to confirm that the deer were "reduced to a dangerous

point." Hunting in the coming year might be eliminated. Nevertheless, they quickly added, recovery of the herd should not exceed recovery of the range. Finally, Wright and Dixon praised the local Forest Service officials' judgment and activities and commended the local Park Service workers for their cooperative spirit.[67]

Park Service officials knew that their Forest Service counterparts might be easily antagonized by demands for changes in administration of the preserve. They were proven correct when an article in the *Federal News* described the Kaibab deer as being at "an admittedly low ebb." This statement could only have come from the Park Service. Upon seeing this report, Stuart undoubtedly thought of Professor Chapman's accusations, which had reached him through Senator Walcott or from Chapman directly. The forester wrote to Albright demanding an explanation for this latest manifestation of Park Service propaganda. Albright checked with his staff and quickly replied that no one had been interviewed for the article and that the information must have come from statements issued in the now-outdated 1932 Annual Report. The director went further in an effort to calm the forester, noting that several items in the article were at "wide variance" with the original report. In this case, he was probably innocent of using the *Federal News* as a sounding board. He made his explanation to Stuart, but made no effort to correct the report. The Forest Service seemed willing to let the matter drop, at least for the time being.[68]

This situation starkly illustrated the expectations of federal officials in making use of scientific data. The Park Service and Forest Service agreed on the need for a clear understanding of the carrying capacity of the range. With a quantitative figure in hand, they hoped to reach a consensus on how many deer should be allowed. Between the lines, however, was the expectation that data on the carrying capacity might simultaneously justify Forest Service policy to Stuart and Park Service policy to Albright. Both expected that the range could ultimately carry more deer. Stuart would have those deer spread in a natural distribution across the plateau; Albright would have them concentrated along the highway, as they had been a decade earlier.

Careful reading of Wright and Dixon's latest report suggested, however, that the meaning of carrying capacity remained open to considerable interpretation. On the one hand, it represented a healthy condition of the range, upon which a specified number of deer could safely graze. On the other hand, carrying capacity was simply a number—in this case a number of deer—that people should expect to find on the plateau, regardless of fluctuating climatic conditions and reproductive factors. Livestock managers had faced this problem of defining carrying capacity on other ranges, but the question dawned anew in game and wildlife management on the Kaibab.[69]

The conflict over protection of the deer came to a head with the advent of an expanded awareness of the complex components of game management. This awareness did not necessarily reflect a real advance in scientific knowledge, but field observers like Walter Mann and Edward Goldman were beginning to work with a younger generation of researchers. These students of game management and ecology, such as D. I. Rasmussen and Odell Julander, employed proven methods on a systematic basis for the first time. As the 1932 conflict suggested, their work would not bring clear resolution to lingering differences of opinion over deer management.

8

The Exception That Proved the Rule

By 1933, Walter Mann and his team of local foresters, park rangers, and state game officials had built a foundation of mutual trust and comparative data. Their annual winter counts enabled them to see the same sections of the plateau at the same time of year with men who could speak their minds around the campfire at the end of the day. Few of them had sufficient training in botany or plant ecology to describe the changes they observed from year to year in quantitative terms. At this intersection of game management and ecology, the language of quadrats remained imprecise, and the connection between recovering vegetation and a fluctuating deer herd continued to present enormous difficulties for the practical tasks of creating hunting limits and adjusting predator control policies.[1] Instead, the men who conducted the annual counts relied on their observations, with increasing attempts to specify how estimates and recommendations grew out of actual counting, particular comparisons, and cooperative experience. These efforts, much easier for Mann to defend on the local level, did not answer the ongoing criticism of outsiders who relied on more general reports of conditions that seemed to perpetuate the worst descriptions of the preserve in the mid-1920s.

The Forest Service and Quantitative Methods

Mann's deer count for 1933 resembled earlier counts and, compared with Odell Julander's more elaborate plans, it offered information on only a single aspect of the Kaibab conditions. Mann, along with a team of local Forest Service, Park Service, and state game officials that included Ben Thompson and Julander, estimated the number of deer on the west-side winter range to be 12,900, nearly identical to the previous year's estimate. They actually saw 4,517 deer and decided that this number represented 35 percent of the total deer on that side of the forest. On the east side, where

riding was more difficult, they estimated that the 309 deer they counted
represented just 10 percent of the total. They concluded that the herd had
nearly doubled in a year, from 1,600 to 3,090. This brought the 1933 total
to approximately 16,000. The forest supervisor also reported that the
team found seventeen dead deer.[2]

The Forest Service hired Odell Julander as a junior range examiner specifically to carry on investigations that Walter Mann and others had conducted over and above their regular tasks. In February 1933, with an eye
toward long-term game management examinations on the Kaibab,
Julander attempted to describe the current methods in sufficient detail to
allow uniformity. The new range examiner noted that in time he would
make improvements in the methods used previously, but in order to make
comparisons with earlier studies he would retain the older methods.

The Forest Service's most general method for gathering comparative
data involved the mapping of individual plant species in what Julander
called "brush plots." On the Kaibab, these were the areas Mann had established in the late 1920s. No doubt inspired by range management
techniques, the plots became somewhat useful only as Mann and others
kept careful records of their contents. They were too few in number to
offer a broad picture of conditions, but Forest Service officials hoped to
improve them each year. Julander described the process of locating and
measuring representative "species of importance" using a compass and
standard surveying tools. The examiner sketched the plants on a map,
and on a separate sheet he recorded "maximum, minimum and average
height, condition and vigor of shrub, etc." The examiner also took a photograph of each plot. These photographs became an enduring legacy of
the range conditions and recovery on the Kaibab.[3]

Julander described experiments with cliff rose plants designed to
simulate browsing by deer. In enclosures that protected the plants from
deer, the examiner clipped newly grown shoots; on some plants 50 percent were clipped, on others 75 percent, and on still others 95 percent.
These clippings represented varying levels of browsing from slight to
moderate to heavy. He conducted similar clipping experiments with aspen trees. Initial clippings of between 25 and 95 percent proved too extreme, so Julander recommended clipping between 15 and 60 percent in
the future. He added, "Detailed records were kept on number and length
of shoots, length clipped, number of leaves and buds left and weights of
clippings." These studies were intended to give a measure of the
"withstandability" of the plants.

In addition to withstandability plots, Julander also established "utilization" plots, where they could measure the actual level of browsing by the deer. In these areas, examiners tied tags onto shoots and measured the growth at regular intervals. These plots gave additional data on withstandability that could be correlated with other plots to establish an index of growing conditions, recovery of the shrubs, and the relative volume of forage produced. Cliff rose, as the primary forage plants for deer, received the most attention in these studies, but plots to investigate other species were established according to the same methods. Examination of ponderosa pine, spruce, and fir—the valuable timber species on the plateau—followed similar procedures, making sure that tagging did not interfere with growth of the tree.

Julander concluded by describing the classification of browsing levels: slight, moderate, and heavy. He determined these categories qualitatively, relative to one another. Slight browsing of a shrub, according to the examiner, involved only a few side twigs. Moderate and heavy browsing involved some combination of either increasing numbers of side twigs, or browsing of larger subordinate branches, or most seriously, browsing of main branches.

By the middle of March 1933, Julander prepared an outline of the ongoing studies along with a summary of his methods. First on the list were carrying capacity studies. These included determination of range conditions, utilization levels, competition between deer and livestock, and deer numbers. With carrying capacity information in hand, the examiner could achieve his second objective, the introduction of plant species that would improve range conditions. The third objective involved managing the preserve "for the best enjoyment of the deer by the people." Julander recommended studies of factors in VT Park, which by then was often referred to as DeMotte Park. Finally, the Forest Service should direct studies toward obtaining data on the life history of the deer. He added an outline of methods for achieving these objectives. For example, determination of carrying capacity included study of general growing conditions as well as plot studies of several different species on both the summer and winter ranges. The least-detailed methods section addressed the issue of bringing deer into DeMotte Park for human amusement. In order to attract deer to the park, Julander suggested studies of climatic conditions, forage, water availability, and "other possible factors." He hoped the Park Service would handle those other factors. Much more

standard were the life history studies of the deer. For those, researchers examined breeding age, twin ratios, the mating season, care of
fawns, longevity, weight, and migration habits. Julander's outline
marked the beginning of a standardized approach to investigations
that had been ongoing for the past several years in a less structured
way under Mann's supervision.[4]

As requests for information continued to reach the Forest Service, officials worked to provide consistent answers. On one occasion, a game
official from the state of Washington asked about the "saturation point"
of the Kaibab National Forest. Assistant Forester Chris Rachford responded by first explaining the Kaibab's carrying capacity in a way that
illustrated precisely how that term was to be interpreted, at least within
his agency. Rachford hoped that the Kaibab ranges could be enhanced,
writing, "The maximum carrying capacity of the area at the present time
is not by any means the potential carrying capacity." Fearing that this
distinction between maximum and potential might leave room for disagreement, the assistant forester explained that vegetation on the range
could maintain the current sixteen thousand deer in the preserve and
continue to improve. That improvement, he suggested, would ultimately
lead to a situation where the range would recover "its original productive-
ness." Rachford then referred to Aldo Leopold's recent description of
saturation point in describing game populations: "As Aldo Leopold in his
book *Game Management* defines these two terms, the saturation point
is a property of a species, while carrying capacity is a property of a unit
of range. Even within the Kaibab there are certain areas on which
heavy concentration occurs, while adjoining range may be somewhat
understocked." This explanation made short work of Leopold's distinction.[5]

Leopold's discussion of saturation point was embedded in a broader
attempt to describe animal "density." Rachford, however, went no further
in exploring the primary issue behind Leopold's use of saturation point
in *Game Management*. Undoubtedly conscious of the studies initiated recently by Mann and Julander, Rachford concluded that "the main problem for some years to come will be to judge carrying capacity by the degree to which vegetation recovers." He was probably also aware that he
was opening—or peeking into an already open—can of worms. In any
case, most of Leopold's discussion involved the game birds he had studied as part of his *Report on a Game Survey of the North Central States*. These
had raised the question of how to determine the carrying capacity of a
range on which animals were unevenly distributed; in other words, where

animal density varied across the range. Rachford was well aware of the uneven Kaibab deer concentration, and he admitted that estimating the potential capacity would be a "broad guess."[6]

National Park Service Wild Life Division Studies

Park Supervisor M. R. Tillotson reported that wildflowers on the North Rim in the past years provided a remarkable display of blooming colors. He attributed this to the nearly complete removal of cattle from Park Service lands, which had finally been accomplished with the help of the Forest Service. Tillotson boasted that the Kaibab might soon "become as famous for its wildflower display as it used to be for its deer before the campaign of hunting was started." The fact that Tillotson publicly blamed hunting for the diminished herd continued to make administration of the preserve difficult for those who hoped the Park Service, the Forest Service, and the state could work harmoniously.[7]

The National Park Service, like the Forest Service, initiated more systematic studies of wildlife on its lands when it began paying heed to its Wild Life Division. Originally funded solely by George Wright, the research group—including Wright, Joseph Dixon, Ben Thompson, and David Madsen—took a more visible role in commenting on agency policies by 1933. Before then, Horace Albright had little use for their recommendations, which sometimes favored Forest Service policies. The Kaibab had been a case in point. Thompson in particular participated in studies of the Kaibab, although all four men visited the plateau to check on conditions there.

During the summer of 1933, the Park Service research group began to support the Forest Service's administration of the deer almost unequivocally. Wright's comments tended to call for long-term study and patience in increasing the deer. For example, Madsen wrote at the end of May, "I am convinced that the [Forest Service] men who are handling this most difficult problem are doing a very good job of it and that it should be our policy to cooperate fully with them in developing an intelligent game management program with the view of building up a larger herd of deer whenever it can safely be done." This was unwelcome advice to Albright, and he often chose to interpret such comments to suit his own views, writing, "It is most pleasing to us to find that the Forest Service officials share with the Park Service the sincere desire to increase the number of deer at the earliest practicable date." Repeated attempts to clarify the Forest Service's position for the director were in vain. To complicate matters further, the Wild Life Division recommended expansion of park boundaries for the improvement of wildlife conditions generally. On the Kaibab, they thought the VT Park area ought to be included in Grand Canyon National Park, much to Albright's delight.[8]

Disagreement over the deer once again reached the highest levels of the federal government when Harold Ickes, President Franklin Roosevelt's new secretary of the Interior, asked Secretary of Agriculture Henry A. Wallace to comment on the proposed Kaibab hunt for 1933. Ickes did not lodge any complaint; he only wanted to bring the hunt to Wallace's attention. Undoubtedly, Park Service officials requested that the new Interior secretary raise the issue again at the cabinet level in the hope of finding sympathy for the park's need of a deer spectacle. Ickes received a response from an assistant to Secretary Wallace, which included a brief history of recent reports from the Kaibab that continued to spell out the need for hunting. The response explained that ever since the deer had increased beyond the carrying capacity of the range, hunting had helped the Forest Service bring the herd down to a number where recovery was possible, and since increasing the number was not yet advisable, hunting should continue. The Department of Agriculture official promised that the Interior Department would be advised of new developments. Indeed, once plans for the hunt were finalized, Secretary Wallace wrote to Ickes reporting that "the ranges generally are still in a very much depleted condition" and that "some overbrowsing and damage are yet occurring." Some improvement had been reported, but hunting remained a part of the Forest Service's plans. In the fall of 1933, hunters removed 820 deer.[9]

Changes in national leadership also included Horace Albright, who resigned from the Park Service at about the same time. Albright's resignation brought an end to Park Service protests at the national level. In August 1933, the director left government service altogether and went to work as an executive of the U.S. Potash Company in New York. His successor was long-time assistant Arno B. Cammerer. Once Albright was gone, Wright and his Wild Life Division enjoyed much better relations with the director's office. They agreed that efforts to increase the deer would wait until the vegetation on the preserve showed signs of significant recovery. Tillotson lacked the patience for this strategy. In a request unprecedented for the park superintendent, he asked the new director for permission to destroy predators that were reportedly harassing and killing deer in the park. Cammerer refused, using Wright's advice to support his decision: policies to increase or even protect the deer would have to wait for range improvement. Tillotson and Albright had always agreed on creating a greater deer spectacle, but their days of conspiring were over. The new director wrote, "Mr. Wright's letter is now before you and we hope that you will see the reasonableness of his point of view." No predators were to be killed.[10]

Edward Goldman reaffirmed his acceptance of the need for predators on the Kaibab when he visited the plateau for three days in June 1933. Homer Shantz and A. A. Nichol from the University of Arizona, Walter Mann and Dave Shoemaker from the Forest Service, and newly appointed state game warden S. L. Lewis accompanied the government biologist. Goldman's own notes suggest that the deer numbers had continued to drop, while the range showed slight improvement. A favorable summer followed by a harsh winter resulted in a few starved deer but not devastation to the herd. The deer reached the high meadows around VT Park during Goldman's visit, and he saw groups ranging in size from fewer than ten up to forty deer. He observed Forest Service studies in open and fenced plots, which suggested that some cutting of aspen might stimulate reproduction. In areas of less intensive browsing, other plant species showed "new growth below the established 'deer line.'" Since the deer seemed sufficiently reduced to allow this recovery, Goldman commented that hunting should continue at about the same rate as the previous year and that neither coyotes nor mountain lions required increased control. While most signs appeared positive for the deer, Goldman advised against allowing them to increase rapidly, since conditions were "not yet very satisfactory." Hunting and an unmolested predator population, he concluded, should remove the annual increase to allow further range improvement.[11]

Ben Thompson represented the Wild Life Division on the 1934 survey of the winter ranges for the second year in a row. Walter Mann provided the official "deer count," while Thompson produced a more detailed narrative document. Both described a mild winter. The deer had scattered widely over the ranges and browsed the cliff rose heavily. Most other plant species showed little browsing. Remnants of the previous year's growth was visible, even on some of the cliff rose, because, according to Mann, heavy snow had not forced deer to concentrate on small areas. The forest supervisor reported a total of 3,166 deer seen on the west side, which translated to an estimate of 12,954 deer based on calculated percentages that ranged from 12 to 50 percent in different areas. Thompson explained that while only deer actually seen were counted, the abundance of tracks gave an indication of how numerous the deer might be in a given section. They made their counts for each area and calculated an estimated total for each. So although they counted fewer deer in this year's survey, the wider scattering of animals in the higher, more forested reaches of the range led the surveyors to assume they had missed more. This was particularly true on the east side. Thompson wrote, "Juniper and piñon growth is so dense in the east side that any sort of census is practically impossible." Although only 382 deer were counted there, Mann reported, as in previous years, that about 90 percent of the 3,500 deer went unseen. The group agreed upon an estimated total of 16,500 total on the plateau, an increase of 500 head over 1933.[12]

Thompson also reported three unanimous opinions of the survey group. There were at least as many deer as the last year, the range still needed further relief, and fawn losses this year would be minimal due to the mild winter. These factors pointed to an increasing deer population and future threats to the range. He insisted that it would be impossible for someone to "visualize the extent of destruction of the Kaibab deer winter range unless he rides over it after a winter's utilization." Thompson's own opinion of the range suggested his desire to see it further protected from deer. In describing the continued damage, especially to the cliff rose, the wildlife expert noted that deer numbers were much easier to bring back than forage plants. In addition, if the range was not restored by reducing the deer even further, "a real deer herd" could never be built up. From his experience on the Kaibab, Thompson drafted a "suggested wild life plan" for the park.[13] This plan was immediately incorporated into a larger report prepared by the Wild Life Division and published by the Park Service.

The Wild Life Division's full agenda became known a few months later when Wright and Thompson's report on their preliminary survey of the wildlife of the national parks appeared. In the introduction they illustrated their intention of presenting "new life-history data and the results of pure scientific research conducted within the national parks and monuments" as well as "the exposition of a developing wilderness-use technique as it affects the biological aspects of the national parks." They hoped to clarify the role of scientists and park officials in determining and performing proper wildlife policy based on the best scientific information available. Wright and Thompson did not presume to give a complete account of wildlife problems in all the national parks. Instead, they described a few cases that would be "representative of the type of wildlife management being developed in the national parks." The cases chosen, not surprisingly, included the northern Yellowstone elk and the deer north of the Grand Canyon. They included a series of short descriptions of wildlife on Mesa Verde National Park, Carlsbad Caverns National Park, and Great Smoky Mountains National Park, but the majority of the discussion focused on the Kaibab deer.[14]

Wright specified three causes that contributed in various ways to the park problems: "First, adverse early influences which operated unchecked in the pre-park period, and continued into the early formative period; second, the failure of parks as independent biotic units by virtue of boundary and size limitations; and, third, the injection of man and his activities into the native animal environments." In some parks, one or two of these causes could explain wildlife problems, but all three causes came into play as Wright described the Grand Canyon National Park. The wildlife expert explained that during the "early park period, the livestock concept of wildlife administration prevailed," and efforts to establish parklike conditions required rangers to trap furbearing animals to earn their salaries. Predatory animals deserved no special protection and were hunted relentlessly in order to protect game animals, which were generally in short supply.

Wright noted that only recently had the Park Service established "the principle of equal protection for all species." He refused to condemn past efforts, recognizing that the early national park concept required exactly such activities. He suggested that the parks needed a broader principle of wildlife protection after the "earlier protect-and-hands-off policy had abundantly shown it could not accomplish [its] objective [of preservation] alone and unaided." The new principle, he suggested, would include "scientific, planned management" and "would be used to perpetuate and restore primitive wildlife conditions." Big game protection had not yet attained much success with management.[15]

To illustrate the situation facing big game, Wright's coauthor Ben Thompson explored the paradox of preserving wild conditions in the face of increasing recreational use. Thompson was influenced by Aldo Leopold's depiction of the paradox of wilderness. Leopold wrote, "The more people are concentrated on a given area, the less is the chance of their finding what they seek." The national parks should provide a balance, he said, between the desire of people for what was familiar and what was unique. The amusements of Coney Island, for example, obviously did not belong in the national parks. Somewhat less obvious, Thompson insisted that the sentiments that led to the protection of seemingly helpless deer on the Kaibab also worked against the intelligent use of wilderness. For thousands of people, the most important part of the national park experience included seeing "the things which are peculiar to the primeval wilderness and, what is more, peculiar to a particular wilderness—such as Glacier or Yellowstone or Grand Canyon or some other one." To achieve this balance of preserving the peculiar in a way that diverse people could appreciate required knowledge of "recreational psychology" as well as "the biological requirements of wilderness management."[16]

Turning explicitly to the Kaibab deer, Thompson described the contradictions in Theodore Roosevelt's actions on the Kaibab over the years. The man who wanted to protect deer and kill mountain lions exemplified the problem of injecting human activities into wilderness settings. Thompson blamed Roosevelt's generation of conservationists for creating "a first-class tangle" by not allowing the Forest Service to kill deer in the early 1920s. The situation he observed a decade later suggested that "it will probably take 50 years of careful management to completely cover the scars of the fiasco." The whole affair had its value for Thompson, however. He recognized the urgent need to move beyond that early park concept to the era of scientific management. He concluded, "It was a conservation fiasco and it opened our eyes to the necessity of wildlife (not game) management."[17]

Thompson maintained that the deer and mountain lion relationship might have been "the main factor in the whole complex problem." However, by itself, in some place unfrequented by humans searching for wilderness values, the Kaibab deer would never have faced the dramatic changes seen in the 1920s. He recognized that a broader view of management must look beyond single factors, such as predators. For Thompson, the national park boundary also contributed significantly to the problem, as deer "wander back and forth, as seasons and quest for food dictate, across refuge or hunting ground, park or forest, as the case may be." Roosevelt's cougar hunt of 1913, he wrote, "was done then with the idea that proper wilderness utilization would consist of killing the bloodthirsty animals so that people could enjoy the gentle ones." In 1934, Thompson criticized that reasoning. In an often-quoted line, he summarized, "Unfortunately, the Kaibab was only the type case; the same thing has happened in many places throughout the West in both national parks and national forests where deer and elk have been protected and their enemies destroyed."[18]

As the type case, Thompson believed the Kaibab could now become the model for successful wildlife management. He cited the annual deer census and "cooperative range reconnaissance," as well as the fenced quadrats, which provided a "more scientific method" for comparison of deer browsing.[19] The Kaibab reflected Thompson's broader hope for the

national parks: "Not only do I believe that such wilderness use is the inevitable solution of the Kaibab type of difficulty, but further, that it is the
only possible utilization of the wilderness areas surrounding the national
parks which can make it possible for us to preserve the wilderness aspects
of the national parks themselves." The recommendations of Wright and
Thompson for the Kaibab reflect those made for other parks. One point
stood out: park officials should "allow the normal predatory animals
equal protection with other forms of the park's wildlife." Although the
National Park Service had favored protection of predators in principle for
several years, the connection between the fiasco on the Kaibab and the
need to protect predators became more entrenched with statements such
as this.[20]

DEER NUMBERS IN THE MID-1930S

In 1935, Walter Mann again led the survey of winter ranges on the Kaibab.
In ten years on the Kaibab, he had earned the unqualified support and
respect of virtually everyone who had participated in a survey of the
ranges or worked with him in understanding the situation. Leaders of the
Arizona Game Protective Association praised him for his "on the spot"
supervision of the forest. The team on the Kaibab in 1935 found that the
range continued to show some improvement. Again, cliff rose was the
most heavily browsed species. Mann even reported that measurable
amounts—from one to four inches—of "last year's growth" remained un-
eaten. An expanded table of deer counted in different areas, estimated
percentages of the total counted, and estimated totals provided a detailed
look at where and how many the deer were on the plateau. At the bottom,
Mann added estimated numbers of deer in two areas that had not been
surveyed. The group made only one ride on the east side but estimated
that there were 500 more deer there than the previous year. All told,
Mann listed 12,540, "or, in round numbers, 13,000" on the west and
4,000 on the east. The estimated herd of 17,000 deer in 1935 was 500
head larger than in 1934.[21]

Later that year, T. Gilbert Pearson, who had served on the Kaibab committees of 1924 and 1931, planned an article on wildlife protection that
would update readers on the situation in northern Arizona. Pearson was
by then president emeritus of the National Association of Audubon Societies and published some of his reminiscences in connection with
wildlife protection. He was anxious to develop the Kaibab story as an example of "over-conservation." He asked the Forest Service for information on hunting and the lawsuits with Arizona over administration of the

deer. Pearson was also curious to know the present condition of the preserve. He was updating a 1926 article he wrote for *Bird Lore* on "over-conservation."[22] In the mid-1930s, especially with Wright and Thompson's
wildlife report, the Kaibab story was taking on new meaning. The deer
began to represent the failings of early Park Service wildlife protection
and the excesses of Forest Service livestock management, and at the same
time the role of predators assumed a level of importance that had not
previously been recognized.

Another mild winter meant that conditions on the ranges in early 1936
were the best Mann and other observers had seen in years. Deer were
scattered widely and the heaviest browse in some places had consumed
only half of the recent growth of cliff rose. Other species were lightly
browsed. Estimates of the number of deer were again placed at seventeen
thousand, based on counts very similar to previous years. In addition,
Mann hoped to experiment with census methods using an airplane.
Counts from the air would be compared to counts on the ground. The
pilot, however, would not agree to fly on less than a week's notice, and
since the trip was usually planned to coincide with clear weather that
could only be forecast a few days ahead, the airplane experiment had to
be abandoned, with hopes that it would take place the next year. Odell
Julander continued to monitor the Forest Service's experimental plots
and had worked on the Kaibab for three years by this time, but had not
yet compiled his studies into any useful form. Julander did accompany
the survey team in 1936, but no one commented on his particular contributions.[23]

The importance of predators, even for livestock, was derived from
retellings of the Kaibab case. In October 1936, A. A. Nichol, a veteran of
Kaibab surveys himself, reported to the *American Cattle Producer* that
some balance in predatory species was needed, even for the good of cattle
ranchers. Killing a mountain lion that might kill a calf seemed like good
policy, but Nichol reminded the reader that on the Kaibab, removal of
over six hundred lions by Uncle Jim Owens "eventually worked a hard-
ship on the cattle interests there, since the removal of lions resulted in an
enormous increase in the deer until there was forage for neither cattle
nor deer." In this case, the Kaibab illustrated the point that predators
served a purpose in the balance of nature, even for cattle producers.[24]

The annual deer counts initiated in the 1930s became the most consistent source of information on the deer and range conditions. Even so,
weather and administrative complications sometimes interfered. No deer

count was made in early 1937, and perhaps even more remarkably, no official reason was given. The Park Service prepared a "wildlife census" in the summer, but it merely listed the large species within the park and gave some estimate of their numbers. No systematic counts were made, and the estimates did not include forestlands. Deer were only one among many species, and without a count that included animals in the National Forest on the Kaibab, the estimate seemed useless.[25]

In 1938, Walter Mann reconvened the winter deer count with new intensity. His team included park rangers Arthur Brown and Warren Hamilton, who had ridden along in previous surveys. The Forest Service contingent included two men who had never been on a deer count. As part of their training, Mann planned to show them the methods of counting deer, estimating percentages of the herd seen, and observing the condition of the ranges. Most importantly, Mann trained them in working with the representatives of other agencies. He described the collegiality fostered by the rides and the great importance of perpetuating that spirit. The seasoned forest supervisor knew very well that if anything came up during the count that might lead to disagreement among the parties present, it might result in far-reaching criticism and added work during the coming year. He concluded, "It is these winter deer counts that have brought the Park Service and Forest Service into unity in deer management on Kaibab North."[26] Because of this high ideal, Mann committed as much time as necessary to the annual survey.

Undoubtedly for the benefit of the less-experienced men, Mann wrote up a list of items that should be noted by each surveyor every day on the ride. He prefaced the list with a comment on their practical goals. They all knew that not all the deer could be counted and that the main point was to decide the percentage that could be counted. That percentage would vary in accordance with topography, weather, and methods of covering the range. As a result of their collective observations, Mann continued, "I should like to have free and open discussions as the work progresses, reserving final decisions until the job is done." Once they had all seen the ranges, the deer, and whatever evidence of predator activity they could find, they would attempt to reach full agreement on the conditions and number of deer on the plateau.[27]

As it turned out, the 1938 survey proved a difficult one. Unseasonable rains and bad weather at times made rides especially unpleasant and observations impossible. To make it worse, Arizona Game Warden J. B. Edwards disagreed with the others at every opportunity. According to

Mann, Edwards finally insisted on a different estimate of the total number of deer—twelve thousand instead of fifteen thousand as agreed by the rest of the participants. Mann was able to compliment the Park Service men, especially Warren Hamilton for his "energy, good thinking and good judgment." Because the estimates came in lower than in 1936, Mann felt compelled to offer an explanation to Park Superintendent Tillotson. The forester claimed the difference was due to "a different crew and varied weather conditions" not that any reduction in deer had actually occurred. Since such ad hoc explanations for changes in the population seemed all too common, Park Service Assistant Director Clifford Presnall was left to question, "How valuable is this type of a count?" This question may have been the beginning of the end of cooperation between the agencies for the next few years. Yet it was precisely "this type of count" that had met the needs of the various agencies in understanding the situation and that Mann had so earnestly endorsed. The park rangers who accompanied Mann each year had agreed with the findings of the survey.[28] Agreement on the use to which those findings could be put was more elusive.

ADJUSTING MANAGEMENT PLANS

Park ranger Arthur Brown noted that regardless of the number of deer counted, the range would now support more deer than it had a decade earlier. In accord with general Park Service policy, he suggested that hunting should be limited somewhat to maintain a large population. He stated that reductions in hunting would make the Kaibab "a hunter's paradise." Tillotson, who was always quick to call for changes that might build up the herd, immediately promoted Brown's comment by informing Park Service Director Arno Cammerer that while experts could give "reasonably accurate" estimates of deer numbers, the Forest Service continued to place too much emphasis on determining the exact deer population.

Rather than counting deer, Tillotson insisted that range conditions should be used to determine plans for management. Tillotson did not claim to be a range expert himself, but Brown, an experienced ranger, had suggested that "the range will support a far greater number than now occupy the area." The superintendent concluded by hinting that the Park Service should demand a change in plans for the fall hunt. He followed this by forwarding Mann's report, which did not definitely state that the range was understocked. Tillotson did not explicitly state his hopes for how the Park Service would use these documents. His previous experience with Albright indicated that the director's office might initiate further inquiries aimed at restricting hunting or otherwise increasing the deer.[29]

Tillotson's letters were reviewed in Park Service headquarters by the assistant director, Clifford Presnall. The assistant director offered a point-for-point rebuttal of what he saw as the superintendent's thinly veiled attempt to involve the Park Service in a struggle with the Forest Service over deer management policy. The assistant director noted that a desire for immense herds of deer to astonish visitors was not an appropriate goal. He suggested that the improvement of the Kaibab range paralleled improvements on ranges elsewhere that had resulted primarily from favorable growing conditions. The news that the deer looked healthy did not translate into a clear mandate to increase their numbers again, because the point where their food would be in jeopardy might be reached all too soon.

Finally, the prospect of hunting on the Kaibab had only recently become a sporting endeavor. Presnall believed that before 1934, "hunting deer on the Kaibab was comparable to shooting range cattle." The fact that some hunters had come up empty-handed in the last few seasons was a sign of improvement for the deer and sport hunters alike. Any reduction in hunting should be left to the discretion of the Forest Service officials who had direct control of issuing permits. With Presnall's comments in hand, Victor Cahalane, acting chief of the Wildlife Division, drafted a letter to Tillotson and had it signed by Assistant Director Bryant. The superintendent was praised for his insight and assured that the "entire question" would be discussed with Forest Service officials. In addition, the finer points of the assistant director's missive were put gently, with the request that further "scientific study of sample plots" be carried out by Brown.[30]

During the summer of 1938, a local forester named Harlen G. Johnson prepared summaries of his observations of the deer. He tried to provide data on the relative numbers of bucks, does, and yearlings around VT Park for comparison with numbers collected in previous deer counts. Mammalogists and zoologists had long collected this kind of life history information, but no one had established its significance for game management on places like the Kaibab. Mann and his teams did not collect this sort of data during their winter counts. In February and March, when the counts took place, bucks had shed their antlers and yearlings had almost reached adult size. In the summer, sex and age differences were readily apparent, but deer could not be systematically observed except in the meadows along the roads, which bucks regularly avoided. Johnson, however, took an interest in the relative numbers of deer in different age classes that summer. Yearling deer were especially interesting, since these represented the replacement of deer taken by hunters and the "natural mortality" of the herd.

Johnson noted that changes in the relative frequency of different deer classes had more to do with behavior than actual loss or gain of numbers. For example, does tended to stay hidden during the early summer—the fawning season. Bucks became scarce as the breeding season approached in the fall. When comparing systematic counts in VT Park, Johnson considered weather and food conditions as variable factors in the number of deer seen. These factors, while particularly uncontrollable, were not the only variables that sometimes made deer scarce. Johnson explained that "every once in a while a tourist will attempt to get a picture of a deer and in order to get a closer shot will run or drive into the meadow with the result that the deer will scamper to the timber." When such events took place, the forester planned an additional count for the next evening to assure accuracy. Johnson did not have similar sets of observations to compare farther back than the previous summer when his own work began. Counts made in the meadows—dating back to the early 1920s—were highly anecdotal. He intended to build on the data each year.[31]

When Park Ranger Arthur Brown visited the North Rim in August, Johnson accompanied him to several areas where they examined the vegetation together. Brown wondered why there were so few fawns and why the aspen and clover showed such remarkable growth. These questions would require further study. Tillotson was not prepared to wait around and let the Forest Service allow hunters to kill more deer in the meantime. In October 1938, the park superintendent wrote to Director Cammerer to report Brown's and his own observations of the range. He enclosed a photograph of "typical Aspen reproduction" and noted how fully the vegetation had recovered at the expense of the deer in recent years. In case Cammerer had forgotten, Tillotson reminded him that there was "no longer any such thing as a great spectacle formed by the large herds of deer grazing in the meadows along the road." The tireless advocate of these spectacles hoped that with the great reductions already made and the satisfactory range improvement, the usual hunting on the Kaibab would be discontinued. However, the Forest Service and the state game commission did not see the matter in this light and had already made plans for hunting in the fall. Tillotson expressed an unmistakable desire to see the Forest Service and the state "do away with hunting altogether." A memo from the director's office suggested that the Park Service should proceed slowly in favoring any modification of hunting since the wet years that had apparently produced the abundant vegetative recovery might soon change to drought years.[32]

Tillotson would have to watch from afar to see whether his desires would be fulfilled. The day he wrote his letter to the director, the Park Service announced changes that made him a regional director in Richmond, Virginia. Tillotson's successor, Harold C. Bryant, would move to Arizona after serving in the director's office, where he had followed the Kaibab case closely. The answer to Tillotson's request that the Park Service recommend cessation of hunting came, coincidentally, from Bryant and was signed by the acting chief of the Wildlife Division, Victor Cahalane. The wildlife official thanked Tillotson for his suggestion, but added, "No immediate action will be taken but your report will be kept available for reference in any future decisions." During the 1938 deer season, hunters with state licenses and federal permits killed 692 deer.[33]

Heavy snows delayed the 1939 winter deer count by one month, and Bryant, as the new park superintendent, joined the group for a few days on the east side of the plateau. He hoped to see groups of deer numbering fifteen or more. When a Forest Service ranger named Shorty Auman spotted tracks, he told Bryant to wait on a small ridge. Auman then spurred his horse around a small stand of juniper trees out of which seventeen deer burst and ran past Bryant. The superintendent reportedly told Auman, "You certainly made good." Bryant found his first experience on the deer count enlightening, both in seeing how the count was conducted and in getting acquainted with Mann and the others. He commented, "Needless to say there is a good deal of difference between meeting a fellow-worker in his office and living a couple of days with him in camp." Nothing was revealed about their level of agreement on this occasion. The superintendent did not sign the official count report, since he had not seen most of the range, but his Park Service representatives, Arthur Brown and W. B. McDougall, did. The total number of deer counted by the group was 2,283—ten more than the previous year. The percentage seen in different areas ranged mostly from 10 to 20 percent. Northwest of Ryan, in the extreme corner of the preserve, they saw ten deer. These represented only 3 percent of the deer in that area, according to the counters, so 300 were included in the estimated number for that area. At

Tablerock Point, the group counted 170 deer and estimated 680, assuming they saw 25 percent of the deer there. The total estimate came to 15,097.[34] The absolute accuracy of this number could still be questioned, but as a point of reference, it showed a slight decline in the herd.

Park Naturalist Brown prepared a copy of the official report for Bryant and Cammerer. Brown's colleague, McDougall, worked as a wildlife technician for the regional Park Service office in Albuquerque and provided a separate report. McDougall's account included details of how the count was conducted as well as his own personal impressions of it and the all-day haul through deep snow that was necessary to cover the twelve miles from Ryan to Slide, where they established the main camp. McDougall described how at the end of each day the men were asked to estimate the percentage of deer actually seen in the areas they covered. At the same time, the men made observations of the range conditions. Those who could compare the vegetation to previous years concluded that the deer had browsed the cliff rose more severely that winter. This, they suggested, was due to the long winter and the fact that according to Harlen Johnson's range studies the cliff rose had grown 36 percent less than during the year before. The wildlife technician praised Johnson's work and predicted an optimistic future for the deer thanks to the deer counts and Supervisor Mann's desire to give "every advantage to the deer herd." McDougall also noted that a lion hunter, Jack Butler, reportedly killed 22 mountain lions on the Kaibab in 1938. In McDougall's opinion, these lions, along with 100 coyotes killed that year and 225 killed in 1937, were predators that might actually have helped the deer population. He wrote, "It is probable that the deer herd would profit by a somewhat larger number of predators, especially mountain lions, although it is realized that these numbers must be kept in check." Once again, there seemed to be no way of explicitly addressing this ongoing question.[35]

McDougall praised the annual deer counts in an extended discussion of the value of making observations of the range and the deer on the same areas at about the same time each year. He recognized that they actually counted only about 15 percent of the deer, and that "no one knows whether that estimated total is within 10 percent or 50 percent or 100 percent correct." The substance of the count, however, derived more from the repeated comparisons. McDougall wrote that the "scientific experimentalist" (Johnson) and the "thoroughly practical men" (Brown, Auman, and Mann) alike agreed that the count was worthwhile. This agreement recommended the method, particularly since it proved to be the best way to address what McDougall called "an ecological problem in game management that is of national interest and importance." He concluded by noting that everyone seemed to agree that the range would support more deer and that "it would be a good thing, as an experiment, to reduce the number of deer taken by hunters during the next open season from that taken last year." This experiment, however, would require the approval of officials who had not participated in the count and had divergent views of the situation.

Park Superintendent Bryant—now appropriating Tillotson's line of reasoning—insisted that the deer had become too scarce and implied that he would like to see large numbers of deer, even if they were starving. When local foresters met with Bryant, they let him do the talking, agreeing as often as possible and keeping quiet otherwise. Harlen Johnson and Walter Mann already planned to discuss a reduction in deer hunting with the state and hoped the Park Service would be gratified.[36]

Their discussions did not take place in time to affect hunting policy that year, however. The hunt resembled previous hunts, with 693 deer taken by 1,085 hunters. Of the deer killed, 391 were bucks, three of which weighed over 250 pounds and one being a new all-time record on the Kaibab at 268 pounds. Johnson provided this information to a local newspaper, reporting that the success rate for hunters was lower than in 1938, when the weather had been moist, but similar to 1937, which had been a dry season.[37]

Despite the strong words in favor of continuing the annual counts by Mann, McDougall, and Bryant alike, no count took place in the winter of 1940, nor was any reason for the second missed survey in four years recorded.[38] A combination of factors—including the lack of an official count—reinvigorated the latent controversy between the Park Service, Forest Service, and state game commission. In addition, an increase in the observed number of coyotes on the plateau and the continued desire of park officials to see more deer along the highway fueled the conflict. This time, disputants referred to carrying capacity and predator control explicitly and repeatedly. Those observers who had been around for a decade or more provided valuable insights on the condition of the range and deer. However, larger concerns again introduced a complex array of conflicting goals, despite what Kaibab veterans considered to be the best management efforts. The intersecting effects of hunting and predation on the deer herd caused a serious clash between the federal agencies.

The Forest Supervisor's report of 1923 states that old-time residents, trappers, hunters and stockmen think his estimate is no more than half the number of deer. In 1924 Forest Ranger Benjamin Swapp's estimate of the number of deer was 50,000. G. W. Findlay, a sheep owner of Kanab, Utah, estimated over 100,000. In 1936 all the local residents of Kanab and Fredonia and the area surrounding the Kaibab Plateau agreed that the present number of deer about one-tenth the number that existed there in 1924. Forest officers now believe that there were more than 100,000 deer in 1924.

Estimates taken from yearly reports of the Forest Supervisor:

```
1908 .............. 4,000 deer
1909 .............. No record.
1910 .............. 9,000
1911 .............. 10,000
1912 .............. 10,000
1913 .............. No record.
1914 .............. No record.
1915 .............. 10,000
1916 .............. 15,000
1917 .............. 15,000
1918 .............. 15,000
1919 .............. 15,000
1920 .............. 20,000
1921 .............. 20,000
1922 .............. No record.
1923 .............. 30,000
1924 .............. 30,000
1925 .............. 30,000
1926 .............. 30,000
1927 .............. 30,000
1928 .............. 30,000
1929 .............. 30,000
1930 .............. 30,000
1931 .............. 20,000
1932 .............. 14,000
1933 .............. 16,000
1934 .............. 16,500
1935 .............. 17,000
1936 .............. 17,000
1937 .............. 15,000
1939 .............. 15,000
1940 .............. 9,000
1941 .............. 9,000
```

(There were probably more than
(100,000 deer during these six
(years.

(Systematic counts not made
(previous to 1930.

(Counts for percentages in VT
(Park in 1930 showed a 50%
(drop in numbers.

These estimates are for the entire area north of the Colorado River up to and including 1918; they cover the area north of the old National Park boundary from 1919 to 1926; and cover the present area from 1927 to 1941.

A range count was not made in 1940. The summer counts in VT Park show a definite drop in numbers during 1939 and 1940. The range count in the spring of 1941 shows a definite drop in number. This drop may be attributed to losses by predatory animals. A systematic program of predatory animal control is now being carried on by The Fish and Wildlife Service.

-26-

Walter Mann assembled deer population data from forest supervisors' reports from 1908 to 1941, including his own estimates in the margin.

CONCERNS OVER COYOTES

In the summer of 1940, Park Service Naturalist William H. Behle and Assistant Chief Ranger Arthur Brown met with Harlen Johnson to gather information on the "coyote-deer situation" in the Kaibab National Forest. They reported their findings to Edwin McKee, the park's chief naturalist. McKee wanted to hear an official response to rumors that the number of deer had dropped while the coyote population in the forest had risen in the past year. Johnson told the park rangers that the opposite was in fact the case, and he cited the smaller number of coyotes trapped as evidence that fewer coyotes existed on the plateau. He had seen a total of only seven coyotes in the forest in the past year himself, and only two deer killed by coyotes had been found. Johnson's observations also suggested that deer were just as abundant as in recent years, although they were tending to stay back in the forest, away from the roads. He had evidence to support the decreased numbers in the open meadows but, according to Behle, nothing supported his claim that more deer could be found in the forest. Johnson did provide a list of reasons why the deer were not frequenting the open areas. Road work involving heavy loads of gravel disturbed the deer, as did increased driving speeds on improved roads constructed in the past few years. In addition, tourists carrying motion-picture cameras chased deer to get "action shots." Finally, greater rainfall and improvement of the range explained the decreased need for deer to concentrate in the meadows.

Behle noted that Johnson did not bring out "detailed field notes and records" to support his claims, but the park naturalist did not doubt that such data would further substantiate these contentions. Behle also reported that the forester opposed predator control. He wrote, "Johnson believes that predators play a beneficial role in nature, that they are not too numerous, and that a campaign of extermination is not justified." Given this, Behle concluded that the rumors about an increasing coyote population might be the result of propaganda started by "local cattlemen who desire the removal of predators for their personal interests" or by predatory animal control people in both the state and federal agencies who hoped to justify their new "Vermin Control" campaigns. Only a few days later, Brown reported that the Biological Survey had indeed employed two coyote trappers and one lion hunter to reduce the number of predators on the Kaibab, presumably at the request of the Forest Service.[39]

The Biological Survey—by then officially renamed the United States Fish and Wildlife Service—employed the three predator-control men for a three-month period to "assist the Forest Service and the Arizona Game and Fish Commission." When word of the Park Service's concern reached W. C. Henderson, then acting director of the Fish and Wildlife Service, he ordered his regional director, John Gatlin, to suspend coyote trapping and lion hunting. Henderson wanted to wait for a thorough investigation, and he also wanted to keep the Park Service's involvement in the matter confidential. However, when Gatlin wrote to the regional forester and state game warden, he plainly stated that the Park Service had "raised an objection." In fact, the Park Service's objection arose directly from McKee's disagreement with the state game commission's assumption that predators were killing deer. McKee had reported on a recent meeting of the Arizona Game Commission, stating, "First the commission attempted to prove that deer are scarce primarily because of predators yet the supposed evidence consists entirely of a *guess* that predators last year destroyed 5,000 deer." Despite a lack of real evidence and the apparent concern that too many deer were being killed, McKee was astonished to see the commission open hunting with over a thousand permits. The park naturalist suggested a continuation of current studies designed to census the deer, determine their food needs, and find out whether predators were killing deer or not.[40]

Knowledge that the Park Service was, in a sense, interfering—with the assistance of the Fish and Wildlife Service—in a long-standing agreement of the Forest Service and state game commission did not sit well with the state game warden, K. C. Kartchner. He complained directly to Secretary of the Interior Harold Ickes, outlining again the increase of the deer in the decades prior to 1928, the year the state began to regulate hunting. Since that time, the warden continued, the Forest Service and the state game commission worked together to reduce the deer. The arrangement succeeded, but a new wrinkle had developed. Kartchner had discovered that the Kaibab deer herd had been reduced "below the carrying capacity of the range, not by legal hunting nearly so much as by predatory animals which have gotten out of control." Where an estimated thirty thousand deer browsed on the range in the late 1920s, Kartchner now believed there to be only five thousand.

Protecting the deer once again meant destroying their enemies. With the range rehabilitated, or at least well on its way, and the hunting arrangement fully in place, Kartchner saw no reason to allow predators to interfere with "maximum deer production," which he noted stood at the head of the list of Forest Service and Arizona priorities. Federal Fish and Wildlife Service hunters and trappers were poised to implement the planned solution. They would systematically remove lions and coyotes in an effort to reverse the decline of deer. Kartchner believed there was "no question but that predators have been responsible." As evidence of the abundance of these animals, the warden reported that 113 coyotes, 11 bobcats, and one lion had been killed recently in a month's time. Meanwhile, the Park Service protest had seemingly suspended this control work. Kartchner insisted that the Park Service was in an "inconsistent and impossible position," demanding that its tourists be able to see deer along the highway in greater numbers than exist today and at the same time protesting the very steps that were needed "to rebuild the herd back to its normal capacity." Park officials had no basis for the current protest, which threatened to obstruct "the efficient management of the most notable Mule Deer herd in the Southwest."[41]

Kartchner explained that management of the herd was aimed at producing an "annual crop" of up to two thousand deer, which would attract hunters from all over the country. In addition, a herd that could sustain such a yield required "proper predator control" and would provide hundreds of deer in the open meadows on top of the plateau where tourists would see them throughout the summer. He concluded with the hope that Ickes would not stand in the way of cleaning up the forest of predators. He added that "it simmers down to a question of whether we are going to raise deer for the meat-eating cats and coyotes or whether we are going to manage the herd on a utilization, sustained-yield basis with its added attraction for tourists during the summer months." Ten years of allowing the predators free range on the Kaibab, for Kartchner, was enough. This strongly worded letter to the secretary of the Interior actually represented restraint on the warden's part. Kartchner allowed more partisan feelings to show in corresponding with his U.S. senators, Carl Hayden and Henry Ashurst: "For some years there has been a smoldering and sinister movement on the part of the National Park Service to take the Kaibab National Forest." He asked Hayden and Ashurst to intervene and hopefully end the Park Service's "greedy designs." Such an effort, the warden believed, would be greatly appreciated by the entire citizenship of Arizona. Excerpts of these letters appeared in the Phoenix newspaper, and Senator Hayden forwarded a copy to the Park Service, asking for an explanation of the "smoldering and sinister" movement.[42]

The Park Service's new superintendent of Grand Canyon National Park, Frank Kittredge, reviewed Hayden's letters. Kittredge had served as the park's chief engineer beginning in the early 1930s and visited the North Rim frequently for over a decade inspecting the roads and making recommendations for improvements. With respect to the deer, he recommended that despite the real need for further study of the predator situation, as Park Naturalist Edwin McKee had suggested, the Park Service should participate in a coordinated trial period during which deer hunters would be restricted and predators would be trapped or killed. Kittredge confirmed that the Forest Service would willingly agree to such a plan.

The state game commission, however, was unlikely to reduce hunting permits for two reasons. First, permits generated income, and second, reducing permits would offend the local hunting associations, groups that had considerable control over the commission's decisions. The superintendent hoped the new Park Service director, Newton Drury, who replaced Arno Cammerer in August 1940, would make some decisions soon. Without reference to actual changes in the weather, Kittredge concluded that "a storm is apt to break any time." Kittredge may have overdramatized the situation, since by 1940 virtually everyone involved in North Rim affairs was too savvy to let the predicament get out of hand. Director Drury, however, had no previous Park Service experience, so the Park Service spent the next month clarifying its position. Officials in Washington explained to everyone involved that no Park Service employee had blocked predator control and no sinister movement was afoot.[43]

Secretary Ickes responded directly to Kartchner, assuring him that the temporary cessation of predator control on the Kaibab did not result from a protest or inappropriate interference between federal agencies. The Fish and Wildlife Service needed time to assess certain "inconsistencies and differences of opinion" that arose out of preliminary reports. Past difficulties in managing the Kaibab deer required that the Park Service proceed all the more prudently. Representatives of the Department of the Interior had recently conferred with Forest Service officials, and they agreed upon a resumption of the predator control program on a practical and fact-finding basis, according to Ickes, "which should insure all participating agencies against harmful criticism." Federal officials would consult Kartchner and other state officials before proceeding with more planning. They promised to consider the needs of tourists and hunters.[44]

Arthur Demaray wrote similar letters on behalf of Drury to the two Arizona senators and the editor of *Arizona Wildlife*, each of whom had received word of the "smoldering plans" from Kartchner. Demaray explained that the information that had passed between the Park Service and Fish and Wildlife Service was part of routine correspondence. He sternly concluded, "The National Park Service has made no recommendations about this predatory animal control program, either officially or unofficially, at any time, and in this particular you have been completely misinformed."[45]

Director of the Fish and Wildlife Service Ira Gabrielson apologized to the Park Service for any misunderstandings that his department had caused in ordering a stop in predator control. By that time, Demaray and others had realized that the bulk of the misunderstanding resulted from Fish and Wildlife Service Regional Director John Gatlin's comment that the Park Service had raised an objection. Whatever Gatlin's personal motivation, his agency concurred with the Park Service on the status of predators on the Kaibab. A six-day survey by officials in the Fish and Wildlife Service, who were accompanied by predator hunters and trappers, found very little sign of lion activity. Coyotes, while present in some areas, did not seem to threaten the vitality of the deer population.[46]

Even with all of this communication, goodwill could not be restored. Kartchner wrote back to Senators Hayden and Ashurst after seeing Demaray's stern denial of interference, enumerating actions by the Park Service that went back to the 1920s, which taken together amounted to a conspiracy theory. His case was built largely on the accusation that the Park Service was incompetent to manage wildlife or to judge proper management techniques and was based more on feelings about past experiences than the current level of expertise in the various divisions. He wanted the Arizona congressional delegation to "prevent further meddling by that Service in a matter it clearly does not understand and which is furthermore outside its jurisdiction." Hayden asked Demaray directly to instruct his field officials not to interfere with predator control on lands beyond their administrative reach.[47]

Before explicitly agreeing to Hayden's request, the Park Service opted to initiate a planned investigation that would include representatives of the concerned government units. The state game commission objected to the participation of the Park Service in any further study of the plateau outside the park, so the Fish and Wildlife Service engaged W. B. McDougall and D. I. Rasmussen to conduct the investigation. In addition to this planned study, Ira Gabrielson wrote to Senator Hayden in a further attempt to clarify the position of his agency in relation to the Park Service with respect to the predator control program on the Kaibab. Gabrielson supported the facts as Demaray had described them previously and insisted that Kartchner's accusations were without justification. He concluded, "In my opinion, this incident should not be taken as an occasion to stir up feeling regarding old controversies that we know have arisen from time to time over this problem and others to which Mr. Kartchner evidently alludes." Finally, Demaray forwarded correspondence between Mann and various Park Service officials to Hayden, which showed the long-term cooperative efforts of the two federal agencies. By the end of the year, the Park Service seemed to be out of the woods.[48]

A Turning Point

The year 1941 marked a kind of turning point, both in studies of the Kaibab and in national attitudes toward management of the situation there. That year, Rasmussen published his dissertation in *Ecological Monographs*, and Aldo Leopold, who had long been concerned about deer management in northern Arizona, finally visited the plateau and saw its vegetation, deer, and terrain firsthand. While some things stayed the same—the Park Service, Forest Service, state game commission, and a new Arizona governor continued to struggle in search of common ground—the consensus of the scientific community regarding what had happened there over the years began to change.[49] Largely due to the efforts of Rasmussen and Leopold, the legacy of the Kaibab deer became ensured in the history of ecology and population biology. Prior to that year the deer seemed especially significant to the nation's nature lovers and a handful of mammalogists, foresters, and game managers, but the legend might have ended with the controversy. It did not.

The deer count for 1941 took place in March, conducted by a group consisting primarily of forest officials. Only one state game representative and no one from the Park Service participated. Notably, Rasmussen joined the group for about half of the survey. They found the deer widely scattered and concluded that a pack of dogs running loose on the east side for the past month and the mild winter had kept the deer from concentrating on the range. During that year's survey, Forest Service Range Examiner Fred

Johnson implemented a new method of estimating the deer, which involved determining the number of deer seen on a known area by covering the area with six or eight riders (rather than just one or two, as with the previous method). He believed that this would give a precise density—the number of deer per square mile or per acre. These densities could then be compared to

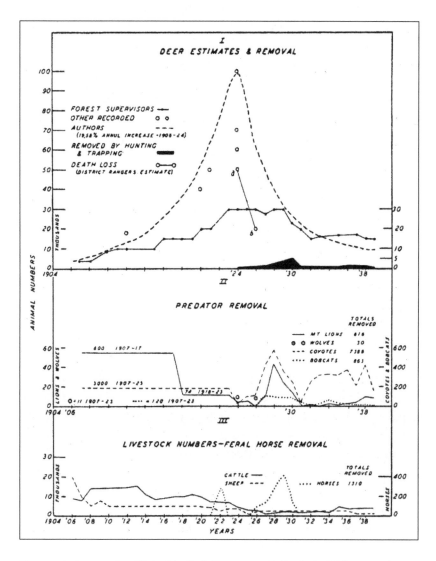

The population graph published by D. I. Rasmussen in Ecological Monographs *included data on predator removal and livestock numbers in addition to the famous deer graph. Reprinted with permission.*

general estimates of the percentage of deer seen (the previous method), in
order to verify these estimates. Johnson hoped this would increase the reli-
ability of estimates on areas where riders believed they saw only 10 to 20
percent of the deer.

Recognizing that deer were not evenly distributed, Johnson managed
to conclude that there were between fourteen and seventy-eight deer per
square mile on the ten areas examined. He divided the west side range
into four larger areas of distinct densities and multiplied density times
acreage and multiplied the product times a conversion factor for the percentage of deer seen. This gave a total of 8,365 deer on the west side. A
similar examination of the east side was deemed too expensive and demanding, particularly with the widely scattered deer. The group agreed
that there were approximately two thousand deer on the east side and
thirteen hundred deer on the west side that had not been ridden due to
heavy snows. This gave an approximate total of twelve thousand deer in
1941.

Johnson described the range as being in good condition with heavy
browsing only in isolated areas. Some of the most critically damaged vegetation from years past now showed notable recovery. Johnson also reported that coyotes seemed more abundant than in previous years, and
that mountain lions could kill adult bucks. Carcasses of six such bucks
were found, probably killed shortly after the mating season when they
were most vulnerable. The range examiner suggested mountain lion control that targeted predators on specific areas of the plateau would be more
effective than reducing hunting permits in increasing deer numbers.
Hunters concentrated their efforts wherever deer were relatively abundant, while predators killed deer in more remote areas where they were
scarcer. Johnson concluded that reducing hunters would lead to overpopulation of congested areas, while removing predatory animals would
allow an overall increase with less threat to the population.[50]

Johnson's report was not the last word on the 1941 count. Walter
Mann, who once again led the survey, objected to several of the range
examiner's conclusions. Making no reference to the new density method
of estimating the deer population, Mann showed that the number seen
closely matched previous counts. He added, however, that improved
knowledge of where to find deer resulted in a much higher percentage of
deer seen. Surveyors knew where to look. Using higher percentages for
the entire range, Mann concluded that the total estimate should be placed
at less than nine thousand deer, rather than nearly twelve thousand, as

Johnson and several others suggested. J. B. Edwards from the state game commission agreed with the forest supervisor. In addition, Mann pointed out that if he was right, the combination of hunting and predation by coyotes and mountain lions would lead to a continuing decrease in the deer population with each passing year. He recommended that a year-round lion hunter be stationed on the Kaibab along with government coyote trappers.

Mann made it clear that the overabundance of deer in the early 1920s resulted from removal of too many predators and a complete prohibition of hunting. Now because the Park Service in particular insisted on protecting predators, and hunters succeeded in killing almost a thousand deer each year, "we find ourselves in a very embarrassing position in management. We have plenty of forage and only a few deer." This conclusion began to gain wider acceptance, and it lent credence to the notion that protection of deer from predators and human hunters led to an opposite extreme, where forage was scarce and deer were abundant. Thus, protection was simply a primitive form of mismanagement. Mann's suggestion that the deer might now number fewer than ten thousand gave wildlife officials pause when they looked at management in the 1930s.[51]

Aldo Leopold visited the Kaibab in July as part of a tour through the West on behalf of the American Wildlife Institute. The veteran forester and by then widely recognized leader in game management wanted to see for himself the area that had endured so much controversy. Leopold's reaction to the Kaibab reflected his wider assessment of deer ranges in the United States. Acknowledging that vegetation on the plateau seemed largely recovered, he was astonished to learn that efforts to build up the herd were again in motion. The wildlife leader regarded this policy as "dangerous and unsound." He noted the naiveté of trying to manage deer through licensed hunting and predator destruction. Leopold compared situations in Utah and Oregon, where prevailing conditions were as bad as the Kaibab at its worst, with mismanagement on the famous preserve. He concluded that changes in deer populations resulting from disruptions in natural checks—now regularly referred to by Leopold as irruptions—posed a greater threat to forests than anything but fire. Moreover, the problem was widespread and a general lack of understanding of how to deal with it continued to plague wildlife managers.[52]

In Utah, Leopold met with Rasmussen. Along with the American Wildlife Institute entourage, they laid plans for an ambitious research program that Leopold later called a "pipe dream." They would find funding for a graduate student to undertake a study similar to Rasmussen's. The researcher would need "impartial" funds in order to conduct the work unhampered by government agencies. The person they had in mind was Richard J. Costley. Costley had been an undergraduate student of Rasmussen's before going to Illinois to complete a master's degree with Victor Shelford in 1936. Since then, he had worked as a range examiner for the Forest Service in northwestern Utah, undoubtedly working closely with Rasmussen once again. In 1941, he returned to Illinois to complete doctoral work with Shelford. He proposed to undertake a study of the deer on Stansbury Mountain in Utah, a herd that then resembled the Kaibab herd in the years just before it reached its peak. Leopold was convinced that Costley needed to gather data from a healthy deer herd and compare it to the Stansbury herd, which was already headed for disaster. The only place to find a healthy herd, the wildlife leader advised, was in Mexico. Leopold also expected that if all the data from the Kaibab and other herds that had suffered a similar fate could be compiled and analyzed, "a common denominator" might emerge. While Costley prepared for more field studies, Leopold began the comparative analysis.[53]

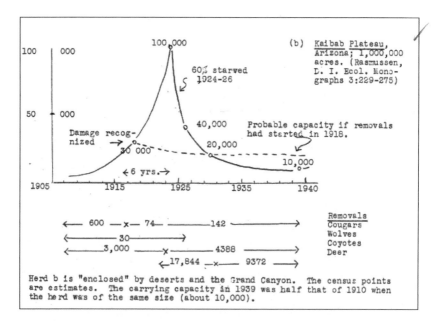

Aldo Leopold drew by hand a copy of Rasmussen's graph for his class lectures, then published the graph to accompany his discussion of deer irruptions.

Between 1941 and the end of his life in 1948, Leopold repeatedly used the Kaibab case to illustrate the hazards of management efforts gone astray. In an article written shortly after his visit and in lectures given in game management classes at Madison, Leopold compared the Kaibab to deer herds in Michigan and Pennsylvania, where hunting had reduced the populations before widespread starvation took place. On the Kaibab, Leopold recounted how starvation followed destruction of vegetation that lowered the carrying capacity of the range. In the other cases, the carrying capacity of the range had been maintained by proactive reduction of deer. Leopold's thesis clearly pointed to the importance of hunting as a means of managing deer and maintaining their populations at levels below the point at which the range would be damaged. His other writings in the 1940s, particularly the essay "Thinking Like a Mountain," which appeared in *A Sand County Almanac* illustrated the plight of deer that faced Kaibab-like conditions. Leopold, more than anyone, used previous studies in northern Arizona to demonstrate the importance of proper management of game.[54]

The first in a series of photographs taken by the Forest Service shows the browse line of trees on the west side of the plateau in 1930. Photo courtesy of Kaibab National Forest.

By the mid-1940s, the Kaibab deer reached true iconic status. What-ever further studies of the deer and range conditions might reveal, the data would be tainted by the widely held opinion that the early irruption on the Kaibab took place at a time when such an event was completely unexpected and probably unavoidable. Events in the 1920s and 1930s further complicated the picture, as mismanagement and ignorance con-tinued. For Leopold and others, it was time for a fresh start. New "all-out" studies on relatively unsullied ground with consistent long-term methods would replace the piecemeal estimates of the beleaguered Kaibab. Leopold's suspicion that predators controlled deer populations would be tested repeatedly, but decades of research did little to change the idea that had taken hold in 1941: the Kaibab had irrupted due to predator removal, and every game range where predator control was practiced was similarly slated for irruption.

This shift was further marked by an article published in *Natural His-tory* in November 1941. Sherman Baker described the killing of coyotes as a traditional pastime of ranchers and game hunters who hoped to protect

Twelve years later, this photo shows that the vegetation was recovering, as can be seen by the rising browse line in 1942. Photo courtesy of Kaibab National Forest.

their respective livestock and prey from predators. He challenged this tradition by noting that except in sheep country, coyotes posed little threat to livestock and big game. The massive toll mountain lions took on deer—one per week—needed to be considered in the context of an alternate disaster sometimes wrought by killing lions. The Kaibab deer served to make Baker's point. He wrote: "Wildlife is not just a simple matter of so many cougars and so many deer, for instance. There exist in nature many complex and subtle relationships that we do not even suspect. It is not possible, for example, to produce more game merely by killing off the predators." Baker paraphrased a long passage from George Wright and Ben Thompson's description of the Kaibab situation to emphasize the official recognition this view had merited. He concluded that people need to "think twice" before meddling in the "dynamic balance" of nature. Coming as it did at a time when some Kaibab officials—notably from the Park Service—wanted to meddle with that balance, Baker's article represented a new level of irony. If biologists had learned anything on the Kaibab, it was that management efforts often had far-reaching and unexpected implications. The proposal to avoid meddling in nature's delicate balance would satisfy no one, however. The goal of more deer in the right places did not seem attainable without some kind of meddling.[55]

Articles like Baker's, which made specific reference to the Kaibab deer without adding substantially to knowledge of either the situation there or the relationship between deer and predators more generally, appeared on a regular basis throughout the 1940s. Leopold in particular used the case to illustrate his own changing ideas about predators. When his own version of Rasmussen's graph began to appear in biology textbooks in the 1950s, the entire history of the Kaibab deer became fixed. Ecologists and wildlife managers no longer questioned the role of their predecessors in understanding the situation. Rather, they used people like Goldman, Mann, and Rasmussen to illustrate the ignorance of an earlier age. More recent scientists attempted to distance themselves as much as possible from those who came before them. They offered definitive accounts of the Kaibab case, and those accounts became increasingly simple. Rasmussen's graph made it possible to describe the entire history in a single figure with just a paragraph of explanation. Thompson had said the Kaibab was the "type case" of what happened to prey species when predators were destroyed. In the minds of Leopold, Sherman Baker, and the readers of their articles, the Kaibab became just that, whatever the richer natural and human history of the situation might actually include.

Epilogue

The oft repeated story of the Kaibab deer in Arizona is another case in point. At one time the deer population was in equilibrium with its environment. A number of predators—wolves, pumas, and coyotes—prevented the deer from outrunning their food supply. Then a campaign was begun to "conserve" the deer by killing off their enemies. Once the predators were gone, the deer increased prodigiously and soon there was not enough food for them. The browse line on the trees went higher and higher as they sought food, and in time many more deer were dying of starvation than had formerly been killed by predators. The whole environment, moreover, was damaged by their desperate efforts to find food.

RACHEL CARSON

Scientists love to tell stories about science, especially stories that neatly illustrate well-established principles. The Kaibab became just such a story, and its retellings continue. In addition to accounts by scientists, the story of the Kaibab deer appears in popular nature writing, hunting lore, and environmental history. The complexities of events on the Kaibab between 1920 and 1945 have made it possible for chroniclers to derive a variety of lessons from two basic narratives. The first narrative is the textbook case, which makes predators essential participants in ecological communities. The second comes from popular and environmental histories that suggest human intervention in the balance of nature generally wreaks unintended havoc. What both narratives do with this complex story is to draw out the facts that best match their preferred lesson. I hope that this book provides a third narrative, which not only explains the existence and purpose of previous accounts but also contains a new lesson about the meaning of such a complex case in the history of science.[1]

Throughout the 1950s and 1960s, textbook writers used the Kaibab story and progressively simpler versions of Aldo Leopold's graph as the key to understanding the important role of predators. Alfred Emerson's version of Leopold's graph appeared in *Principles of Animal Ecology* primarily to illustrate how predators benefit an animal community. In 1957, George Gaylord Simpson used the example and the graph to point out "the unforeseen and disastrous possibilities of ignorant interference in natural communities." Ten years later, William T. Keeton suggested that the Kaibab deer illustrated the "cardinal fact of ecology" regarding the importance of predators, but this fact was "frequently overlooked by well-meaning but misguided people who consider parasites and predators repugnant and evil."[2]

Graeme Caughley attempted to call a halt to the proliferation of Kaibab stories in ecology and general biology textbooks in 1970. He explained that textbook writers had constructed the progression of increasingly simplified graphs based on assumptions rather than evidence. "Data on the Kaibab deer herd in the period 1906–39 are unreliable and inconsistent," he insisted, "and the factors that may have resulted in an upsurge of deer are hopelessly confounded."[3] For readers of *Ecology*, Caughley offered a crushing critique, and most textbook authors chose to eliminate the case from their discussions of populations and predator-prey relations altogether.[4]

Not all biology textbooks expunged the Kaibab deer story, but while some retained it out of apparent ignorance of Caughley's critique, at least one embraced both the case and Caughley's point to demonstrate the pitfalls of general biology texts.[5] Jeffrey Baker and Garland Allen, in the third edition of their widely used introductory text, *The Study of Biology*, moved the Kaibab story into a supplement, which appeared alongside a discussion of ecological relationships in the main text. The first two editions of the book had used the Kaibab story almost verbatim as it appeared in Simpson's text. Baker and Allen redrew the graph with permission from Simpson. Those editions were published in 1967 and 1971. By the time their third edition came out in 1977, Caughley's critique was well known. The supplement ran under the bold-faced headline, "The Kaibab Deer Case: Myth or Reality?" Like Caughley, Baker and Allen illustrated their new discussion of the story with drawings of the earlier versions of the graph, specifically Rasmussen's, Leopold's, and Davis and Golley's. The supplement briefly related the facts of the case as presented in earlier editions, but emphasized that various assumptions about causes and a lack of critical reexamination had established a more "convenient" story of the importance of predators. They added, "Textbooks (the present not excepted) are often notorious for perpetuating accepted dogma in a field without reexamining the original data." Particularly in ecology, they noted, experiments are not easy to replicate. Students, therefore, should join these textbook authors in being "especially critical of ecological reports that 'overinterpret' limited sets of data."[6]

More recently, textbook authors are embracing reforms in science education, which have been prompted in part by historians and philosophers of science. In biology, Michael Mix, Paul Farber, and Keith King provide the most notable example by insisting that students should be exposed to the "process of science" throughout the text, rather than introduced to the "scientific method" in the beginning as an explanation for how science is done. The process of science en-

The Forest Service completed its series showing the recovery of the vegetation on the west side of the plateau with this 1948 photo. Photo courtesy of Kaibab National Forest.

gages students to think about how questions arise, are answered, and give rise to new questions. This also demonstrates the dynamic nature of scientific investigation. Such an approach requires attention to the history of science that goes well beyond the typical vignettes that describe contributors to scientific ideas as precursors to modern concepts. Science educators need better models for presenting more accurate histories of science.[7]

Daniel Botkin's *Discordant Harmonies* is a different kind of ecology textbook that reaches out to a popular audience with lessons about nature. Botkin uses the Kaibab case to illustrate how naturalists have perceived an order in nature since the beginning of recorded history. The balance between predator and prey, as demonstrated on the Kaibab and predicted by common logic, could be disrupted by human interference. Although this simple perception of order cannot be demonstrated historically, the Kaibab recalls for Botkin as a scientist (and not a historian) how nineteenth- and early-twentieth-century naturalists imagined a "divine order" in nature. The deer and mountain lions of the Kaibab illustrate how "species were perceived to interact in a highly ordered way." Leopold's view represents that of scientists, naturalists, and conservationists, who Botkin asserts shared a common view of nature's balance. When Caughley proposed a more diffuse explanation for the Kaibab irruption, ecologists saw that nature may not consist of a divinely ordered scheme. Caughley's claim spoke against what Botkin sees as "deep-seated beliefs about the necessity for the existence of predators as well as all other creatures on the Earth."[8] The consequence for modern ecology is profound. If ecologists cannot demonstrate the necessity of mountain lions—or any other particular species for that matter—on what basis can they argue for environmental action? Botkin hopes for an international ecological survey justified by the need for ongoing refinement of positive scientific knowledge.

One might hope that a clear account of the Kaibab story would emerge eventually, based on a complete scientific study of the ecological history of the plateau. Botkin's approach advocates such a hope. A team of researchers working with Dan Binkley at Colorado State University hopes to unravel at least a part of the Kaibab story by examining the age structure of aspen stands across the plateau. They hypothesize that if the classic story is true, they will find substantially fewer cohorts of aspen that date from between 1915 and 1925. If they can find enough old stands, they will also look to see if regeneration in what was reportedly the peak livestock period—around 1890—was lower than in the 1880s or after 1900. Binkley, who has used the Kaibab lesson in his classroom, speculates that while historical information may never solve the mystery, adding to our knowledge of the case makes it an even more useful opportunity for teaching students about the complexity of nature and management.[9]

Most popular accounts of the Kaibab case connect the story with Leopold's description of wolf extermination in *A Sand County Almanac*. Leopold's discussion of a deer irruption in the Southwest has become one of his most quoted essays. In "Thinking Like a Mountain," he coined the phrase "a fierce green fire" in reference to the dying glow in a wolf's eyes after Leopold shot her. The broader point of his story, which evoked the Kaibab deer in particular, hinged on the destruction of vegetation to the height of a saddlehorn. The recovery of this vegetation—shown graphically in a series of Forest Service photographs taken between 1930 and 1948 on the Kaibab—suggested the aptness of Leopold's metaphor of a mountain that feared its deer in the absence of predators. As a young

Rachel Carson described the Kaibab case briefly in Silent Spring, *and this drawing by Lois and Louis Darling appeared on the opening page of chapter 15, entitled "Nature Fights Back." From* Silent Spring *by Rachel Carson. Copyright © 1962 by Rachel L. Carson, renewed 1990 by Roger Christie. Reprinted by permission of Houghton Mifflin Company. All rights reserved.*

hunter, "full of trigger-itch," he had hoped and believed that if fewer
wolves meant more deer, "no wolves would mean a hunters' paradise." By
the untimely end of his life, he had come to see wolves, deer, and mountains in a new light.[10]

If Leopold's essays signaled a new way of thinking about human effects
on natural communities for a broader audience, Rachel Carson's *Silent
Spring* launched those ideas into a political movement. Her meticulously
researched argument and beautifully written prose echoed in a more
practical sense the philosophical writings of Leopold. Although the most
memorable symbols of her silent spring were songbirds muted by pesti-
cide use run amok, Carson's complex argument called for the replacement of chemicals with biological pest control strategies. As an example
of nature's ability to regulate itself, she cited the Kaibab deer and explained how human interference had wreaked its havoc there too. The
fluidity with which the case could teach lessons only increased in the
1960s, as the environmental movement Carson set in motion gained
momentum and consequently championed Leopold's own "land ethic" as
one of its foundational precepts.

Conservationists, environmental historians, and some wildlife managers—armed with the lessons taught by Leopold and Carson—continue to
use the Kaibab story to make the more general point that humans often
disrupt the balance of nature and that predators play an important role in
animal communities.[11] Donald Worster was the first environmental historian to resurrect the Kaibab case, and he retold it in its simplest form.
He explained that misguided efforts to protect the deer led to rapid
growth of the population, which resulted in starvation of tens of thousands of deer. He completely overlooked Caughley's critique. Following
Worster, many historians perpetuate the Kaibab's simple lesson.

For the most part, environmental historians want to explore the ways
humans view and interact with nature. In many cases they connect scientific knowledge with sentimental beliefs about nature, and they are very
careful not to privilege science. This restraint is important in avoiding an
overly simplistic view of society, which might assume that people's beliefs
and actions are shaped by scientific information alone. They use
Leopold's version of the Kaibab (as told by Worster) as an example of how
popular awareness of ecological principles in the 1960s "trickled down"
from scientists in the 1930s. These accounts, however, add nothing to an
understanding of scientists' efforts to investigate nature's complexity. In
fact, this trickle-down theory of scientific knowledge misrepresents

progress in the history of ecology as an accumulation of facts followed by inevitable dissemination. Efforts to avoid privileging science too often end in ignoring its content entirely. In the end, most environmental historians admit that their accounts remain inadequate to answer the question of what wildlife means in human society. Small wonder.[12]

One environmental historian, Thomas Dunlap, provides a more sophisticated analysis of the role of science and our beliefs about nature. He suggests that the persistence of the Kaibab story as an instructive myth resulted from an ongoing need to illustrate the importance of predators, even if the story had to be oversimplified to do it. The story of the Kaibab deer became "the most durable myth in American forest and game management." Wildlife managers used the Kaibab as an example of "a conservation horror story, a classic wildlife disaster," in order to convince policymakers, hunters, and the general public of the need to preserve predators along with deer in order to ensure the proper management of both. Dunlap suggests that Caughley's challenge to the story reflected a growing confidence on the part of scientists that predators were worthy of preservation and no longer an evil force to be exterminated. While the general public has been slower to come to the same conclusion, scientists by 1970 could provide sufficient evidence without the Kaibab story.[13]

I want to emphasize again that the Kaibab situation, for all of its later meaning, did not suggest an answer to the predator question. For every argument against predator control based on the Kaibab example, opponents offered a corresponding rational denial of the significance of predators in the mismanagement of the deer. Try as they might to derive a clear-cut lesson, neither scientists nor government wildlife officials were able to make a solid case based on that single example. Yet, in countless ways, the Kaibab continued to define the debate. Disagreements continued because everyone could look back and argue over one or another aspect of the deer population growth, habitat degradation, livestock conflict, climatic complexity, hunting regulations, and predator control. We must then conclude that the Kaibab framed many subsequent debates over wildlife management, even if it did not offer answers to specific questions.

Furthermore, the Kaibab does not support the thesis that humans shared a common view of nature—at least before the intrusion of human activity—as a balanced system. Botkin cannot use history as a bulwark for an international program to increase ecological research

This Kaibab doe on Walhalla Plateau browsed on scrub oak just fifty yards from one of the busiest parking lots on the North Rim. Photo by the author.

if he assumes that a proper understanding of nature relies solely on advancements in knowledge. In my view, hope for the beneficial contributions of science depends as much on an awareness of the complex relationships between the motivations, activities, and audiences of scientists as on the seemingly progressive content of science. Scientists contributed to widely praised management on the Kaibab in providing models of cooperative examination of conditions and public access to information about ongoing efforts. Rarely did they make breakthrough discoveries about the state of nature, and those discoveries generally failed to gain audiences outside the scientific community. Rasmussen's detailed research and Mann's long-term studies, in and of themselves, had little effect on broader perceptions of the problems and their solution. At the height of the controversy, in the mid-1920s, nothing that scientists or naturalists offered could serve to satisfy the disparate constituents of wildlife enthusiasts. It was during that period, when solutions were most desperately needed, that scientists could only begin to speculate what those solutions might look like. Even with hindsight, their speculations varied.

In the end, history is much like science. We hope to find answers by
looking to "the past" or to "the data." We typically discover that history
and science offer, instead of answers, innovative ways of framing our
questions. Recall the process-of-science approach exemplified in the
biology textbook by Mix, Farber, and King. Ecologists and wildlife managers have learned to frame their questions in terms of communities of
plant and animal species, rather than in terms of protection of individual
species. They have succeeded in convincing the broader public that
predators are valuable tools in managing deer, elk, and other game animals. The questions, however, continue to change and challenge wildlife
managers in new ways. Now we find overpopulated deer in our suburbs,
sometimes accompanied by large predators. Looking to the Kaibab for a
solution to this problem may be fruitless, but if we examine the features
of that controversy, we may yet find clues for how to proceed.

The first task lies in educating the public about the complexity of wildlife problems. In this, the Kaibab may yet hold its most valuable lesson.
Nature's balance—however real or imagined by scientists, nature lovers,
and government land managers—does not rest on a wide fulcrum, a broad
plank laid over a low, stable support. Perturbations in the systems of nature do not merely shift one species up and another down. If the balance
metaphor is useful at all, it is as compared to a spinning plate atop a long
pole resting on the nose of a talented performer. In the small patches of
wilderness we hope to maintain, that performer might even be imagined
in the guise of a circus clown.

The argument of the 1920s, as to whether nature's balance could be
restored generally, gave way to the insistent voice of wildlife managers—
nature would have to be managed if it was to persist. Scientists began arguing over the changed role of predators on the Kaibab after they had
apparently been almost completely removed, and by then the debaters
could not say with any certainty whether the role had become more or
less significant. In an attempt to shed more light on the issue, they studied the vegetation—not the absent predators. Those who were in a position to decide found that when they spent more time together on the plateau, generally agreeable solutions became easier to find than when they
relied on secondhand reports. Similarly today, trying simply to enumer-
ate essential facts will likely prove counterproductive, especially when
experts disagree over what is essential. Constructing links between government agencies that enhance cooperation rather than draw boundaries
is a crucial step. Adding flexibility to any management plan may be the

most important step. As situations evolve and more information becomes available, managers need to adjust their schemes.

The complex features of the Kaibab controversy emerged slowly and sometimes painfully for the key participants. The lesson of the Kaibab, therefore, runs deeper than an increased awareness of predators, carrying capacity, or irruptions. It points out that our knowledge about nature will perhaps always be entangled with our beliefs about the value of certain species, about order in natural systems, and about balance in ecological communities. Untangling these beliefs from our knowledge is part of seeing the connections between nature and human culture. It is not a task the interested public can expect scientists to undertake for us, nor should we want to be left out of the process.

We continue to embrace the stories that explain the principles of nature, because just as scientists love to tell them, we love the simplicity these stories offer.

Notes

Introduction

1. Leopold, *Sand County Almanac*, 137–41. See also, Leopold, "Deer Irruptions"; and Leopold, Sowls, and Spencer, "Survey of Over-Populated Deer Ranges." Susan Flader, in *Thinking Like a Mountain*, discusses this aspect of Leopold's thinking in detail.
2. Allee, Emerson, Park, Park, and Schmidt, *Animal Ecology*, 706. Emerson is credited in the book's preface with writing the chapter wherein this lesson is found (viii).
3. Bauer, *Mule Deer*, 93. Bauer's chapter on the Kaibab deer is entitled, "The Terrible Lesson of the Kaibab." It is also published, with the same title, as an article in the journal *Mule Deer*.
4. The display also includes a video of predators and prey, which carries the same message with the Kaibab as its central example. My thanks to Mark Alvey at the Field Museum for his assistance in getting a copy of this video, which was not viewable the first time I visited the exhibit, and to Teri Cleeland of the U.S. Forest Service for alerting me to the existence of the exhibit. The Milwaukee exhibit was created around 1970, with a buck and fawn taken from the Kaibab Plateau by museum collectors William Schultz and Walter Pelzer and a mountain lion reportedly purchased from a professional hunting guide in the Kaibab area (Floyd Easterman, personal communication, March 6, 2001).
5. Caughley, "Eruption of Ungulate Populations." Conservationists and environmentalists have generally ignored Caughley's critique, preferring the common-sense simplicity of predator-prey relations demonstrated by the case. Ecologist Don Siniff wonders if Caughley had offered his criticism of the Kaibab case as a less-than-serious attempt to uproot a closely held assumption of academic or theoretic ecologists (Donald Siniff, personal communication, August 8, 1997, St. Paul MN). Wildlife biologist Dave Brown says that only academic ecologists took Caughley to heart, while wildlife managers have gone on using the Kaibab deer

case to illustrate the need to consider predators in management plans. Brown's comment is supported by references to the Kaibab as a "hallmark" in the history of predators and deer in wildlife biology (David E. Brown, personal interview, March 21, 1996, Tempe AZ; McShea, Underwood, and Rappole, eds., *Science of Overabundance*, especially pages 3, 72–73, and 185). Thomas Dunlap offers a brief account of how the Kaibab story helped change popular attitudes toward predators in "Kaibab Myth."

6. I owe special thanks to Tom Dunlap for insisting on this point about the role of the West in this story. For more, see White, *New History of the American West*; Cronon, Miles, and Gatlin, eds., *Under an Open Sky*. On Zane Grey, see Jackson, *Zane Grey*; Kimball, *Ace of Hearts*; and May, *Zane Grey*.

7. On "controversies of facts" and "controversies of theories," see McMullin, "Scientific Controversy," 49–91.

8. Early in the twentieth century, scientists sometimes divided their fact gathering from their more practical research by distinguishing activities as "pure" and "applied" science. Mark Largent has proposed the thesis that pure and applied activities were identified by scientists in order to justify funding basic research and legitimate their scientific expertise using the example of Vernon Kellogg, Stanford entomologist and tireless advocate for a variety of social concerns. Largent demonstrates that Kellogg was an important exemplar of a much broader phenomenon in the biological sciences between the turn of the century and World War II. He cites numerous additional examples, including David Starr Jordan, Raymond Pearl, and Charles Davenport (Largent, "'These are Times of Scientific Ideals'"). For additional examples of how research was classified as distinctly pure or applied, see Cooke, "From Science to Practice"; Kimmelman, "A Progressive Era Discipline"; and Tobey, *American Ideology of National Science*.

9. The history of ecology and wildlife protection begins in the early twentieth century, which immediately raises the possibility that it can be fit into the larger history of conservation in the Progressive Era. In fact, the connection is undeniable; but the history of ecology and wildlife protection suggests a revision of that historiography, rather than an apt example of it. Forty years ago, Samuel Hays and A. Hunter Dupree concluded that, especially during the Progressive Era, scientific expertise contributed enormously to government reform of natural resource use, including water reclamation, forestry, and agriculture. Two generations of conservation and environmental historians have used this thesis to examine controversies over water and land use (Hays, *Conservation and the Gospel of Efficiency*; Dupree, *Science in the Federal Government*). Richard Judd offers the first serious alternative to Hays in en-

vironmental history. His discussion of local conservation efforts around the turn of the century departs from the reliance on federal bureaucracy as an explanation for failed expertise (Judd, *Common Lands*). For examples of those historians who consistently characterize ecology as pure science and resource management (of game, forests, fisheries, and others) as applied science, see Dunlap, *Saving America's Wildlife*; Worster, *Nature's Economy*; and Langston, *Forest Dreams*. Most recently, and dealing directly with wildlife protection, Kurkpatrick Dorsey describes the role of scientists in the creation of treaties between the United States and Canada. For Dorsey, whose information comes primarily from correspondence between scientists and bureaucrats and rarely from original scientific reports, science provided evidence that proved useful when debates "moved to rational economics and politics," but Dorsey relies on changing sentiments about nature to explain how and why that move took place. Science (basic knowledge) is presented as coming in a gift box, carefully packaged and wrapped by technical experts, to be opened only when the time is right (and then useful in assessing what is important); see Dorsey, *Dawn of Conservation Diplomacy*, especially 236–46.

10. For example, Lackey, "Restoration of Pacific Salmon."

11. I am indebted to John Beatty for helping me articulate this view of science and particularly for emphasizing the point that scientists do not speak with one voice in the midst of controversy.

12. For examples of how pure and applied science are used to describe the history of ecology, see Robert McIntosh and Frank Egerton. Both distinguish between pure and applied ecology. The two influenced each another in portraying applied areas of ecology as separate and derivative of pure ecology (McIntosh, *Background of Ecology*, 297; Egerton, "History of Ecology, Part One" and "History of Ecology, Part Two"). This unidirectional model of ecology and conservation was chastened somewhat in this period by Ronald Tobey, who suggested that ecological research was often derived from "utilitarian and scientific problems" (Tobey, *Saving the Prairies*).

13. In a brief note published in 1982 ("Science-Technology Relationship"), Barry Barnes refers to the "major reorientation in our thinking about the science-technology relationship" that had taken place in the previous dozen years or so. The primary component of that reorientation was a change in the tendency to consider technology as subordinate to science. With the two as equals rather than ordered in a hierarchy, Barnes observes that both fields consist of their own cultures that can be extended independently and also interactively. He refers to histories dating from before the 1970s as the "bad old days" for an understanding of technology and science.

More recently within science and technology studies, Bruno Latour (*Science in Action*) has adopted the term "technoscience" as a shorthand for the complex nexus of science and technology. While this term has been adopted by many scholars, its usefulness is limited (or enhanced, depending upon one's perspective) by a lack of clear demarcations. See also Layton, "Technology as Knowledge" and "Mirror-Image Twins"; and the introduction to Krohn, Layton, and Weingart, eds., *Dynamics of Science and Technology*. For discussion of the specific problems of equating technology with applied science, see Staudenmaier, *Technology's Storytellers*, especially pages 83–120. Some historians and sociologists have simply argued against the distinction between pure and applied science on the grounds that any distinction between the two—or between science and technology—is necessarily ambiguous. According to John Ziman, "these categories merge into one another, and confound most of the distinctions between a 'science' and a 'technology'" (*Introduction to Science Studies*, especially chapters 9 and 10).

14. Gregg Mitman has recently called attention to the connections between science, hunting, and folk knowledge needed to capture nature on film (*Reel Nature*, chapter 3). With both pure and applied motivations, science has "dual legitimation," where "interaction" and "mutual invigoration" between pure science and applied science characterize the research. Alan Beyerchen suggests that the dismantling of the traditional model of science-technology relationships, as Layton does, has consequences for applied science. Beyerchen writes that if science and technology are given equal footing, "'[a]pplied science' seems to fall through the cracks as historians of technology do not consider it technology and historians of science regard it as derivative and thus less worthy of immediate attention" ("Stimulation of Excellence," 142).

15. Maarten Heyboer ("Grass-Counters") refers to these criteria as the "dual orientation" of science.

16. For an amusing, sad-but-true account of the challenges faced by two scientists, see Kirkpatrick and Turner, "Urban Deer Contraception," 515–19. Thanks to Bess Frank for bringing this article to my attention.

17. William Cronon ("Uses of Environmental History") has argued (and I tend to agree) that environmental history teaches lessons—in the form of parables—about the way the world works and about human responsibilities within that natural order.

1. BUCKSKIN MOUNTAIN

1. Powell, *Exploration of the Colorado River*, 185. For more on Powell's travels in this region, see Stegner, *Beyond the Hundredth Meridian*, especially pages 90–96, 161–98. Donald Worster (*River Running West*) has recently supplanted the classic work on Powell by Stegner.

2. Hughes, *In the House of Stone and Light*, 88–90.

3. Roosevelt, "Cougar Hunt on the Rim of the Grand Canyon."

4. Some accounts in wildlife management textbooks even suggest that the site was chosen as a perfect location to conduct a massive "wildlife management" experiment. Such a claim, however, is putting the cart before the horse, in the sense that Roosevelt and other early conservationists had no interest in learning how to "manage" the deer—they simply wanted to protect them (Baker, *American Hunting Myth*, 71; and Trippensee, *Wildlife Management*). The name VT Park came from an early ranch run by the Thompson and Van Slack families with the cattle brand vt. The current name is after Harvey DeMotte, a professor at Illinois Wesleyan University who accompanied Powell on his explorations of the area (Maurer, ed., *Kaibab National Forest Visitor's Guide*, 6; Emerson Hough, "The President's Forest," *Saturday Evening Post*, January 14, 1922, 6–7, 65, 69, 72, 75, and January 21, 1922, 23, 57–58, 60, 63).

5. For a recent and excellent history of the natural and human history of the Grand Canyon, see Pyne, *How the Canyon Became Grand*.

6. Euler, "Willow Figurines from Arizona"; Fairley, "Prehistory." Special thanks to Teri Cleeland for providing me with a complete copy of this report. Much of the following account of the early history of the Grand Canyon region is based on Donald Hughes's text (*In the House of Stone and Light*).

7. Fowler, Euler, and Fowler, "John Wesley Powell and the Anthropology of Canyon Country." Less reliable but nevertheless influential accounts of Indian activities in the area prior to white settlement were passed along by the forest supervisor in the 1930s, Walter G. Mann (*Kaibab Deer*; available at the Brigham Young University Library). Population estimates are from Stoffle and Evans, "Resource Competition and Population."

8. Hughes, *In the House of Stone and Light*, 30; Stegner, *Mormon Country*.

9. Hughes, *In the House of Stone and Light*, 33–35; Judge, "Retracing John Wesley Powell's Historic Voyage."

10. Hughes, *In the House of Stone and Light*, 43. See also Crampton, *Land of Living Rock*. Sources of water and grazing land were few and far between. One of the closest and earliest settled in northern Arizona was at Pipe Spring. See Olsen, "Windsor Castle." For more on ranching in Utah, see Walker, "Cattle Industry of Utah."

11. Mann, *Kaibab Deer*. Settlement of Utah and lands north of the Grand Canyon followed a relatively consistent pattern. See Alexander, *Rise of Multiple-Use Management*, 4–7.

12. John Reiger's thesis, that the efforts of sport hunters were the single most important source of conservation thinking, requires a rather

narrow view of conservation. While he provides a useful corrective to thinking only of forestry as the origin of conservation, I agree with critics like Dunlap that he overstates the case (Reiger, *American Sportsmen*). See also Dunlap, "Sport Hunting and Conservation" and *Saving America's Wildlife*, 8–9. An earlier book that emphasized the role of hunting in conservation is Trefethen, *Crusade for Wildlife*, 12, 17.

13. Roosevelt, *Hunting Trips of a Ranchman*.

14. Trefethen, *Crusade for Wildlife*, 2–7. See also Smith, *Politics of Conservation*, chapter 6. Also of interest is Cutright's *Theodore Roosevelt*. The early encounters between Roosevelt and Grinnell are described by Reiger, *American Sportsmen*, 114, 118–19; and Trefethen, *Crusade for Wildlife*, 15–19. Trefethen also reprinted the Boone and Crockett Club constitution (356–57).

15. Roosevelt's involvement is discussed to varying degrees in many historical accounts. A sampling of the most important includes: Nash, *Wilderness and the American Mind*; Schmitt, *Back to Nature*; Lutts, *Nature Fakers*; Barrow, *Passion for Birds*; and Fox, *American Conservation Movement*.

16. First quoted in the *New York Sun*, May 7, 1903, according to Hughes, *In the House of Stone and Light*, 66 (also quoted in part, for example, in Garrett, "Grand Canyon," 2). The quote also appears on a marker on Roosevelt Point, on the North Rim of the canyon between Point Imperial and Cape Royal. Elsewhere, Roosevelt described the canyon as "beautiful and terrible and unearthly. It made me feel as if I were gazing at a sunset of strange and awful splendor" (Roosevelt to John Hay, August 9, 1903, *Letters of Theodore Roosevelt*, 557). Also in 1903, Roosevelt visited Yellowstone National Park and compared what he saw with recent reports by Buffalo Jones. The president concluded that Jones was "not always an accurate observer, and his report on the elk was all wrong." Roosevelt himself saw, in one day, between three and four thousand elk on the north side of the park, and he observed that elk numbered "at least fifteen thousand." Few cougars managed to kill elk, and the president thought that the cougars around watering holes ought to be exterminated (Roosevelt to C. Hart Merriam, April 16, 1903, *Letters* 3:461).

17. Senator Smoot served on the executive committee of Roosevelt's Commission on the Conservation of Natural Resources, organized in 1908 (*Letters* 6:1068). Roosevelt discussed conservation with Smoot and found the senator "favorable to the cause" (Roosevelt to Isaac Franklin Russell, February 4, 1911, *Letters* 7:223). Smoot helped create and guide congressional policy on conservation of natural resources throughout his twenty-eight years in the Senate. See Alexander, "Senator Reed Smoot." Smoot was eventually responsible for introducing legislation that created Zion National Park in 1919.

18. *Congressional Record*, 59th Cong., 1st sess., 1906, 40, pt. 1; *Congressional Record*, 59th Cong., 1st sess., 1906, 40, pt. 9: 8462; *Congressional Record*, 59th Cong., 1st sess., 1906, 40, pt. 10: 9385; *Congressional Record*, 59th Cong., 1st sess., 1906, 40, pt. 10: 9507.

19. This potentially apocryphal connection between Jones and the establishment of the game preserve is proposed in Easton and Brown, *Lord of Beasts*, 132–35. Jones was an influential, if eccentric, early conservationist. See also Mitman, *Reel Nature*, 9, 14; and Pritchard, *Preserving Yellowstone's Natural Conditions*, xv–xvi.

20. Roosevelt, "The Mule-Deer, or Rocky Mountain Blacktail," reprinted in Roosevelt, *Outdoor Pastimes*, 224–55.

21. Roosevelt, "Cougar Hunt on the Rim of the Grand Canyon"; Grey, *Roping Lions in the Grand Canyon*.

22. Palmer, *Chronology and Index*. See Reiger, *American Sportsmen*, especially pages 114–51. On wolves and cattle, see O. W. Williams quoted in Brown, ed., *Wolf in the Southwest*, 21.

23. Walker, "Cattle Industry of Utah"; Freeman, "North Kaibab Revisited," 33. Freeman cites Mann, *Kaibab Deer* (1941).

24. See Joseph Howell, comments from House debate of Grand Canyon Forest Reserve, *Congressional Record*, 59th Cong., 1st sess., 1906, 40, pt. 10: 9385. See also Knack, "Interethnic Competition."

25. Historians have repeatedly described Mather's boosterism. See extensive accounts in Shankland, *Steve Mather*; and Sellars, *Preserving Nature*. On the North Rim specifically, see Klein, "Frontier Products."

26. Emerson Hough, "The President's Forest," *Saturday Evening Post*, January 14, 1922; Mather, "Kaibab Deer Doomed?" 14–17, 59, 61, 63–65. For an account of Mather's Kaibab companion, see Shankland, *Steve Mather*, 271–73.

27. Hal Rothman ("Regular Ding-Dong Fight") has provided an excellent account of how the similarities and differences between the two agencies contributed to ongoing conflict.

2. BEASTS IN THE GARDEN

1. Layne and Hoffmann, "Presidents," 22–70; Zahniser, "Vernon Orlando Bailey," 6–7; Vernon Bailey, U.S. Senate Committee on Agriculture and Forestry, *Control of Predatory Animals*, 71st Cong., 2nd and 3rd sess., 1931, 49. For an overview of the relationship between Bailey and Merriam, see Sterling, "Zoological Research," 19–65.

2. Vernon Bailey, "The Rocky Mountain Mule Deer: A Preliminary Report on the Mule Deer of the Grand Canyon Region of Arizona," April 8, 1930, Box 2, KNF.

3. On the relationship between nineteenth- and twentieth-century natural history, the most recent and in many ways most coherent account is Pauly, *Biologists and the Promise of American Life*. See also numerous selections in Rainger, Benson, and Maienschein, eds., *American Development of Biology*; Benson, Maienschein, and Rainger, eds., *Expansion of American Biology*; and Farber, *Finding Order in Nature*. See also Farber, "Transformation of Natural History." This topic was recently the focus of a conference organized by Farber entitled "The Naturalist Tradition," Oregon State University, March 9, 1998. Another important book on the history of biological traditions in this period is Maienschein, *Transforming Traditions*. For specific examination of ornithology and ecology, see Barrow, *Passion for Birds*; Worster, *Nature's Economy*; and Tobey, *Saving the Prairies*. The connection between changes in the Western frontier and transitions in biology has not been examined. See Turner, *Frontier in American History*; and recent critiques of the closing of the frontier in Cronon, Miles, and Gatlin, eds., *Under an Open Sky*.

4. Dupree, *Science in the Federal Government*. On scientists as bird protectionists see Barrow, *Passion for Birds*, chapter 6. On the way ornithologists contributed to attempts to solve insect problems in agriculture, see Evenden, "Laborers of Nature."

5. See excerpts of naturalists' reports and legislation collected in McIntyre, ed., *War against the Wolf*. For a more synthetic history that includes a discussion of bounties, see Cronon, *Changes in the Land*.

6. Cameron, *Bureau of Biological Survey*.

7. Bailey, "Wolves in Relation," 5.

8. A survey of scientific and natural historical literature bears this out. Secondary support comes from the *Oxford English Dictionary*, 2nd ed., s.v. "predator" and "predatory animal."

9. Bailey, "Destruction of Wolves and Coyotes," 5; and Cameron, *Bureau of Biological Survey*, 46.

10. Hornaday, *Vanishing Wild Life*.

11. On Leopold's earliest introduction to Hornaday's work, see Meine, *Aldo Leopold*, 128–29, 148–50.

12. Leopold, "The Varmint Question," *Pine Cone* 1 (December 1915), reprinted in Flader and Callicott, eds., *River of the Mother of God*, 47–48.

13. Cameron, *Bureau of Biological Survey*, 42–65. See also Dunlap, *Saving America's Wildlife*, chapter 3; and McIntyre, ed., *War against the Wolf*, chapters 3, 4, and 8. Otero also happened to be Leopold's brother-in-law. See Meine, *Aldo Leopold*.

14. Meine has suggested this most forcefully in *Aldo Leopold*, 167–70, and 253–56.

15. Leopold, *Game Management*.

16. The general outline of the history of game management is found in Dunlap, *Saving America's Wildlife*. Leopold's own account appeared as the first chapter of *Game Management*, "A History of Ideas in Game Management." Also valuable are Meine, *Aldo Leopold*; and Flader, *Thinking Like a Mountain*.

17. Grey, *Roping Lions in the Grand Canyon*; Roosevelt, "Cougar Hunt on the Rim of the Grand Canyon."

18. J. C. Roak, "Annual Report, 1920," November 30, 1920, Box 3, KNF.

19. S. B. Locke, "Memorandum for District Forester [Leon F. Kneipp]," [Spring 1920], Box 14, RG 95, NA.

20. S. B. Locke, "Memorandum."

21. Leon F. Kneipp to Chief Forester [William B. Greeley replaced Henry Graves as chief forester during this period], August 12, 1920, Box 14, RG 95, NA. Kneipp was the grazing chief for the Forest Service from 1910 to 1915. See Rowley, *Forest Service Grazing*.

22. Acting Forester [Will C. Barnes] to Biological Survey Chief [Edward W. Nelson], August 27, 1920; Will C. Barnes to Leon F. Kneipp, August 27, 1920; A. K. Fisher to William B. Greeley, September 7, 1920, Box 14, RG 95, NA.

23. Mather, "Kaibab Deer Doomed?" 14–17, 59, 61, 63–65. For an account of Mather's Kaibab companion, see Shankland, *Steve Mather*, 271–73.

24. Emerson Hough, "The President's Forest," *Saturday Evening Post*, January 14, 1922, 6–7, 65, 69, 72, 75, and January 21, 1922, 23, 57–58, 60, 63.

25. Emerson Hough, "The President's Forest," *Saturday Evening Post*, January 14, 1922, 72.

26. Ernest Winkler, "Report," July 8, 1921, files compiled by Christopher Rachford, 1931, KNF.

27. It is interesting to note the close association of the Biological Survey and the American Society of Mammalogists between 1915 and the early 1920s. The predatory animal control issue served to alienate certain individuals, but founding members of the society who were also officials in the bureau remained faithful members throughout their careers (Hoffmeister and Sterling, "Origin," 1–21; and Layne and Hoffmann, "Presidents," 22–70). See also Cameron, *Bureau of Biological Survey*; Sterling, "Builders"; and Dunlap, *Saving America's Wildlife*, chapter 4.

28. W. C. Henderson to Joseph Dixon, October 33, 1921; Henderson to Dixon, October 17, 1921, W. C. Henderson Correspondence, MVZ.

29. George Holman to Joseph Dixon, October 25, 1921; Dixon to Holman, October 28, 1921; Holman to Dixon, November 5, 1921; Dixon to Holman, November 10, 1921; Holman to Dixon, December 10, 1921;

Dixon to Holman, December 15, 1921, George Holman Correspondence, MVZ.

30. George Holman to Joseph Dixon, December 10, 1921; Dixon to Holman, December 15, 1921, George Holman Correspondence, MVZ.

31. J. C. Roak to district forester [unnamed], April 10, 1922, Box 18, RG 95, NA.

32. For emphasizing the literal meaning of "dilemma" and its relevance in controversy, I am indebted to William Downing.

3. A Deer Dilemma

1. Stanley P. Young, "Edward Alphonso Goldman"; Layne and Hoffmann, "Presidents."

2. H. L. Bentley was the first to use the term explicitly in a Department of Agriculture publication. No earlier uses have been found (Bentley, "Cattle Ranges of the Southwest," 7). An excellent account of the situation in and around Yellowstone is found in Pritchard, *Preserving Yellowstone's Natural Conditions*. On Leopold, see Meine, *Aldo Leopold*, 134.

3. Edward A. Goldman and S. B. Locke, "Report on the Summer and Fall Deer Range Examination: Memorandum Regarding Grand Canyon National Game Preserve," October 19, 1922, Box 3, KNF. For a history of carrying capacity in wildlife biology, see Christian C. Young, "Defining the Range." For a more detailed history of range science, see Heyboer, "Grass-Counters." On range management in the Forest Service, see Rowley, *Forest Service Grazing*; and Alexander, "Rule of Thumb." Scientists repeatedly describe the importance of carrying capacity in wildlife biology. See Edwards and Fowle, "Concept of Carrying Capacity"; and Caughley, "What is This Thing Called Carrying Capacity?"

4. Christopher E. Rachford to Chief Forester [William B. Greeley], November 24, 1922, Box 18, RG 95, NA. On Leopold, see Meine, *Aldo Leopold*; and Flader, *Thinking Like a Mountain*.

5. Will C. Barnes to Chief Forester [William B. Greeley], December 28, 1922, Box 18, RG 95, NA.

6. Edward A. Goldman, "Memorandum Regarding Grand Canyon National Game Preserve," April 10, 1923, Box 2, KNF.

7. Edward W. Nelson, "Memorandum on the Grand Canyon National Game Preserve and Methods of Utilizing its Surplus Deer," September 4, 1923, Box 2, KNF.

8. Nelson, "Memorandum on the Grand Canyon," 26.

9. R. W. Williams to Edward W. Nelson, August 21, 1923, KNF. Williams's career is described briefly in an obituary, "Robert White Williams," *Auk*

58, no. 1 (January 1941): 135. Thank you to Mark Barrow for alerting me to this reference.

10. Robert Sterling Yard to Hubert Work, October 17, 1923; Work to Yard, October 10, 1923, Box 2008, RG 48, NA.

11. Hubert Work to Henry C. Wallace, October 10, 1923, Box 2008, RG 48, NA.

12. Hubert Work to Henry C. Wallace, November 1, 1923; William B. Greeley to Robert Sterling Yard, October 11, 1923, Box 2008, RG 48, NA.

13. Henry C. Wallace to Robert Sterling Yard, February 1, 1924, Box 17, RG 95, NA.

14. Two environmental historians have pioneered our understanding of the changing value of varmints, and I am indebted to them for breaking ground and laying the foundation of this important conceptual change in human attitudes toward nature (Dunlap, *Saving America's Wildlife*, chapter 3; and Worster, *Nature's Economy*).

15. Edward Nelson to Joseph Grinnell, December 1, 1920; Nelson to Grinnell, December 10, 1920, Edward Nelson Correspondence, MVZ. On the broader history of the balance of nature, see Egerton, "Changing Concepts."

16. "Sixth Annual Meeting of the American Society of Mammalogists," 218. See, for example, Dice, "Scientific Value of Predatory Mammals," 25–27. As long as there had been game laws, there was conflict between federal and state governments over game regulation. For a brief discussion of how developments around the turn of the century contributed to later conflict, see Belanger, *Managing American Wildlife*.

17. Goldman, "Predatory Mammal Problem," 28–29.

18. Goldman, "Predatory Mammal Problem," 31.

19. Goldman, "Predatory Mammal Problem," 33.

20. Goldman, "Predatory Mammal Problem," 33.

21. Goldman, "Predatory Mammal Problem," 33.

22. Dixon's paper was published as "Food Predilections of Predatory Mammals."

23. Fisher's work is described in Evenden, "Laborers of Nature."

24. Dixon included estimates of the value of mink and marten, animals that were "just as truly predatory" as wolves or mountain lions in that they ate other animals. Mink and marten were often classed as "furbearing mammals." Dixon chose to conflate the two classes.

25. Although Dixon does not mention George Holmon specifically, the biologist undoubtedly used information from the predatory-animal inspector based on their correspondence (Dixon, "Food Predilections," 46).

26. Adams, "Conservation of Predatory Mammals," 83–85.

27. Adams, "Conservation of Predatory Mammals," 89, 93–94.
28. Adams, "Conservation of Predatory Mammals," 90 (original emphasis).
29. Adams, "Conservation of Predatory Mammals," 91.
30. For alternative accounts of the development of ecological concepts relating to predators, see Worster, *Nature's Economy*; and Dunlap, *Saving America's Wildlife*.

4. Getting to the Bottom of Things

1. John B. Burnham et al., "Report of the Kaibab Investigating Committee," October 1, 1924, Box 15, RG 95, NA; also in Kaibab Deer filing cabinet, KNF, 6; also published in *Outdoor Life* (December 1924): 436–37.
2. Burnham et al., "Report of the Kaibab Investigating Committee."
3. Burnham et al., "Report of the Kaibab Investigating Committee."
4. E. A. Sherman to R. W. Williams, September 22, 1924, Box 16, RG 95, NA. The letter was marked "Withdrawn and matter taken up personally with Solicitor," and signed "CER" (Christopher E. Rachford).
5. Mather, "Kaibab Deer Doomed?" 14–17, 59, 61, 63–65; Will H. Dilg, editorial comment published with Mather, "Kaibab Deer Doomed?" 14.
6. Mather, "Kaibab Deer Doomed?"
7. See, for example, Shankland, *Steve Mather*, 273.
8. Shankland, *Steve Mather*, 263.
9. Stephen S. Johnson, "No Deer Starving"; editorial from the *Phoenix Gazette*; both in *Outdoor America* 3, no. 5 (November 1924): 61–65.
10. George W. P. Hunt, "Prevent Slaughter"; letter from Henry C. Wallace to John B. Burnham; Charles McCormick, "Increase Boundary Lines"; all in *Outdoor America* 3, no. 5 (November 1924): 61–65.
11. Arno B. Cammerer to J. R. Eakin, November 6, 1924, Box 278, RG 79, NA.
12. M. E. Musgrave, "Report of George McCormick Kaibab Deer Drive," December 20, 1924, Box 278, RG 79, NA. An extensive collection of magazine and newspaper articles was collected in "Kaibab Deer Drive," Kaibab Deer Files, KNF. George W. P. Hunt to Henry C. Wallace, October 18, 1924; and "Agreement" signed by G. M. Willard and George McCormick, October 20, 1924, Kaibab Deer Files, KNF.
13. R. H. Rutledge to Forest Service Headquarters, October 22, 1924, "Deer Drive" File, KNF.
14. George W. P. Hunt to C. F. Marvin, October 24, 1924; and Marvin to Hunt, October 25, 1924, "Deer Drive" File, KNF.
15. Henry C. Wallace to John B. Burnham, October 1, 1924, Box 2008, RG 48, NA; George W. P. Hunt to Wallace, October 20, 1924; C. F. Marvin to T. E. McCullough, October 25, 1924; and McCullough to Marvin, October 24, 1924, "Deer Drive" File, KNF.

16. R. H. Rutledge to Chief Forester [William B. Greeley], November 3, 1924, "Deer Drive" File, KNF; and Arno B. Cammerer to J. R. Eakin, November 14, 1924, Box 278, RG 79, NA.

17. For telegrams regarding the hunt and arrests, including J. R. Eakin to Stephen T. Mather, November 23, 1924, see Box 278, RG 79, NA. The case is examined in Foster, "Deer of Kaibab." For a comparison of federal and state resource management in forestry, see Robbins, *American Forestry*.

18. R. H. Rutledge to Editor, *Arizona Republican*, November 22, 1924, "Deer Drive" File, KNF.

19. "Report of George McCormick Kaibab Deer Drive," M. E. Musgrave, December 22, 1924, Box 278, RG 79, NA.

20. Later readers, not knowing where to separate fact from fiction, assumed that the whole plot was a product of Grey's imagination. David Balstad, a retired biology teacher who used the Kaibab deer example for twenty-five years in his classroom and knew of the seemingly apocryphal deer drive, slapped his knee in disbelief when the present author assured him that McCormick and Grey actually attempted the drive (Grey, *Deer Stalker* and "The Deer Stalker," *Country Gentleman* 40 (28 March–6 June 1925): 13–23). On Grey, see Kant, *Zane Grey's Arizona*.

21. In reality, that motion picture company, owned by Jesse L. Lasky, formerly of Paramount Pictures, responded to Grey's appeal for a contract that would promote his book. For more on Grey's efforts to make movies, see May, *Zane Grey*, 108.

22. Musgrave, "Report of George McCormick Kaibab Deer Drive."

23. Grey, "Kaibab Deer Refuse to Herd," *Arizona Republican*, December 19, 1924, Box 16, RG 95, NA.

24. William A. Du Puy, "Forest Reserve Becomes a Range of Death: Great Deer Herd, Isolated On an Arizona Plateau, Is Dying Rapidly of Starvation," *New York Times Magazine*, February 15, 1925, 8. The article was reprinted in the *Kansas City Times* the following week; see Box 278, RG 79, NA.

25. Stephen S. Johnson to Arno B. Cammerer, February 16, 1925, Box 278, RG 79, NA.

26. Stephen T. Mather to Stephen S. Johnson, February 19, 1925, Box 278, RG 79, NA. Mather also wrote to R. S. McAllister, a friend in Kanab, asking him to write to the *New York Times* and discredit the story. McAllister supported the notion that the deer were not dying, as the *Times* had indicated. However, the local man replied to Mather, "I see from the tone of your letter that you really do not realize the true conditions." McAllister was very concerned that the deer were so crowded

and hungry that a disease could easily break out and make the *Times* story true after all (R. S. McAllister to Stephen T. Mather, March 30, 1925, Box 278, RG 79, NA).

27. Stephen S. Johnson, "The Kiabab [*sic*] Deer," [Johnson misspelled Kaibab throughout his letter], Letter to the Editor, *New York Times*, February 20, 1925. Copy of original draft in Box 278, RG 79, NA.

28. Johnson, "The Kiabab [*sic*] Deer."

29. Louis A. Wagner to Calvin Coolidge, March 9, 1925; Christopher E. Rachford to Wagner, March 24, 1925, Box 16, RG 95, NA.

30. E. T. Scoyen to J. R. Eakin, February 26, 1925; James DeLong to Stephen T. Mather, January 1, 1925; Mather to Will H. Dilg, February 28, 1925, Box 278, RG 79, NA.

31. Edward W. Nelson to William B. Greeley, February 21, 1925, Box 15, RG 95, NA.

32. On range science in the Forest Service in Utah during this period, see Alexander, "Rule of Thumb"; W. C. Henderson to William B. Greeley, March 30, 1925, Box 15, RG 95, NA.

33. Goldman, "Surplus Game," listed in "Seventh Annual Meeting of the American Society of Mammalogists," 213–16. The paper was later published under the same title in *American Game*. Nelson anticipated the importance of this presentation in a letter to Chief Forester William B. Greeley (Edward W. Nelson to Greeley, March 12, 1925, Box 15, RG 95, NA).

34. E. T. Scoyen to J. R. Eakin, April 9, 1925; Hough, "Phantom Herd," 5–7; Hough to Stephen T. Mather, April 15, 1925; and Arno B. Cammerer to Hough, April 15, 1925, Box 278, RG 79, NA.

5. Taking Notice of the Kaibab Deer

1. Edward A. Goldman, "Report on Conditions Affecting Deer of Kaibab Plateau, Arizona, in June 1925," September 22, 1925, Box 2, KNF.

2. Goldman, "Surplus Game," 28–31.

3. E. Raymond Hall, "Kaibab Deer," Report, 1925, Box 2, KNF.

4. Christopher E. Rachford, "Memorandum the Forester," June 23, 1925, Box 14, RG 95, NA.

5. G. M. Willard to R. H. Rutledge, July 28, 1925; Rutledge to Willard, August 3, 1928; Rutledge to Chief Forester [William B. Greeley], September 24, 1925, Box 16, RG 95, NA.

6. Walter G. Mann, "Game Report," August 26, 1925, Box 14, RG 95, NA.

7. Charles C. Adams to Joseph Dixon, February 11, 1925; Adams wrote of his visit there: "Had a wonderful trip at the Grand Canon [*sic*] and learned some remarkable points on that Deer problem on the north

rim." Adams to Dixon, August 8, 1924, Charles Adams Correspondence, MVZ; Adams to J. R. Eakin, October 6, 1925; Arno B. Cammerer to Eakin, October 19, 1925, Box 278, RG 79, NA. Adams also published a widely cited paper on the role of parks and forests as preserves for predators ("Ecological Conditions in National Forests and in National Parks").

8. J. R. Eakin to Arno B. Cammerer, October 26, 1925; Stephen T. Mather to Arthur E. Demaray, October 31, 1925, Box 278, RG 79, NA.

9. C. L. Harrison to Arthur E. Demaray, December 3, 1925; Demaray to Harrison, January 9, 1926; a memo from the War Department, Office of the Chief of Ordnance, accompanied Harrison to Demaray, January 15, 1926, Box 278, RG 79, NA.

10. War Department memorandum, approximately January 15, 1926, Box 278, RG 79, NA.

11. Arthur E. Demaray to C. L. Harrison, January 19, 1926, Box 278, RG 79, NA.

12. Will C. Barnes to C. L. Harrison, January 26, 1926, Box 278, RG 79, NA. On Barnes, see Rowley, *Forest Service Grazing*, 58; and Will C. Barnes, *Apaches and Longhorns* (n.p., 1941).

13. For more on Leopold and his formulation of this project, see Flader, *Thinking Like a Mountain*, and Meine, *Aldo Leopold*. Leopold was consulted by Chris Rachford regarding management plans on the Kaibab in November 1924 (Christopher E. Rachford to Chief Forester [William B. Greeley], November 24, 1922, Box 18, RG 95, NA). Leopold received a copy of the 1924 Investigating Committee report by special request from Barnes (Will C. Barnes to Aldo Leopold, October 10, 1924). Leopold reviewed another report sent to him by Locke, on February 10, 1925 (Leopold to S. B. Locke, December 27, 1926; Leopold to Locke, June 1, 1926, "Deer Data on Census, etc. 1923–29," Box 1, 9/25/10–4, AL).

14. Will C. Barnes to Aldo Leopold, January 24, 1927, Box 1, 9/25/10–4, AL. Leopold's later reflection appeared, among other places, in his "Thinking Like a Mountain," written in 1944 and published after his death in *Sand County Almanac*. For more on wolves, see Brown, ed., *Wolf in the Southwest*.

15. Will C. Barnes to Aldo Leopold, January 24, 1927, Box 1, 9/25/10–4, AL.

16. Elton's work was important as game managers continued to work out procedures, but Cox, Dunlap, and others tend to neglect the varied and decidedly nontheoretical work of those who translated or reinterpreted Elton's research for application in management. The sources of Elton's ideas, in addition, were not purely theoretical. Too many historians have implied that the science of ecology had, from the outset, a set of fundamental ecological ideas at its core. The source of these ideas is assumed to be rational thought, direct observation of natural systems, and con-

trolled experimentation. While these features match our idealized notions of science, they do not reflect the thinking and action of scientists and naturalists at the time ecology became a science. They also rely on the anachronism of concepts being in place at the same time they were being developed. Along with Adams, Grinnell, Goldman, Bailey, and Barnes, Elton serves as an example of the complex origins of ecological ideas.

The importance of Elton's *Animal Ecology* has been variously insisted upon—by historian Frank Egerton—and downplayed, by Elton himself. See Cox, "Charles Elton," 80. Historians and other scientists have often cited Elton as an ecologist who provided fundamental scientific and ecological knowledge that could be applied to conservation problems. This simplistic, one-way model of knowledge transfer remains untenable here. Sharon Kingsland (*Modeling Nature*, 53–55) notes Elton's interest in economic applications, suggesting that he was also aware of deeper, more fundamental issues in his work, but she does not comment on the influence of previous "applied" work on his thinking. Joel Hagen places Elton into the history of the ecosystem concept. Hagen notes Elton's personal emphasis on "the importance of . . . detailed field research as a foundation for ecology." Elton actually relied on a "relatively small body of empirical evidence" in forging his "basic ecological principles," according to Hagen (*Entangled Bank*, 55). Assumptions that Elton provided the basis for one-way knowledge transfer to game management abound. Thomas Dunlap suggests that Elton's writings on animal ecology helped replace "cut and try" methods that had failed in previous management efforts. Dunlap (*Saving America's Wildlife*, 70–72) says game managers like Aldo Leopold and Herbert Stoddard used methods "recognized and approved" by Elton and other ecologists. Donald Worster (*Nature's Economy*, 294–301) also writes that Elton "laid the foundations for the New Ecology."

17. Elton, *Animal Ecology*, 115. Elton cited T. Gilbert Pearson, "Conservative Conservation," *The National Association of Audubon Societies*, Circular 9 (1924).
18. Elton, *Animal Ecology*, 70. Darwin's "web of complex relations" is discussed in Hagen, *Entangled Bank*. Leopold (*Sand County Almanac*, 251–58) described the pyramid of numbers for the next generation of ecologists and the conservation-minded public in his popular style.
19. Elton, *Animal Ecology*, 143.
20. On carrying capacity, see Christian C. Young, "Defining the Range."
21. Elton, *Animal Ecology*, 102.
22. Special thanks to Mark Largent, who insists upon this distinction. It deserves to be developed in more detail. According to Cox, "[Elton] was

much more interested in what animals were doing than in efforts to construct mathematical metaphors for the phenomena" (Cox, "Charles Elton," 43, 51).

23. Elton, *Animal Ecology*, vii–viii.

24. This case occupies a place of prominence in the history of game legislation and legal battles between state and federal governments. For details on the action of the courts, see Foster, "Deer of Kaibab." Foster suggests that the Forest Service was basing its actions on the best knowledge available, while the state, led by Governor Hunt and Game Warden Willard, followed purely political motivations. Because of the rational superiority of the Forest Service argument, the court decided for the federal government. This interpretation, however, oversimplifies the respective positions of the state and federal governments and inappropriately privileges scientific knowledge for this case.

25. R. W. Williams to William B. Greeley, October 24, 1927; Will C. Barnes to Greeley, October 25, 1927; and Greeley to Barnes, October 25, 1927, Box 16, RG 95, NA.

26. Earl V. Storm, "Deer and Range Studies Plan," February 21, 1928, files compiled by Christopher Rachford, 1931, KNF.

27. Vernon Bailey, "Mammals of the Grand Canyon, Arizona," January 16, 1929, Box 2, KNF.

28. Bailey, "Mammals of the Grand Canyon," 8.

29. The term "deer line" appeared first in the published literature the same year, where former chair of the Kaibab Investigating Committee John Burnham compared it to the load-line markings on ocean-going cargo ships, named after Samuel Plimsoll (Burnham, "Plimsoll Line in White Cedars," 43–47).

30. R. H. Rutledge, "Memorandum," October 15, 1928, files compiled by Christopher Rachford, 1931, KNF. A later summary report recorded that hunters killed 1,005 deer in 1927 (Mann, *Kaibab Deer*).

31. R. H. Rutledge to Chief Forester [William B. Greeley], August 27, 1928, Box 16, RG 95, NA; U. S. Swartz to Rutledge, October 4, 1928; C. B. Morse to Rutledge, October 5, 1928, files compiled by Christopher Rachford, 1931, KNF.

32. R. H. Rutledge to Chief Forester [William B. Greeley], October 15, 1928, files compiled by Christopher Rachford, 1931, KNF.

33. *Hunt, Governor of Arizona, et al. v United States*, 278 US 99 (November 19, 1928).

34. Press Release, "Solution of Kaibab Deer Problem Now Expected," December 17, 1928, Box 16, RG 95, NA.

35. R. E. Gery, "Memorandum for District Forester," December 27, 1928; Walter G. Mann, "Government Killing Report, 1928," January 19, 1929,

filing cabinet KNF. For more on what it meant to protect wild animals, see Mighetto, *Wild Animals*; and Isenberg, *Destruction of the Bison*.

36. Earl V. Storm and Walter G. Mann, "Kaibab Deer and Range Studies Progress Report for Season of 1928," January 22, 1929, KNF.

37. S. B. Locke, "Memorandum," January 28, 1929; Locke to Aldo Leopold, June 25, 1928, Box 1, 9/25/10–4, AL. Ligon served as head of the Biological Survey's predatory animal control program in New Mexico and Arizona from its beginning in 1915. He informed Leopold that exact dates and counts of control efforts on the Kaibab were unknown (J. Stokely Ligon, "Chapter VIII [See old draft No. 2]" in an early draft of Leopold's "Deer Management in the South West," approximately March 20, 1929, Box 10, 9/25/10–6, AL). Flader notes that Leopold apparently provided the conceptual framework for the book, "based on the analogies with forestry and range cattle management that he had begun to work out in his early published articles." The three never brought the book project to completion, for reasons that are not known (Flader, *Thinking Like a Mountain*, 71–72; and Meine, *Aldo Leopold*, 150, 224, 240–41, 270–71).

38. Aldo Leopold, "Outline for Chap. VIII. The Kaibab Deer Herds. By S. B. Locke, U.S. Forest Service, Ogden, Utah," Box 10, 9/25/10–6, AL.

39. Edward A. Goldman, "The Deer of the Kaibab Plateau, Arizona, June 1929 (Excerpts), III. General Conditions," October 3, 1929, Rachford compilation, KNF.

40. M. R. Tillotson to Stephen T. Mather, June 13, 1929; E. E. Brownell to Horace M. Albright, December 3, 1929, Box 278, RG 79, NA.

41. Paul G. Redington to R. L. Bayless, June 28, 1929, Box 15, RG 95, NA.

42. Committee, "Report," June 30, 1929, Box 14, RG 95, NA.

43. R. H. Rutledge, "Memorandum of Kaibab Deer Conference," July 5, 1929, Box 14, RG 95, NA.

44. Homer L. Shantz to John C. Phillips, July 23, 1929, Box 2, KNF.

45. "Kaibab Deer," in Minutes of 123rd Meeting of Service Committee, August 22, 1929; Anonymous, "Settlement of Kaibab Deer Problem in Sight," *Bulletin* 13, no. 35 (September 2, 1929), Box 14, RG 95, NA.

46. In retirement, Mather had continued to correspond with Albright regarding conditions on the Kaibab, including efforts to introduce antelope in Grand Canyon National Park near the North Rim ("Stephen Mather Dies in Boston," *Berkeley Daily Gazette*, January 23, 1930, Stephen T. Mather Correspondence, MVZ). See also Shankland, *Steve Mather*; and Sellars, *Preserving Nature*.

6. SCIENTIFIC EXPERTISE IN THE MIDST OF CONTROVERSY

1. Horace M. Albright to Paul G. Redington, October 31, 1929, Box 278, RG 79, NA; Paul G. Redington to R. Y. Stuart, November 13, 1929, Box 15, RG

95, NA; Christopher E. Rachford to Frank Stokes, Jr., January 16, 1930, Box 14, RG 95, NA.

2. See for example, January 24, 1930, and April 1, 1930, A. Brazier Howell Correspondence, MVZ.

3. Harold E. Anthony to E. L. Sumner, October 23, 1930; Anthony to Paul G. Redington, August 14, 1930, Harold Elmer Anthony Correspondence, MVZ; A. Brazier Howell to E. Raymond Hall, September 5, 1930, A. Brazier Howell Correspondence, MVZ. Anthony increasingly opposed Redington and the survey's policies and insisted that the society present a united front. He even called Dixon and Storer, who began to cooperate more extensively with the survey—"weak 'sisters'" who began to wobble despite their earlier convictions. He asked Hall and Grinnell to "get after" them (Anthony to E. Raymond Hall, January 23, 1931, Harold Elmer Anthony Correspondence, MVZ).

4. Twelfth Annual Meeting of the American Society of Mammalogists, American Museum of Natural History, New York, May 21–24, 1930, published as "Symposium on Predatory Animal Control," in *Journal of Mammalogy* 11, no. 3 (August 1930). Contributions from participants at this symposium suggest that a vocal minority of ASM members and government biologists had strong feelings about predatory animal control. The differences between these participants may not, in fact, have pervaded both organizations. The presence of a few members of the society complaining about federal policies and the attitudes of a few survey officials defending those policies did not necessarily create a national crisis in the biological sciences or conservation policies.

5. Goldman, "Coyote—Archpredator."

6. Henderson, "Control of the Coyote."

7. Hall, "Predatory Mammal Destruction." A. Brazier Howell explained that in fourteen years the Biological Survey had not spent a thousand dollars on publishing the evidence that Goldman and others claimed was so abundantly in favor of the bureau's policies. During the same time, millions of dollars had been spent on destruction (Howell, "At the Cross-Roads").

8. Adams, "Rational Predatory Animal Control."

9. Hall reported conversations with Bailey to Grinnell (E. Raymond Hall to Joseph Grinnell, May 20, 1930, E. Raymond Hall Correspondence, MVZ); Vernon Bailey, "The Rocky Mountain Mule Deer: A Preliminary Report on the Mule Deer of the Grand Canyon Region of Arizona," April 8, 1930, 1, Box 2, KNF.

10. Bailey, "Rocky Mountain Mule Deer," 10.

11. Bailey, "Rocky Mountain Mule Deer," 34.

12. "Nothing to Get Excited About," *Arizona Silver Belt*, April 1, 1930, Box 268, RG 79, NA.

13. Park Superintendent M. R. Tillotson was the most likely source of rumors that the park would be expanded onto forest lands.

14. It is not necessary to claim that Demaray was thinking "ecologically" here. He merely pointed out that a wider jurisdiction would allow the Park Service to protect more wildlife—the same kind of thinking that established the preserve in the first place (Arthur E. Demaray to Henry F. Ashurst, May 16, 1930, Box 278, RG 79, NA).

15. Arthur E. Demaray to Edmund Seymour, May 16, 1930, Box 278, RG 79, NA.

16. Walter G. Mann to R. H. Rutledge, June 13, 1930; R. H. Rutledge to R. Y. Stuart, June 16, 1930, Box 14, RG 95, NA.

17. Horace M. Albright to NPS files, July 8, 1930, Box 14, RG 95, NA.

18. R. Y. Stuart to D. S. Spencer, August 10, 1930, Box 14, RG 95, NA; W. S. Basinger to Horace M. Albright, August 13, 1930, Box 278, RG 79, NA; Jack Tooker, "The Dollar Sign on Arizona Game," manuscript for *Outdoor Life* attached to M. R. Tillotson to Albright, August 8, 1930, Box 278, RG 79, NA.

19. Edmund Seymour to Horace M. Albright, August 18, 1930, Box 278, RG 79, NA.

20. M. R. Tillotson to Horace M. Albright, August 14, 1930; Albright to W. S. Basinger, August 29, 1930, Box 278, RG 79, NA.

21. Walter G. Mann to R. H. Rutledge, February 28, 1930, Box 14, RG 95, NA.

22. Walter G. Mann, "Main Points to Be Covered in the Biological and Game Management Research on the Kaibab National Forest," April 1930, Box 1, 9/25/10–4, AL.

23. "Committee Report," attached to R. H. Rutledge to R. Y. Stuart, May 29, 1930, Box 14, RG 95, NA.

24. Walter G. Mann to H. D. Ruhl, June 30, 1930, Box 278, RG 79, NA, original emphasis.

25. Walter G. Mann to Naomi R. Martin, July 19, 1930, Box 278, RG 79, NA, original emphasis.

26. Freeman, "North Kaibab Revisited," 48; Walter G. Mann, "Memorandum," August 14, 1930, Box 14, RG 95, NA. As studies of vegetative growth continued, they began to resemble the work of plant ecologists who began plot comparisons around the turn of the century. Neither Mann nor the men who conducted this work had any direct connection to Frederic Clements and the Nebraska school, but the influence of Clements's work was clearly being felt in range management and forestry by the late 1920s. On Clements, see Tobey, *Saving the Prairies*; and

on the connections between plant ecology and range management, see Heyboer, "Grass-Counters."

27. Walter G. Mann to Edmund Seymour, August 26, 1930, Box 14, RG 95, NA.

28. The suggestion that Shelford encouraged students to conduct research in familiar areas comes from Rasmussen's son, David Rasmussen, personal interview, March 21, 1996. For more on Shelford as an advisor during this period, see comments from his students in Croker, *Pioneer Ecologist*, 93–106.

29. David Rasmussen, personal interview, March 21, 1996; Dale Jones, correspondence with the author; William Hurst, correspondence with the author; Christopher E. Rachford to R. H. Rutledge, June 26, 1929, Box 14, RG 95, NA.

30. D. Irvin Rasmussen, "Deer Report," undated, approximately September 1, 1930, Box 278, RG 79, NA.

31. Aldo Leopold to E. Raymond Hall, July 1, 1930; Hall to Leopold, July 11, 1930; Leopold to Hall, July 18, 1930, Aldo Leopold Correspondence, MVZ. S. B. Locke to Aldo Leopold, August 7, 1930, Box 10, 9/25/10–3, AL. The symposium was held in Ames, Iowa, January 1, 1930. Locke, "Study of Big Game Ranges," 770.

32. S. B. Locke, "Wild Life Management," manuscript, presented at American National Livestock Association Meeting, Seattle, January 30, 1931, Box 10, 9/25/10–3, AL.

33. R. N. Dunlap to A. Larsson, February 20, 1930, Box 14, RG 95, NA. For more on the development of "carrying capacity," see Christian C. Young, "Defining the Range."

34. Walter G. Mann, "Trapping Mule Deer at Big Springs Ranger Station," December 9, 1930; Mann, "Report on Catching and Raising Fawns," December 12, 1930, Box 278, RG 79, NA.

35. "Tillotson Raps Statements About Deer in Kaibab Area," *Arizona Daily Star*, November 30, 1930; "The Kaibab Deer—Again," *Tucson Daily Citizen*, December 9, 1930.

36. Anon. [via Chris Rachford] to R. Y. Stuart, December 16, 1930; Stuart to Horace M. Albright, December 16, 1930; Albright to Stuart, December 19, 1930; Albright to M. R. Tillotson, December 19, 1930, Box 16, RG 95, NA.

37. Tillotson was referring to a dispute between Western novelist Zane Grey and state game authorities. The writer and avid sportsman threatened never again to return to or write about the state of Arizona after the state refused to exempt him from certain regulations. Grey believed that his status as a writer who brought great visibility to the state earned him

special consideration (Jackson, *Zane Grey*). See also Kant, *Zane Grey's Arizona*.

38. "Mr. Tillotson's Admissions," *Tucson Daily Citizen*, December 11, 1930; M. R. Tillotson to Horace M. Albright, December 30, 1930, Box 279, RG 79, NA.

39. Walter G. Mann, February 18, 1931, Box 278, RG 79, NA.

40. Walter G. Mann, "Kaibab Deer Count," March 1, 1931, Box 2, KNF.

41. Walter G. Mann, March 3, 1931, Box 278, RG 79, NA.

42. Walter G. Mann, March 23, 1931, Box 278, RG 79, NA.

43. S. B. Locke, "Wild Life Management," (manuscript, presented at American National Livestock Association Meeting, Seattle, January 30, 1931), Box 10, 9/25/10–3, AL.

44. James P. Brooks to M. R. Tillotson, April 13, 1931, Box 278, RG 79, NA.

7. Big Game Management Plans on the Kaibab

1. Christopher E. Rachford to R. H. Rutledge, January 28, 1931, Box 2, KNF. *Outdoor America* was published by the Izaak Walton League and edited by the outspoken conservationist Will Dilg; *American Game* was published by the American Game Protective Association; *Bird Lore* was published by the National Association of Audubon Societies and regularly included essays by T. Gilbert Pearson. The *Journal of Mammalogy*, published by the American Society of Mammalogists, regularly included reference to the Kaibab deer in its pages. The American Bison Society published a report, including an essay that described the Kaibab situation for members (Edmund Seymour, "Arizona Problems," *Report of the American Bison Society, 1927–30*, American Bison Society, 1931, 32–39).

2. Christopher E. Rachford, Collected Documents, Box 278, RG 79, NA. Recent histories of the Kaibab deer continue to rely on Rachford's collected documents almost exclusively.

3. Karl T. Frederick, draft report to Camp Fire Club, March 2, 1931, Box 278, RG 79, NA.

4. Edmund Seymour to Horace M. Albright, March 31, 1931, Box 278, RG 79, NA; Seymour to Christopher E. Rachford, May 1, 1931, Box 2, KNF.

5. Horace Albright to R. Y. Stuart, April 7, 1931, Box 278, RG 79, NA.

6. A. Brazier Howell to Harold C. Bryant, March 1, 1931, Box 278, RG 79, NA; Howell to Harold E. Anthony, March 8, 1931, A. Brazier Howell Correspondence, MVZ.

7. A. Brazier Howell to R. Y. Stuart, April 22, 1931, Box 19, RG 95, NA.

8. A. Brazier Howell to Joseph Grinnell, May 17, 1931, A. Brazier Howell Correspondence, MVZ. For more on the passage of the bill funding the Biological Survey's poison program, see Dunlap, *Saving America's Wildlife*, chapter

4; Dunlap, "Values for Varmints"; and Worster, *Nature's Economy*, chapter 13.

9. F. E. Mullin to R. Y. Stuart, April 16, 1931, Box 19, RG 95, NA.

10. Horace Albright to M. R. Tillotson, May 25, 1931, Box 278, RG 79, NA.

11. Christopher E. Rachford to R. H. Rutledge, May 21, 1931, Box 2, KNF.

12. R. H. Rutledge to Christopher E. Rachford, May 26, 1931, Box 19, RG 95, NA; Rachford to Rutledge, June 4, 1931, Box 2, KNF.

13. Henry B. Ward to Christopher E. Rachford, May 28, 1931; Fred Gibson to R. Y. Stuart, June 3, 1931, Box 19, RG 95, NA.

14. "Kaibab Investigative Committee," June 25, 1931, Box 278, RG 79, NA.

15. M. R. Tillotson to Horace Albright, June 26, 1931, Box 278, RG 79, NA.

16. M. R. Tillotson, "Résumé of statement made before Kaibab Investigative Committee," June 14, 1931, Box 278, RG 79, NA.

17. Harold E. Anthony to E. Raymond Hall, July 7, 1931, Harold E. Anthony Correspondence, MVZ; Harold Bryant to Horace M. Albright, September 30, 1931, Box 278, RG 79, NA.

18. E. Raymond Hall to Joseph Grinnell and Jean Linsdale, June 15, 1931, E. Raymond Hall Correspondence, MVZ.

19. "Kaibab Group Finishes U.S. Range Study," *Salt Lake City Tribune*, June 19, 1931, Box 269, RG 79, NA. The quotations in the following paragraphs are from the report, unless otherwise noted ("Kaibab Investigative Committee," June 25, 1931, Box 278, RG 79, NA).

20. The importance of the combination-of-both principle has been described by John W. Alchemy, M.D., personal communication.

21. For an overview of national-level events, see Dunlap, *Saving America's Wildlife*, chapter 4; Dunlap, "Values for Varmints"; and Worster, *Nature's Economy*, chapter 13. While the predator debate represents the dawning of a new ecological consciousness for both of these scholars, I consider that debate to be the outcome of conflicting beliefs about the amount of control humans hoped to exert over nature. The evidence, as Dunlap suggests, was scant on both sides of the issue. It came down to a question of how game managers would employ that evidence to argue for more hunting of deer rather than allowing predators to do the killing.

22. Edmund Seymour to Horace Albright, June 22, 1931, Box 278, RG 79, NA.

23. D. I. Rasmussen to E. Raymond Hall, July 10, 1931, D. I. Rasmussen Correspondence, MVZ; Hall to A. Brazier Howell, July 10, 1931, and Hall to Howell, July 20, 1931, A. Brazier Howell Correspondence, MVZ.

24. E. Raymond Hall to Aldo Leopold, June 29, 1931, and Leopold to Hall, July 6, 1931, Aldo Leopold Correspondence, MVZ.

25. D. L. Vasbinder to R. H. Rutledge, June 27, 1931, Box 2, KNF.

26. Editorial, "Kaibab Report," *American Game* 20, no. 4 (July–August, 1931): 50; Anon., "The Kaibab Deer Problem," *Bird Lore* 33, no. 4 (July–August, 1931): 304.

27. M. R. Tillotson to Horace M. Albright, July 25, 1931; Tillotson to Albright, July 27, 1931, Box 278, RG 79, NA.

28. R. Y. Stuart to R. H. Rutledge, September 19, 1931, Box 2, KNF.

29. R. Y. Stuart to T. Gilbert Pearson, September 19, 1931, Box 2, KNF. Identical letters to seven other members of the committee were reportedly sent but not saved in the surviving files.

30. George Pratt to R. Y. Stuart, September 21, 1931; John MacFarlane to Stuart, September 26, 1931; Joseph Dixon to Stuart, October 7, 1931, Box 19, RG 95, NA.

31. R. H. Rutledge to Paul Redington, December 24, 1931; E. A. Sherman to Redington, Box 15, RG 95, NA.

32. Virtually all later sources referred to the published version. Apparently only Shelford cited the dissertation before 1941. All references here are from the dissertation manuscript unless otherwise noted (Rasmussen, "Biotic Communities of the Kaibab Plateau," Ph.D. diss., University of Illinois, 1932); Rasmussen, "Biotic Communities" (1941); Clements and Shelford, *Bio-Ecology*.

33. Rasmussen referred specifically to the studies with which he was most familiar, those of fellow students of Shelford: Weese, "Animal Ecology of an Elm-Maple Forest"; Blake, "Comparison of the Animal Communities of Coniferous and Deciduous Forests"; Blake, "Further Studies"; Smith, "Animal Communities of a Deciduous Forest Succession"; Shackleford, "Animal Communities of an Illinois Prairie"; Bird, "Biotic Communities."

34. The Ecological Society of America attempted to increase its visibility in human relationships with nature, but the status of this work in academic studies remains uncertain. See Tjossem, "Preservation of Nature and Academic Respectability."

35. Taylor stressed the practical significance of life-history studies along with the great general interest of such work (Taylor, "Outlines for Studies of Mammalian Life-Histories").

36. Rasmussen, "Biotic Communities" (1932), 19.

37. Shelford, "Improving Quality of Investigations and Publications in Animal Ecology," 235.

38. Rasmussen, "Biotic Communities" (1932), 6–7; graph follows p. 140.

39. Rasmussen, "Biotic Communities" (1932), 10.

40. Rasmussen, "Biotic Communities" (1932), 38–39.

41. Rasmussen, "Biotic Communities" (1932), 42.

42. Rasmussen, "Biotic Communities" (1932), 116. Rasmussen cited an article by Allan Brooks on mountain lions in British Columbia to support the potential impact of the predator population on the deer. Brooks was a supporter of Edward Goldman and opposed the "sentimental" views of predators espoused by Joseph Dixon and Lee Dice. His work never received the wide notice of Rasmussen's (Brooks, "Past and Present Big-Game Conditions," 37–40).

43. Rasmussen, "Biotic Communities" (1932), 108–9. These issues were discussed at the Matamek Conference, a report of which Rasmussen cited (Huntington, "Matamek Conference on Biological Cycles"). For more on population fluctuations, see Egerton, "Changing Concepts."

44. Victor E. Shelford to Charles C. Adams, undated, received May 25, 1932; Charles C. Adams to Victor E. Shelford, May 25, 1932, Box 34, CA. Adams also indicated that he doubted whether Leopold would back a "scientific study" because "he will want a game study, as his interest is from the other end of the problem" (Daniel Irvin Rasmussen, Curriculum Vitae, provided by David I. Rasmussen, April 28, 1998).

45. Other members of the count survey were Robert Park and Odell Julander, Forest Service; R. H. Betts, Arizona Fish and Game Department; and Arthur Brown and R. E. Laws, National Park Service (Walter G. Mann, "Kaibab Deer Count," January 30, 1932, Box 2, KNF; and Mann, "Estimate of the Number of Deer on East Side, Kaibab National Forest," March 22, 1932, Box 279, RG 79, NA).

46. M. R. Tillotson to Horace M. Albright, August 8, 1932, Box 278, RG 79, NA; F. W. Robinson to Horace M. Albright, August 22, 1932, Box 279, RG 79, NA.

47. Maria (Mrs. C. S.) Jackson to Horace M. Albright, September 3, 1932; Harold C. Bryant to Maria Jackson, September 14, 1932, Box 279, RG 79, NA. For more on the increasing protection for predators, see Pritchard, *Preserving Yellowstone's Natural Conditions*; and Sellars, *Preserving Nature*.

48. M. R. Tillotson to Horace M. Albright, September 13, 1932, Box 279, RG 79, NA.

49. Harold C. Bryant to Horace M. Albright, September 27, 1932; Albright to George Pratt, September 30, 1932, Box 279, RG 79, NA.

50. Pritchard, *Preserving Yellowstone's Natural Conditions*; and Sellars, *Preserving Nature*.

51. T. Gilbert Pearson to R. Y. Stuart, October 4, 1932; Chris Rachford to Pearson, October 5, 1932, Box 14, RG 95, NA; Harold C. Bryant to Horace M. Albright, October 10, 1932, Box 279, RG 79, NA.

52. David Madsen to Horace M. Albright, October 13, 1932; "Utah Deer Areas Equal to Kaibab, Declares Madsen," *Salt Lake City Tribune*, October 13, 1932, Box 279, RG 79, NA.

53. Handwritten comments on David Madsen to Horace M. Albright, October 13, 1932, Box 279, RG 79, NA.

54. There is no direct evidence that Bryant or Albright had forwarded news of increased predator control to Hall, but given the earlier letter to Pratt, it seems likely (E. Raymond Hall to Walter G. Mann, October 25, 1932; Mann to Hall, October 29, 1932; Hall to Mann, November 3, 1932; Mann to Hall, November 18, 1932, Walter Mann Correspondence, MVZ).

55. Goldman, "Management of Our Deer Herds."

56. Walter G. Mann to Regional Forester [Ernest Winkler], November 12, 1932, Box 14, RG 95, NA; Mann, "Game Report, 1932," December 20, 1932, Walter Mann Correspondence MVZ.

57. George M. Wright to Horace M. Albright, November 22, 1932, Box 279, RG 79, NA.

58. Handwritten memoranda, Arthur Demaray, Harold C. Bryant, Arno B. Cammerer, undated; M. R. Tillotson to Horace M. Albright, undated, Box 279, RG 79, NA.

59. Horace M. Albright to R. Y. Stuart, December 2, 1932, Box 16, RG 95, NA.

60. R. Y. Stuart to Horace M. Albright, December 13, 1932, Box 279, RG 79, NA.

61. Arthur Demaray to Horace M. Albright, December 21, 1932, Box 279, RG 79, NA.

62. Horace M. Albright to R. Y. Stuart, December 23, 1932, Box 16, RG 95, NA. See also Pritchard, *Preserving Yellowstone's Natural Conditions*; and Sellars, *Preserving Nature*.

63. R. Y. Stuart to Regional Forester [Ernest Winkler], January 12, 1933; Stuart to Horace M. Albright, January 13, 1933, Box 14, RG 95, NA.

64. George M. Wright to Horace M. Albright, January 24, 1933, Box 1023, RG 79, NA.

65. Horace M. Albright to George M. Wright and Joseph Dixon, February 2, 1933, Box 1023, RG 79, NA.

66. Herman H. Chapman to Frederic C. Walcott, February 1, 1933, Box 10, 9/25/10–3, AL.

67. George M. Wright to Horace M. Albright, March 9, 1933, Box 1023, RG 79, NA.

68. "Peak Activities Faced by Staff of U.S. Park Service," *Federal News*, March 18, 1933, clipping; R. Y. Stuart to Horace M. Albright, March 22, 1933; Albright to Stuart, April 3, 1933, Box 16, RG 79, NA. That Stuart saw Chapman's letter is suggested by the fact that a copy of the letter appeared in Aldo Leopold's files. It was probably forwarded to both Stuart and Leopold by Chapman, who made specific references to his former students.

69. For a more detailed discussion of this point, see Christian C. Young, "Defining the Range."

8. The Exception That Proved the Rule

1. Ronald Tobey (*Saving the Prairies*, 65–75) describes an epistemological shift in plant ecology, which occurred around the turn of the century around Frederic Clements at Nebraska. This shift toward quantifying vegetation in ways that revealed long field experience as largely erroneous did not take hold on federal lands where intensive grazing by livestock was not the primary use of the range.

2. Walter G. Mann to Regional Forester [Ernest Winkler], March 21, 1933, Box 14, RG 95, NA.

3. Odell Julander, "Methods Used in Game Management Studies on the Kaibab National Forest," February 20, 1933, Box 1, KNF.

4. Odell Julander, "Outline of Biological and Game Management Studies and Methods Used," March 20, 1933, Box 1, KNF.

5. S. F. Rathburn to the Biological Survey, May 31, 1933, forwarded to the Forest Service, June 6, 1933; Chris Rachford to S. F. Rathburn, June 14, 1933, Box 14, RG 95, NA.

6. Leopold, *Game Survey of the North Central States*. See also, Leopold, *Game Management*, 49–51.

7. M. R. Tillotson to Horace M. Albright, August 11, 1933, Box 1022, RG 79, NA.

8. George Wright to Horace M. Albright, March 9, 1933; Harold C. Bryant to Wright, April 7, 1933; Wright to M. R. Tillotson, April 13, 1933; Bryant to Wright, April 19, 1933; David Madsen to Albright, May 28, 1933; Bryant to Wright, June 2, 1933; Albright to Madsen, June 9, 1933; Joseph Dixon to Albright, July 17, 1933; Wright to Bryant, July 19, 1933, Box 1023, RG 79, NA. For more on the role of the Wild Life Division within the National Park Service, see Sellars, *Preserving Nature*.

9. Harold L. Ickes to Henry A. Wallace, August 22, 1933; C. V. Marvin to Ickes, August 28, 1933; Henry A. Wallace to Ickes, October 5, 1933, Box 552, RG 48, NA; Mann, *The Kaibab Deer: A Brief History and the Present Plan of Management* (copy to the author provided by William Hurst, July 25, 1998).

10. M. R. Tillotson to Arno B. Cammerer, January 6, 1934; George Wright to Cammerer, January 10, 1934; Cammerer to Tillotson, January 22, 1934, Box 1024, RG 79, NA.

11. Edward A. Goldman, "Notes on Deer of Kaibab Plateau, Arizona," June 10, 1933, forwarded by W. C. Henderson to Horace M. Albright, August 2, 1933, Box 1023, RG 79, NA.

12. Other members of the count survey were Robert Park and Dave Shoemaker, Forest Service; J. B. Edwards and Charles Murray, Arizona Fish and Game Department; and Warren Hamilton, National Park Service (Walter G. Mann, "Kaibab Deer Count," March 18, 1934, Box 2, KNF; Ben Thompson to Arno B. Cammerer, March 28, 1934, Box 1023, RG 79, NA).

13. Ben H. Thompson, "Suggested Wild Life Management Plan for Grand Canyon National Park," April 18, 1934, Box 1023, RG 79, NA.

14. Wright and Thompson, *Fauna*, vii–viii.

15. Wright and Thompson, *Fauna*, 13, 15, 27.

16. Wright and Thompson, *Fauna*, 39, 55; Leopold, "Conservation Economics."

17. Wright and Thompson, *Fauna*, 39, 47, 49.

18. Wright and Thompson, *Fauna*, 49, 51.

19. Wright and Thompson, *Fauna*, 50, 51.

20. Wright and Thompson, *Fauna*, 52, 89.

21. W. B. Raudebaugh, A. J. Mackey, T. C. McCullough to F. A. Silcox, August 15, 1934, Box 14, RG 95, NA; Walter Mann, "Kaibab Deer Count," February 16, 1935, Box 2, KNF.

22. T. Gilbert Pearson to F. A. Silcox, November 4, 1935; Pearson to Chris Rachford, November 7, 1935, Box 14, RG 95, NA; Pearson, "A Problem of Over-Conservation," 88–90.

23. Walter G. Mann to M. R. Tillotson, January 25, 1936, Box 1023, RG 79, NA; Robert P. Boone to Dave Shoemaker, March 10, 1936, Box 2, KNF.

24. Nichol, "Hunters."

25. Arthur L. Brown, "Wildlife Census," September 30, 1937, Box 1023, RG 79, NA.

26. Walter G. Mann to regional forester, February 2, 1938, Box 2, KNF.

27. Walter G. Mann, "Winter Deer Counting," February 11, 1938, Box 2, KNF.

28. Walter G. Mann to Regional Forester [Ernest Winkler], April 1, 1938, Box 2, KNF; Mann to M. R. Tillotson, April 4, 1938; Clifford C. Presnall, handwritten note (undated) on Mann to Tillotson, Box 1023, RG 79, NA.

29. Arthur L. Brown, "Annual Deer Count, Kaibab Forest North," April 12, 1938; M. R. Tillotson to Arno B. Cammerer, April 22, 1938; Tillotson to Cammerer, April 29, 1938, Box 1023, RG 79, NA.

30. Clifford C. Presnall to Victor H. Cahalane, May 3, 1938; Victor H. Cahalane for Harold C. Bryant to M. R. Tillotson, May 4, 1938, Box 1023, RG 79, NA.

31. Harlen G. Johnson to Walter G. Mann, July 16, 1938; Johnson, "Factors Influencing Deer Counts in DeMotte Park," August 1, 1938, Box 2, KNF.

32. Arthur Brown to M. R. Tillotson, August 18, 1938; Tillotson to Arno B. Cammerer, October 10, 1938, Box 1024, RG 79, NA.

33. "New Park Chief Named in Santa Fe: Changes Also Made at Grand Canyon," *Albuquerque Journal*, October 10, 1938, Box 1006; Clifford C. Presnall, undated memo; Harold C. Bryant to M. R. Tillotson, October 18, 1938, Box 1024, RG 79, NA.

34. Harold C. Bryant to Arno B. Cammerer, March 28, 1939, Box 1023, RG 79, NA; Walter G. Mann to Regional Forester [C. N. Woods], March 28, 1939, Box 2, KNF.

35. W. B. McDougall, "Special report: The Annual Deer Count on the Kaibab National Forest," April 6, 1939, Box 1023, RG 79, NA.

36. Robert P. Boone to Regional Forester [C. N. Woods], April 21, 1939; Regional Forester to Walter G. Mann, July 29, 1939; Harlen G. Johnson to Mann, August 5, 1939, files KNF.

37. "247 [sic] Pound Buck Taken by Hunter in North Kaibab," *Williams News*, November 23, 1939, Box 1023, RG 79, NA.

38. Mann noted without explanation that no count had taken place in 1940 (Mann, *Kaibab Deer*).

39. William H. Behle to Edwin McKee, July 24, 1940; Brown's report was passed on by the acting superintendent in J. V. Lloyd to Arno B. Cammerer, August 7, 1940, Box 1023, RG 79, NA.

40. W. C. Henderson to John C. Gatlin, August 16, 1940; Gatlin to Regional Forester, August 30, 1940; Edwin McKee, "Memorandum Regarding Deer Problem on North Rim," August 26, 1940, Box 1023, RG 79, NA.

41. K. C. Kartchner to Harold L. Ickes, September 4, 1940, Box 1023, RG 79, NA.

42. K. C. Kartchner to Carl Hayden, September 4, 1940; Kartchner to Henry F. Ashurst, September 4, 1940; "Game Warden Seeks U.S. Deer Protection," *Arizona Republican*, September 5, 1940; Hayden to Hillary A. Tolson, September 6, 1940, Box 1023, RG 79, NA.

43. Frank A. Kittredge to Director [Newton B. Drury], September 6, 1940, Box 1023, RG 79, NA.

44. Harold L. Ickes to K. C. Kartchner, September 16, 1940, Box 1024, RG 79, NA.

45. Arthur E. Demaray to Henry F. Ashurst, September 18, 1940; Demaray to Carl Hayden, September 18, 1940; Demaray to James R. Wilson, September 17, 1940, Box 1024, RG 79, NA.

46. Ira N. Gabrielson to Director [Newton B. Drury], September 16, 1940; E. M. Mercer, "Report of Depredations on Deer in the Kaibab National Forest by Coyotes and Mountain Lions," September 6, 1940, Box 1023, RG 79, NA.

47. K. C. Kartchner to Carl Hayden, September 30, 1940; Kartchner to Henry F. Ashurst, September 30, 1940, Box 1024, RG 79, NA; Hayden to Arthur E. Demaray, October 2, 1940, Box 1023, RG 79, NA.

48. W. B. Bell to D. I. Rasmussen, September 13, 1940; Ira N. Gabrielson to Carl Hayden, October 16, 1940; Arthur E. Demaray to Hayden, December 27, 1940, Box 1023, RG 79, NA.

49. Frank A. Kittredge to Director [Newton B. Drury], January 14, 1941, Box 1023, RG 79, NA. The new governor was Sidney Osborn.

50. Fred W. Johnson to Regional Forester [C. N. Woods], March 28, 1941, Box 2, KNF.

51. Walter G. Mann to Regional Forester [C. N. Woods], April 18, 1941, Box 2, KNF.

52. Aldo Leopold, "Report to the American Wildlife Institute on the Utah and Oregon Wildlife Units," August 10, 1941, Box 1, 9/25/10–2, AL. Quoted in Meine, *Aldo Leopold*, 417.

53. Leopold wrote several letters trying to track down a source of funding for Costley (Aldo Leopold to Homer L. Shantz, August 15, 1941; Leopold to Ira N. Gabrielson, August 15, 1941; Leopold to Shantz, October 15, 1941; Leopold to Richard J. Costley, September 13, 1941, Box 2, 9/25/ 10–2, AL). Costley wrote up a detailed plan for the study, which repeatedly highlighted connections with earlier Kaibab studies (Richard J. Costley, "A Study of the Rocky Mountain Mule Deer with a Special Reference to the Biotic Relationships of the Stansbury Mountain Herd of Central Utah," December 15, 1941, Box 2, 9/25/10–2, AL).

54. Aldo Leopold, "Deer Irruption Study," November 24, 1941, Box 2, 9/25/ 10–2, AL. This manuscript gave rise to two widely cited articles on the crisis of deer management that had emerged across the country (Leopold, "Deer Irruptions"; Leopold, Sowls, and Spencer, "Survey of Over-Populated Deer Ranges"). Leopold's lecture notes included a hand-drawn version of the Kaibab irruption that later appeared in his published articles. Thanks to Dale McCullough at the University of California, Berkeley, for sharing this graph with the author.

55. Sherman Baker, "Nature Balanced, Nature Unbalanced." Baker was listed as a "Deputy Game Warden, State of Arizona." This nonsalaried position made Baker unqualified to offer official statements for the state game commission. K. C. Kartchner stripped him of the title and informed Bryant, who had cited the article as support for Park Service policy, of the fact (Harold C. Bryant to Director [Newton B. Drury] and Victor H. Cahalane, November 28, 1941; K. C. Kartchner to Sherman Baker, December 8, 1941; Kartchner to Bryant, December 8, 1941, Box 1006, RG 79, NA).

Epilogue

1. I am indebted once again to Mark Largent for pointing out the similarity between this conclusion and that of Stephen J. Gould, who has argued persuasively about the use of scientific ideas in widely ranging assertions of human prejudice, especially including claims about racial differences (see Gould, "Racism and Recapitulation," 216).

2. Allee et al., *Animal Ecology*, 706–7; Simpson, Pittendrigh, and Tiffany, *Life*, 654; Keeton, *Biological Science*, 740.

3. Caughley, "Eruption of Ungulate Populations," 56. Caughley spelled irruption differently than Leopold, but suggested no different meaning for the word (Davis and Golley, *Principles in Mammalogy*).

4. Burk, "Kaibab Deer Incident."

5. I have, at various stages of writing this book, toyed with the idea of creating a definitive table of textbook uses of the Kaibab, but I feared that the point of such an exercise would amount to simply pointing out that some authors were farther out of touch with certain realities of the situation than others. Because it is a relatively small point in the larger scope of what biology textbooks writers and compilers are attempting to present, and because most of those authors would readily admit their deficiencies in one or more areas, the effort seemed fruitless.

6. My thanks to Gar Allen, a historian of science, for his willingness to discuss this episode with me. It should be noted that he was quick to deny any involvement in both the initial overinterpretation of the Kaibab case and the later enlightened discussion of it. (His contributions to the text focused on genetics and evolution, not ecology.) He remains primarily concerned that—as the supplement suggests—students and educators take a critical view of introductory texts that are mass produced under tremendous pressures from publishers, tenure-review committees, and sometimes state education departments, to name a few. The fourth edition (1982) of the book retained the supplement (Baker and Allen, *Study of Life Biology*, 1034–36). Examples of such textbook cases are probably more numerous than we would like to admit. One recent example involves the recapitulation theory of Ernst Haeckel. For specific reference to this case being propagated in textbooks, see Gould, "Abscheulich!" 42–49.

7. Mix, Farber, and King, *Biology*.

8. Botkin, *Discordant Harmonies*, 76–78.

9. Dan Binkley, Colorado State University, personal communication, July 26, 2001.

10. Leopold did not describe the Kaibab deer explicitly in the posthumously published *Almanac*, but he had discussed the case in detail elsewhere.

11. Conservationists include Chase, *Playing God in Yellowstone*, 14–70; Bauer, *Mule Deer*, 79–93; Shabecoff, *Fierce Green Fire*, 88–89; and also Botkin, *Discordant Harmonies*, 76–80. Environmental historians include Nash, *Wilderness and the American Mind*, 182–99; Worster, *Nature's Economy*, 269–75; Flader *Thinking Like a Mountain*, 84–104, 175–84, 242–52; and Meine, *Aldo Leopold*, 240–41, 254–55, 270–71, 366, 369, 440, 442. Wildlife managers include Russo, *Kaibab North Deer Herd*; Brown, ed., *Wolf in the Southwest*, 24; and Bolen and Robinson, *Wildlife Ecology*, 16–17.

12. Most recently, see Isenberg, "Moral Ecology of Wildlife." Other examples include, Mike Davis, *Ecology of Fear*, 233–36; Dorsey, *Dawn of Conservation Diplomacy*; and MacEachern, "Canadian National Parks Predator Policy," 197–212.

13. Dunlap, "Kaibab Myth," 60–61. According to Dunlap, a myth is "a piece of common wisdom, legend, or example, whether true false, or in-between." He has also aptly noted that "myths are shorthand, the things we never learned but we all know." Dunlap does not intend his use of the word *myth* to be pejorative. Rather, he explores this myth as an example of the changes that took place in American wildlife conservation ideology. The myth, for him, illustrates that society can choose to apply or ignore scientific evidence, depending on what suits its political, economic, and ideological needs (Dunlap, *Saving America's Wildlife*, ix, 65, 77–78).

Bibliography

Manuscript Collections

Resources for Documents, Reports, and Photographs

Charles Adams Papers (CA), Western Michigan University Archives, Kalamazoo MI

Kaibab National Forest (KNF), Williams AZ

Aldo Leopold Papers (AL), University of Wisconsin–Madison, Special Collections, Madison WI

Museum of Vertebrate Zoology (MVZ), University of California, Berkeley CA

National Archives (NA), College Park MD

    RG 22   Records of the Fish and Wildlife Service

    RG 48   Records of the Office of the Secretary of the Interior

    RG 79   Records of the National Park Service

    RG 95   Records of the Forest Service

D. I. Rasmussen, "Biotic Communities of the Kaibab Plateau," Ph.D. diss., University of Illinois, Champaign-Urbana, 1932, Special Collections.

Utah State University, Special Collections, Logan UT

Secondary Sources

Adams, Charles C. "The Conservation of Predatory Mammals." *Journal of Mammalogy* 6, no. 2 (May 1925): 83–96.

——— "Ecological Conditions in National Forests and in National Parks." *Scientific Monthly* 20 (1925): 561–93.

——— "Rational Predatory Animal Control." *Journal of Mammalogy* 11, no. 3 (August 1930): 353–57.

Alexander, Thomas G. "From Rule of Thumb to Scientific Range Management: The Case of the Intermountain Region of the Forest Service." *Western Historical Quarterly* 18, no. 4 (October 1987): 409–28.

———— *The Rise of Multiple-Use Management in the Intermountain West: A History of Region 4 of the Forest Service*. FS-399. Salt Lake City: Brigham Young University and MESA Corporation, 1987.

———— "Senator Reed Smoot and Western Land Policy, 1905–1920." *Arizona and the West* 13, no. 3 (Autumn 1971): 245–64.

Allee, W. C., Alfred E. Emerson, Orlando Park, Thomas Park, and Karl P. Schmidt. *Principles of Animal Ecology*. Philadelphia: W. B. Saunders, 1949.

Allen, Durward L. *Our Wildlife Legacy*. Rev. ed. New York: Funk and Wagnalls, 1974.

Allen, Garland. *Life Science in the Twentieth Century*. New York: John Wiley and Sons, 1975.

Altschul, Jeffrey H., and Helen C. Fairley, eds. *Man, Models, and Management: An Overview o the Archaeology of he Arizona Strip and the Management of Its Cultural Resources*. Washington DC: U.S. Forest Service and U.S. Bureau of Land Management, 1989.

Bailey, Vernon. "Destruction of Wolves and Coyotes: Results Obtained during 1907." *Bureau of Biological Survey Circular* 63 (29 April 1908): 1–11.

———— "Wolves in Relation to Stock, Game, and the National Forest Reserves." *Forest Service Bulletin* 72 (January 19, 1907): 3–31.

Baker, Jeffrey J. W., and Garland E. Allen. *The Study of Life Biology*. 3rd ed. Philippines: Addison-Wesley, 1977.

Baker, Ron. *The American Hunting Myth*. New York: Vantage, 1985.

Baker, Sherman. "Nature Balanced, Nature Unbalanced." *Natural History* 48, no. 4 (November 1941): 212–15.

Barnes, Barry. "The Science-Technology Relationship: A Model and a Query." *Social Studies of Science* 12 (1982): 166–72.

Barrow, Mark V., Jr. *A Passion for Birds: American Ornithology after Audubon*. Princeton: Princeton University Press, 1998.

Bauer, Erwin A. *Mule Deer: Behavior, Ecology, Conservation*. Stillwater MN: Voyager, 1995.

———— "The Terrible Lesson of the Kaibab." *Mule Deer* 2, no. 4 (Fall 1996): 22–25.

Belanger, Dian Olson. *Managing American Wildlife: A History of the International Association of Fish and Wildlife Agencies*. Amherst: University of Massachusetts Press, 1988.

Benson, Keith R., Jane Maienschein, and Ronald Rainger, eds. *The Expansion of American Biology*. New Brunswick NJ: Rutgers University Press, 1991.

Bentley, H. L. "Cattle Ranges of the Southwest: A History of the Exhaustion of the Pasturage and Suggestions for Its Restoration." *Farmers' Bulletin* no. 72. Washington DC: United States Department of Agriculture, 1898.

Beyerchen, Alan. "On the Stimulation of Excellence in Wilhelmian Science." In *Another Germany: A Reconsideration of the Imperial Era*, edited by Jack R. Dukes and Joachim Remak, 139–68. Boulder CO: Westview, 1988.

Bird, Ralph. "Biotic Communities of the Aspen Parkland of Central Canada." *Ecology* 11 (1930): 356–442.

Birney Elmer C., and Jerry R. Choate, eds. *Seventy-Five Years of Mammalogy*. Norman OK: American Society of Mammalogists, 1994.

Blake, Irving. "A Comparison of the Animal Communities of Coniferous and Deciduous Forests." *Illinois Biological Monographs* 10 (1927).

———. "Further Studies on Decidious Forest Animal Communities." *Ecology* 12 (1931).

Blum, Ann Shelby. *Picturing Nature: American Nineteenth-Century Zoological Illustration*. Princeton: Princeton University Press, 1993.

Bolen, Eric G., and William L. Robinson. *Wildlife Ecology and Management*. 3rd ed. Upper Saddle River NJ: Prentice-Hall, 1995.

Botkin, Daniel B. *Discordant Harmonies: A New Ecology for the Twenty-First Century*. New York: Oxford University Press, 1990.

Bowers, Janice Emily. *The Life and Work of Forrest Shreve*. Tucson: University of Arizona Press, 1988.

Boyce, Mark S., and Larry D. Hayden-Wing, eds. *North American Elk: Ecology, Behavior, and Management*. Laramie: University of Wyoming, 1979.

Brooks, Allan. "Past and Present Big-Game Conditions in British Columbia and the Predatory Mammal Question." *Journal of Mammalogy* 7, no. 1 (February 1926): 37–40.

Brown, David E., ed. *The Wolf in the Southwest: The Making of an Endangered Species*. Tucson: University of Arizona Press, 1983.

Burk, C. John. "The Kaibab Deer Incident: A Long Persisting Myth." *BioScience* 23, no. 2 (1973): 113–14.

Burnham, John B. "The Plimsoll Line in White Cedars." *Journal of Mammalogy* 9, no. 1 (February 1928): 43–47.

Cameron, Jenks. *The Bureau of Biological Survey: Its History, Activities, and Organization*. Service Monographs of the United States Government, No. 54. Baltimore: Institute for Government Research, 1929.

Carson, Rachel. *Silent Spring*. Boston: Houghton Mifflin, 1962.

Cartmill, Matt. *A View to a Death in the Morning: Hunting and Nature through History*. Cambridge: Harvard University Press, 1993.

Caughley, Graeme. "Eruption of Ungulate Populations, with Emphasis on Himalayan Thar in New Zealand." *Ecology* 51, no. 1 (December 1970): 53–72.

——— "What is This Thing Called Carrying Capacity?" In *North American Elk: Ecology, Behavior, and Management*, edited by Mark S. Boyce and Larry D. Hayden-Wing, 2–8. Laramie: University of Wyoming Press, 1979.

Chase, Alston. *Playing God in Yellowstone: The Destruction of America's First National Park*. New York: Harcourt Brace, 1986.

Clements, Frederic E., and Victor E. Shelford. *Bio-Ecology*. New York: John Wiley and Sons, 1939.

Cooke, Kathy J. "From Science to Practice, or Practice to Science: Chickens and Eggs in Raymond Pearl's Agricultural Breeding Research, 1907–1916." *Isis* 88 (1997): 62–86.

Cox, David L. "Charles Elton and the Emergence of Modern Ecology." Ph.D. diss., Washington University, 1979.

Crampton, C. Gregory. *Land of Living Rock: The Grand Canyon and the High Plateaus: Arizona, Utah, Nevada*. New York: Alfred A. Knopf, 1972.

Croker, Robert A. *Pioneer Ecologist: The Life and Work of Victor Ernest Shelford, 1877–1968*. Washington DC: Smithsonian Institution Press, 1991.

Cronon, William. *Changes in the Land: Indians, Colonists, and the Ecology of New England*. New York: Hill and Wang, 1983.

——— "The Uses of Environmental History." *Environmental History Review* 17 (Fall 1993): 1–22.

Cronon, William, George Miles, and Jay Gatlin, eds. *Under an Open Sky: Rethinking America's Western Past*. New York: W. W. Norton, 1992.

Crowcroft, Peter. *Elton's Ecologists: A History of the Bureau of Animal Population*. Chicago: University of Chicago Press, 1991.

Cutright, Paul Russell. *Theodore Roosevelt: The Making of a Conservationist*. Champaign-Urbana: University of Illinois Press, 1985.

Davis, D. E., and F. B. Golley. *Principles in Mammalogy*. New York: Reinhold, 1963.

Davis, Mike. *Ecology of Fear: Los Angeles and the Imagination of Disaster*. New York: Metropolitan, 1998.

Dice, Lee R. "The Scientific Value of Predatory Mammals." *Journal of Mammalogy* 6, no. 1 (February 1925): 25–27.

Dixon, Joseph. "Food Predilections of Predatory Mammals." *Journal of Mammalogy* 6, no. 1 (February 1925): 34–46.

Dorsey, Kurkpatrick. *The Dawn of Conservation Diplomacy: U.S.-Canadian Wildlife Protection Treaties in the Progressive Era*. Seattle: University of Washington Press, 1998.

Dunlap, Thomas R. *Nature and the English Diaspora: Environment and History in the U. S., Canada, Australia, and New Zealand*. Cambridge, England: Cambridge University Press, 1999.

———— *Saving America's Wildlife: Ecology and the American Mind, 1850–1990*. Princeton: Princeton University Press, 1988.

———— "Sport Hunting and Conservation, 1880–1920," *Environmental Review* 12, no. 1 (Spring 1988): 51–60.

———— "That Kaibab Myth," *Journal of Forest History* 32, no. 2 (April 1988): 60–68.

———— "Values for Varmints: Predator Control and Environmental Ideas, 1920–1939." *Pacific Historical Review* 53 (1989): 141–61.

Dupree, A. Hunter. *Science in the Federal Government: A History of Policies and Activities*. Cambridge: Harvard University Press, 1957.

Easton, Robert, and Mackenzie Brown. *Lord of Beasts: The Saga of Buffalo Jones*. Tucson: University of Arizona Press, 1961.

Edwards, R. Y., and C. David Fowle. "The Concept of Carrying Capacity." In *Transactions of the Twentieth North American Wildlife Conference*, edited by James B. Trefethen, 589–602. Washington DC: Wildlife Management Institute, 1955.

Egerton, Frank N. "Changing Concepts of the Balance of Nature." *Quarterly Review of Biology* 48, no. 2 (June 1973): 322–50.

———— "The History of Ecology: Achievements and Opportunities, Part One." *Journal of the History of Biology* 16 (1983): 259–310.

———— "The History of Ecology: Achievements and Opportunities, Part Two." *Journal of the History of Biology* 18 (1985): 103–43.

Elton, Charles. *Animal Ecology*. New York: Macmillan, 1927.

Euler, Robert C. "Willow Figurines from Arizona." *Natural History* 75 (March 1966): 62–67.

Evenden, Matthew D. "The Laborers of Nature: Economic Ornithology and the Role of Birds as Agents of Biological Pest Control in North American Agriculture, ca. 1880–1930." *Forest and Conservation History* 39 (October 1995): 172–83.

Fairley, Helen C. "Prehistory." In *Man, Models, and Management: An Overview of the Archaeology of the Arizona Strip and the Management of Its Cultural Resources*, edited by Jeffrey H. Altschul and Helen C. Fairley. Washington DC: U.S. Forest Service and U.S. Bureau of Land Management, 1989.

Farber, Paul L. *Discovering Birds: The Emergence of Ornithology as a Scientific Discipline, 1760–1850*. Baltimore: Johns Hopkins University Press, 1997; New York: D. Reidel, 1982.

———— "Discussion Paper: The Transformation of Natural History in the Nineteenth Century." *Journal of the History of Biology* 15 (1982): 145–52.

———— *Finding Order in Nature: The Naturalist Tradition from Linnaeus to E. O. Wilson*. Baltimore: Johns Hopkins University Press, 2000.

Flader, Susan L. *Thinking Like a Mountain: Aldo Leopold and the Evolution of an Ecological Attitude toward Deer, Wolves, and Forests*. 2nd ed. Madison: University of Wisconsin Press, 1994.

Flader, Susan L., and J. Baird Callicott, eds. *The River of the Mother of God and Other Essays by Aldo Leopold*. Madison: University of Wisconsin Press, 1991.

Ford, Andrew. *Modeling the Environment: An Introduction to System Dynamics Models of Environmental Systems*. Washington DC: Island Press, 1999.

Foster, James C. "The Deer of Kaibab: Federal-State Conflict in Arizona." *Arizona and the West* 12 (Autumn 1970): 255–68.

Fowler, Don D., Robert C. Euler, and Catherine S. Fowler. "John Wesley Powell and the Anthropology of Canyon Country: A Description of John Wesley Powell's Anthropological Fieldwork, the Archeology of the Canyon Country, and Extracts from Powell's Notes on the Origins, Customs, Practices, and Beliefs of the Indians of that Area." *Geological Survey Professional Paper 670*. Washington DC: Government Printing Office, 1969.

Fox, Stephen. *The American Conservation Movement: John Muir and His Legacy*. Madison: University of Wisconsin Press, 1981.

Freeman, Duane R. "The North Kaibab Revisited: A Look at Policies and Management." Master's thesis, Colorado State University, 1983.

Garrett, W. E. "Grand Canyon." *National Geographic* 154, no. 1 (July 1978): 2–51.

Goldman, Edward A. "The Coyote—Archpredator." *Journal of Mammalogy* 11, no. 3 (August 1930): 325–34.

———— "Management of Our Deer Herds." *Transactions of the Nineteenth American Game Conference* (1932): 49–58.

———— "Predatory Mammal Problem." *Journal of Mammalogy* 6, no. 1 (February 1925): 28–33.

———— "Surplus Game—A Problem in Administration." *American Game* 15, no. 1 (January 1926): 28–31.

Golley, Frank Benjamin. *A History of the Ecosystem Concept in Ecology: More Than the Sum of the Parts*. New Haven CT: Yale University Press, 1993.

Gould, Stephen Jay. "Abscheulich! (Atrocious!) Haeckel's Distortions did not Help Darwin." *Natural History* 109, no. 2 (March 2000): 42–49.

———— "Racism and Recapitulation." In *Ever Since Darwin*, 214–221. New York: W. W. Norton, 1977.

Grey, Zane. *Roping Lions in the Grand Canyon*. New York: Grossett and Dunlap, 1924.

———— *The Deer Stalker*. New York: Harper, 1949.

Hagen, Joel B. *An Entangled Bank: The Origins of Ecosystem Ecology*. New Brunswick NJ: Rutgers University Press, 1992.

Hall, E. Raymond. "Predatory Mammal Destruction." *Journal of Mammalogy* 11, no. 3 (August 1930): 362–69.

Hays, Samuel P. *Conservation and the Gospel of Efficiency: The Progressive Conservation Movement, 1890–1920*. Cambridge: Harvard University Press, 1959.

———— *Explorations in Environmental History*. Pittsburgh: University of Pittsburgh Press, 1998.

Henderson, W. C. "The Control of the Coyote." *Journal of Mammology* 11, no. 3 (August 1930): 336–50.

Heyboer, Maarten. "Grass-Counters, Stock-Feeders, and the Dual Orientation of Applied Science: The History of Range Science, 1895–1960." Ph.D. diss., Virginia Polytechnic Institute and State University, 1992.

Hoffmeister, Donald F., and Keir B. Sterling. "Origin." In *Seventy-Five Years of Mammalogy*, edited by Elmer C. Birney and Jerry R. Choate, 1–21. Norman OK: American Society of Mammalogists, 1994.

Hornaday, William T. *Our Vanishing Wild Life: Its Extermination and Preservation*. New York: New York Zoological Society, 1913.

Hough, Donald. "The Phantom Herd of the Kaibab." *Outdoor America* 3, no. 12 (July 1925): 5–7, 72–73.

Howell, A. Brazier. "At the Cross-Roads." *Journal of Mammalogy* 11, no. 3 (August 1930): 377–89.

Hughes, J. Donald. *In the House of Stone and Light: A Human History of the Grand Canyon*. Grand Canyon Natural History Association, 1978.

Huntington, Ellsworth. "The Matamek Conference on Biological Cycles, 1931." *Science* 74, no. 1914 (September 4, 1931): 229–35.

Isenberg, Andrew. *The Destruction of the Bison: An Environmental History, 1750–1920*. Cambridge, England: Cambridge University Press, 2000.

———— "The Moral Ecology of Wildlife." In *Representing Animals*, edited by Nigel Rothfels. Bloomington: University of Indiana Press, in press.

Jackson, Carlton. *Zane Grey*. Rev. ed. Boston: Twayne, 1989.

Judd, Richard. *Common Lands, Common People: The Origins of Conservation in Northern New England*. Cambridge: Harvard University Press, 1997.

Judge, Joseph. "Retracing John Wesley Powell's Historic Voyage Down the Grand Canyon." *National Geographic* 135, no. 5 (May 1969): 668–713.

Kant, Candace C. *Zane Grey's Arizona*. Flagstaff AZ: Northland, 1984.

Keeton, William T. *Biological Science*. New York: W. W. Norton, 1967.

Kimball, Arthur G. *Ace of Hearts: The Westerns of Zane Grey*. Fort Worth: Texas Christian University Press, 1993.

Kimmelman, Barbara. "A Progressive Era Discipline: Genetics at American Agricultural Colleges and Experiment Stations, 1890–1920." Ph.D. diss., University of Pennsylvania, 1987.

Kingsland, Sharon. *Modeling Nature: Episodes in the History of Population Ecology*. 2nd ed. Chicago: University of Chicago Press, 1995.

Kirkpatrick, Jay F., and John W. Turner. "Urban Deer and Contraception: The Seven Stages of Grief," *Wildlife Society Bulletin* 25, no. 2 (1997): 515–19.

Klein, Kerwin L. "Frontier Products: Tourism, Consumerism, and the Southwestern Public Lands, 1890–1990." *Pacific Historical Review* 62 (1993): 39–71.

Knack, Martha C. "Interethnic Competition at Kaibab during the Early Twentieth Century." *Ethnohistory* 40, no. 2 (Spring 1993): 212–45.

Krohn, Wolfgang, Edwin T. Layton Jr., and Peter Weingart, eds. *The Dynamics of Science and Technology: Social Values, Technical Norms and Scientific Criteria in the Development of Knowledge*, Yearbook in the "Sociology of the Sciences" Series, Vol. 2. Dordrecht, Holland: D. Reidel Publishing, 1978.

Lackey, Robert T. "Restoration of Pacific Salmon: The Role of Science and Scientists." In *What Is Watershed Stability?*, edited by Sari Sommarstrom, 35–40. Water Resources Center Report No. 92. Berkeley: University of California Press, 1997.

Langston, Nancy. *Forest Dreams, Forest Nightmares: The Paradox of Old Growth in the Inland West*. Seattle: University of Washington Press, 1995.

Largent, Mark Aaron. "'These are Times of Scientific Ideals': Vernon Lyman Kellogg and Scientific Activism, 1890–1930." Ph.D. diss., University of Minnesota, 2000.

Latour, Bruno. *Science in Action: How to Follow Scientists and Engineers through Society*. Cambridge: Harvard University Press, 1987.

Layne, James N., and Robert S. Hoffman. "Presidents." In *Seventy-Five Years of Mammalogy*, edited by Elmer C. Birney and Jerry R. Choate, 22–70. Norman OK: American Society of Mammalogists, 1994.

Layton, Edwin T. Jr. "Mirror-Image Twins: The Communities of Science and Technology in Nineteenth-Century America." *Technology and Culture* 12 (1971): 562–80.

———. "Technology as Knowledge." *Technology and Culture* 15 (1974): 31–41.

Leopold, Aldo. "Conservation Economics." *Journal of Forestry* 32, no. 5 (1934): 537–44.

——— "Deer Irruptions." *Wisconsin Conservation Bulletin* 8, no. 8 (August 1943): 3–11.

——— *Game Management*. New York: Charles Scribners' Sons, 1933.

——— *Report on a Game Survey of the North Central States*. Madison WI: The Democrat Press for the Sporting Arms and Ammunition Manufacturers' Institute, 1931.

——— *A Sand County Almanac and Sketches Here and There*. New York: Oxford University Press, 1949.

Leopold, Aldo, Lyle K. Sowls, and David L. Spencer. "A Survey of Over-Populated Deer Ranges in the United States." *Journal of Wildlife Management* 11 (April 1947): 162–77.

Locke, S. B. "The Study of Big Game Ranges." *Ecology* 11 (1930): 770.

Lorbiecki, Marybeth. *Aldo Leopold: A Fierce Green Fire*. Helena MT: Falcon, 1996.

Lutts, Ralph H. *Nature Fakers: Wildlife, Science, and Sentiment*. Golden CO: Fulcrum, 1990.

MacEachern, Alan. "Rationality and Rationalization in Canadian National Parks Predator Policy." In *Consuming Canada: Readings in Environmental History*, edited by Chad Gaffield and Pam Gaffield, 197–212. Mississaugua, Ontario: Copp Clark, 1995.

Maienschein, Jane. *Transforming Traditions in American Biology, 1880–1915*. Baltimore: Johns Hopkins University Press, 1991.

Mann, Walter G. *The Kaibab Deer: A Brief History and Present Plan of Management*. Kaibab National Forest AZ: U.S. Forest Service, 1931, amended 1934 and 1941.

Mather, Stephen T. "Are Kaibab Deer Doomed?" *Outdoor America* 3, no. 5 (November 1924): 14–17, 59, 61, 63–65.

Matthiessen, Peter. *Wildlife in America*. New York: Viking, 1959.

Maurer, Stephen G., ed. *Kaibab National Forest Visitor's Guide*. Albuquerque: Southwest Natural and Cultural Heritage Association, 1990.

May, Stephen J. *Zane Grey: Romancing the West*. Athens: Ohio University Press, 1997.

McIntosh, Robert P. *The Background of Ecology: Concept and Theory*. Cambridge, England: Cambridge University Press, 1985.

McIntyre, Rick, ed. *War against the Wolf: America's Campaign to Exterminate the Wolf*. Stillwater MN: Voyageur, 1995.

McMullin, Ernan. "Scientific Controversy and Its Termination." In *Scientific Controversies: Case Studies in the Resolution and Closure of Disputes in Sci-*

ence and Technology, edited by H. Tristram Engelhardt Jr. and Arthur L. Caplan, 49–91. New York: Cambridge University Press, 1987.

McShea, William J., H. Brian Underwood, and John H. Rappole, eds. *The Science of Overabundance: Deer Ecology and Population Management*. Washington DC: Smithsonian Institution Press, 1997.

Meine, Curt. *Aldo Leopold: His Life and Work*. Madison: University of Wisconsin Press, 1988.

Mighetto, Lisa. *Wild Animals and American Environmental Ethics*. Tucson: University of Arizona Press, 1991.

Mitman, Gregg. *Reel Nature: America's Romance with Wildlife on Film*. Cambridge: Harvard University Press, 1999.

——— *The State of Nature: Ecology, Community, and American Social Thought, 1900–1950*. Chicago: University of Chicago Press, 1992.

Mix, Michael C., Paul Farber, and Keith I. King. *Biology: The Network of Life*. 2nd ed. New York: Harper Collins, 1996.

Nash, Roderick. *Wilderness and the American Mind*. 3rd ed. New Haven CT: Yale University Press, 1982.

Nelson, Richard. *Heart and Blood: Living with Deer in America*. New York: Alfred A. Knopf, 1997.

Nichol, A. A. "Hunters, Conservationists, Game, and Cattlemen." *American Cattle Producer* 18, no. 5 (October 1936): 6–7.

Oeschlager, Max. *The Idea of Wilderness: From Prehistory to the Age of Ecology*. New Haven CT: Yale University Press, 1991.

Olsen, Robert W. Jr. "Windsor Castle: Mormon Frontier Fort at Pipe Spring." *Utah Historical Quarterly* 34 (Summer 1966): 218–26.

Palmer, Theodore S. *Chronology and Index of the More Important Events in American Game Protection, 1776–1911*. Washington DC: U.S. Biological Survey Bulletin, no. 41, 1912.

Pauly, Philip J. *Biologists and the Promise of American Life: From Meriwether Lewis to Alfred Kinsey*. Princeton: Princeton University Press, 2000.

Pearson, T. Gilbert. "A Problem of Over-Conservation." *Bird Lore* 28 (1926): 88–90.

Penna, Anthony N. *Nature's Bounty: Historical and Modern Environmental Perspectives*. New York: M. E. Sharpe, 1999.

Powell, John Wesley. *Exploration of the Colorado River of the West and Its Tributaries: Explored in 1869, 1870, 1871, and 1872, under the Direction of the Secretary of the Smithsonian Institution*. Washington DC: Government Printing Office, 1875.

Pritchard, James A. *Preserving Yellowstone's Natural Conditions: Science and the Perception of Nature*. Lincoln: University of Nebraska Press, 1999.

Prudden, T. Mitchell. *On the Great American Plateau: Meanderings among Canyons and Buttes, in the Land of the Cliff-Dweller, and the Indian of To-Day*. New York: G. P. Putnam's, 1906.

Pyne, Stephen J. *Fire in America: A Cultural History of Wildland and Rural Fire*. Princeton: Princeton University Press, 1982.

——— *Fire on the Rim: A Firefighter's Season at the Grand Canyon*. Seattle: University of Washington Press, 1995.

——— *How the Canyon Became Grand: A Short History*. New York: Penguin, 1998.

Rainger, Ronald, Keith R. Benson, and Jane Maienschein, eds. *The American Development of Biology*. New Brunswick NJ: Rutgers University Press, 1988.

Rasmussen, D. Irvin. "Biotic Communities of the Kaibab Plateau." Ph.D. diss., University of Illinois, 1932.

——— "Biotic Communities of the Kaibab Plateau, Arizona." *Ecological Monographs* 11, no. 3 (July 1941): 229–75.

Reiger, John F. *American Sportsmen and the Origins of Conservation*. Rev. ed. Norman: University of Oklahoma Press, 1986.

Robbins, William G. *American Forestry: A History of National, State, and Private Cooperation*. Lincoln: University of Nebraska Press, 1985.

Roosevelt, Theodore. "A Cougar Hunt on the Rim of the Grand Canyon." *Outlook* 105 (4 October 1913): 259–66.

——— *Hunting Trips of a Ranchman: Sketches of Sport on the Northern Cattle Plains*. New York: G. P. Putnam's, 1886; reprint, Upper Saddle River NJ: Literature House, 1970.

——— *The Letters of Theodore Roosevelt*, edited by Elting E. Morison. Vol. 3. Cambridge: Harvard University Press, 1954.

——— *Outdoor Pastimes of an American Hunter*. New York: Charles Scribner's, 1908.

Rothman, Hal K. "'A Regular Ding-Dong Fight': Agency Culture and Evolution in the NPS-USFS Dispute, 1916–1937." *Western Historical Quarterly* 20 (May 1989): 141–61.

Rowley, William D. *U.S. Forest Service Grazing and Rangelands: A History*. College Station: Texas A & M University Press, 1985.

Runte, Alfred. *National Parks: The American Experience*. 2nd ed. Lincoln: University of Nebraska Press, 1987.

Russo, John P. *The Kaibab North Deer Herd: Its History, Problems, and Management*. Phoenix: Arizona Game and Fish Department, 1964.

Schmitt, Peter J. *Back to Nature: The Arcadian Myth in Urban America*. Baltimore: Johns Hopkins University Press, 1990.

Scott, James C. *Seeing Like a State: How Certain Schemes to Improve the Human Condition Have Failed*. New Haven CT: Yale University Press, 1998.

Sellars, Richard West. *Preserving Nature in the National Parks: A History*. New Haven CT: Yale University Press, 1997.

"Seventh Annual Meeting of the American Society of Mammalogists." *Journal of Mammalogy* 6, no. 3 (August 1925): 213–16.

Shabecoff, Philip. *A Fierce Green Fire: The American Environmental Movement*. New York: Hill and Wang, 1993.

Shackleford, Martha. "Animal Communities of an Illinois Prairie." *Ecology* 10 (1929): 126–54.

Shankland, Robert. *Steve Mather of the National Parks*. 3rd ed. New York: Alfred A. Knopf, 1970.

Shelford, Victor E. "Ways and Means of Improving the Quality of Investigations and Publications in Animal Ecology." *Ecology* 11 (1930): 235–37.

Sheridan, Thomas E. *Arizona: A History*. Tucson: University of Arizona Press, 1995.

Simpson, George Gaylord, Colin S. Pittendrigh, and L. H. Tiffany. *Life: An Introduction to Biology*. New York: Harcourt Brace and Company, 1957.

"Sixth Annual Meeting of the American Society of Mammalogists." *Journal of Mammalogy* 5, no. 3 (August 1924): 218–21.

Smith, Frank E. *The Politics of Conservation*. New York: Pantheon, 1966.

Smith, Vera. "Animal Communities of a Deciduous Forest Succession." *Ecology* 9 no. 4 (October 1928): 479–500.

Staudenmaier, John M. *Technology's Storytellers: Reweaving the Human Fabric*. Cambridge: MIT Press, 1985.

Steen, Harold K, ed. *Forest and Wildlife Science in America: A History*. Asheville NC: Forest History Society, 1999.

Stegner, Wallace. *Beyond the Hundredth Meridian: John Wesley Powell and the Second Opening of the West*. Boston: Houghton Mifflin, 1954; reprinted New York: Penguin, 1992.

——— *Mormon Country*. New York: Bonanza Books, 1942.

Sterling, Keir B. "Builders of the U. S. Biological Survey, 1885–1930." *Journal of Forest History* 33 (October 1989): 180–87.

——— "Zoological Research, Wildlife Management, and the Federal Government." In *Forest and Wildlife Science in America: A History*, edited by Harold K. Steen, 19–65. Durham NC: Forest History Society, 1999.

Stoffle, Richard W., and Michael J. Evans. "Resource Competition and Population: A Kaibab Paiute Ethnohistorical Case." *Ethnohistory* 23, no. 2 (1976): 173–97.

Taylor, Walter P. "Outlines for Studies of Mammalian Life-Histories." *United States Department of Agriculture Miscellaneous Publications* 86 (1930): 1–12.

Tjossem, Sara Fairbank. "Preservation of Nature and Academic Respectability: Tensions in the Ecological Society of America, 1915–1979." Ph.D. diss., Cornell University, 1994.

Tobey, Ronald C. *The American Ideology of National Science, 1919–1930.* Pittsburgh: University of Pittsburgh Press, 1971.

——— *Saving the Prairies: The Life Cycle of the Founding School of American Plant Ecology, 1895–1955.* Berkeley: University of California Press, 1981.

Trefethen, James B. *Crusade for Wildlife: Highlights in Conservation Progress.* Harrisburg PA: Stackpole, 1961.

Trippensee, R. E. *Wildlife Management: Upland Game and General Principles.* New York: McGraw-Hill, 1948.

Turner, Frederick Jackson. *The Frontier in American History.* New York: Holt Rinehart & Winston, 1920.

Walker, Don D. "The Cattle Industry of Utah, 1850–1900, An Historical Profile." *Utah Historical Quarterly* 32 (Summer 1964): 182–97.

Weese, Asa. "Animal Ecology of an Elm-Maple Forest." *Illinois Biological Monographs* 9 (1924): 345–438.

White, Richard. *"It's Your Misfortune and None of My Own": A New History of the American West.* Norman: University of Oklahoma Press, 1991.

Worster, Donald. *Nature's Economy: A History of Ecological Ideas.* 2nd ed. New York: Cambridge University Press, 1995.

——— *A River Running West: The Life of John Wesley Powell.* New York: Oxford University Press, 2001.

——— *The Wealth of Nature: Environmental History and the Ecological Imagination.* New York: Oxford University Press, 1993.

Wright, George M., and Ben H. Thompson. *Fauna of the National Parks of the United States: A Preliminary Survey of Faunal Relations in National Parks.* Fauna Series No. 2. Washington DC: Government Printing Office, July 1934.

Young, Christian C. "Defining the Range: Carrying Capacity in the History of Wildlife Biology and Ecology." *Journal of the History of Biology* 31, no. 1 (Spring 1998): 61–83.

——— "A Textbook History: Use of the Kaibab Lesson in Teaching Biology." *American Biology Teacher* 62, no. 8 (October 2000): 559–64.

Young, Stanley P. "Edward Alphonso Goldman." *Journal of Mammalogy* 28 (1947): 91–109.

Zahniser, Howard. "Vernon Orlando Bailey, 1864–1942." *Science* 96, no. 2479
        (3 July 1942): 6–7.

Ziman, John. *An Introduction to Science Studies: The Philosophical and Social As-
        pects of Science and Technology*. Cambridge, England: Cambridge Uni-
        versity Press, 1984.

Index

Page references for illustrations appear in italics.

Adams, Charles, 52, 58–60, 66, 88–89, 114, 159
administrative philosophies, of federal agencies, 19, 191
Albright, Horace, 109, 110, 119, 121, 130, 136, 139, 142, 143, 161–62, 166–68, 169–70, 177–78
Alchemy, John W., 239 n.20
Allen, Garland, 207–8, 247 n.6
alliance of ranchers, sporthunters, and conservationists, 27–28
American Bison Society, 135–37, 148
American Forestry Association, 137
American Game, 84, 150
American Game Protective Association, 85, 135–37
American Indians, 20; in balance of nature, 58, 156–57
American National Livestock Breeders Association, 61, 136–37, 139
American Society of Mammalogists, 35, 52–60, 84, 88, 110–12, 137–38, 144–45, 225 n.27, 235 n.4
Anasazis, 12
Anderson, Mark, 140
Anthony, Harold E., 110, 138
Arizona: and administration of hunting, 48, 70–71, 73, 96–98, 101, 106–7, 109, 123–24, 128, 131, 150–52, 183–84, 188–89, 197–98; and statehood, 19
Arizona Daily Star, 129
Arizona Game and Fish Department, 121, 194, 197–98

Arizona Game Protective Association, 135–37, 147, 183
Arizona Republican, 76
Arizona Strip, 13
Arizona Territory, 17
Arizona Wildlife, 197
arms and ammunition manufacturers, 53
Ashurst, Henry F., 19, 116, 195, 197
Auman, Shorty, 189–90

Bailey, Vernon, 22, 24–25, 52, 98–100, 113, 115–17, 118
Baker, Jeffrey, 207–8
Baker, Sherman, 204–5
balance of nature, 1, 53, 58, 65–67, 75, 76, 78, 83, 87, 92–93, 105, 112, 124, 158, 184, 205, 206, 209, 211, 212, 214
Balstad, David, 229 n.20
Barnes, Will C., 44, 90–93
basketmakers, 12
Bayless, R. Lee, 106–7, 118–19, 123, 149
bears, 11, 16
Behle, William H., 193
Big Saddle, 132
Big Springs, 14
Binkley, Dan, 209–10
Bird Lore, 150, 184
bison, 16, 18
bobcats. *See* predators
Boone and Crockett Club, 16, 61
Botkin, Daniel, 209, 212–13
bounty system(s), 23, 24
Bright Angel Creek, 10
Brooks, James P., 121, 131–33, 139
Brown, Art, 131–32, 185, 186–91, 193
browse line, *203, 204, 208. See also* vegetation

Bryant, Harold, 137, 161–62, 167–68, 187, 189–91
Bryce National Park, 21
Buckskin Mountain, 8, 27, 73–74, 76
buffalo. *See* bison
Bureau of Biological Survey, 23–24, 26, 28, 40, 113; and advising Forest Service, 33, 43–44, 50, 51, 67, 86, 116, 147, 164; and advising National Park Service, 33, 51, 67, 110–11; field naturalist program of, 22; predatory animal control by, 20, 76, 83, 87, 147, 193–98, 225 n.27
Burnham, John B., 61, 69
Butler, Jack, 190

Calahane, Victor, 187, 189
Cammerer, Arno, 67, 77, 88, 163, 178, 186, 188, 196
Camp Fire Club (of America), 135–37
Cape Royal. *See* Greenland Point
carnivores, 11–12, 18, 57. *See also* predators; predatory animals
carrying capacity, 6, 40–46, 64, 80, 95, 99–100, 102, 104, 105, 116, 122–23, 127–28, 147, 167–72, 175–76, 191, 194
Carson, Rachel, 211
cattle. *See* grazing; livestock; ranching
Caughley, Graeme, 207, 209, 212, 217 n.5
Chapman, Herman H., 170–71
Cincinnati Zoological Gardens, 89
combination-of-both principle, 146, 239 n.20
Committee on Wild Life Sanctuaries (American Society of Mammalogists), 54
communities of scientists, 5, 137, 145, 198
conservationists, 2, 15
control of nature, 53, 55–56, 58, 112, 116, 214. *See also* balance of nature
Coolidge, Calvin, 78
Costley, Richard J., 202
cougar. *See* mountain lion
cowboy(s), 16, 45, 160
coyotes, 11, 37, 87, 112–13, 115, 147, 158, 205; control of, as predatory animals, 24–25, 45, 85, 111, 163, 190; food habits of, 57
Cutting, Heyward, 61

Darwin, Charles, 94, 96
deer, 16, *213*; behavior of, 4, 8, 45, 46, 83–85, 157; competition, with cattle, 32, 41, 140, 146; condition of, 38, 41–46, 62, 79–80, 83, 85, 98–101, 105–6, 124, 127, 154–55, 187–88; court cases relating to, 69–98, 100–103, 83, 85, 98–99; estimate of numbers of, 30, 39, 41, 62, 63, 83, 89–91, 99, 100, 102, 116, 122, 125, 132, *155*, 155–57, 160, 163–64, 170–71, 173–74, 179–80, 183–86, 189–90, *192*, 193, *199*, 199–201, *202*; habitat of, 9, 126, 154; number of, killed by predatory animals, 98; migration of, 10, 32, 42, 45, 102; opposition to government killing of, 77; starvation of, as limiting factor, 95, 98, 157, 169; studies of, 47, 50, 79, 83–85, 99–100, 103–7, 117–18, 121–25, 127, 131, 143, 152–57, 159, 173–76, 179–81; trapping and shipping of, 64, 74, 88, 106–7, 129; utilization of (commercial hunting), 46–48. *See also* game; VT Park
deer drive, 71–75
deer herd: calls for counts of, 31, 194; calls for reduction of, 63–65, 67, 101, 116, 148; factors affecting size of, 20, 51, 65, 83, 85, 86, 102, 127, 138, 158, 160, 169, 179, 182, 212
deer line. *See* browse line; vegetation
The Deer Stalker (Grey), 72, *72*–75
DeLong, James, 79
Demaray, Arthur E., 89, 90, 117–19, 168, 197–98
DeMotte, Harvey C., 13, 221 n.4
DeMotte Park, 10, 34, 175. *See also* VT Park
density, population, of deer, 95, 176–77, 199–200
Department of Agriculture, 23, 40, 69, 97–98, 101
Department of Wildlife Management (Utah State Agricultural College), 159
Dice, Lee, 111
Dilg, Will H., 65, 79
Division of Biological Survey. *See* Bureau of Biological Survey
Dixon, Joseph, 36–37, 52, 56–58, 111, 113, 137–38, 152, 162, 170–71, 177

Downing, William, 226 n.32
Drury, Newton, 196–97
Dry Park, 132
Dunlap, Thomas, 212
DuPuy, William, 76–77, 79
Dutton Point, 145

Eakin, J. R., 67, 88–89
Ecological Monographs, 198, 199
ecology, as "pure" science, 5, 93, 96, 218
    n.8, 219 n.12
economic relations, between animals, 23,
    24
economy of nature, 96. See also balance of
    nature
Edwards, J. B., 185–86, 201
elk, 16. See also Yellowstone National Park
Elton, Charles, 93–96, 158, 231–32 n.16
Emerson, Alfred, 207
Esperanza Cattle Company, 90
experts, 40, 50, 80, 112, 218–19 n.9; call
    for, 47, 51, 62–64, 67, 76. See also
    Goldman, Edward A.; Mann, Walter

Farber, Paul, 208, 214
federal game preserves, 16
Field Museum of Natural History
    (Chicago), 2
Fish and Wildlife Service, 194–98. See also
    Bureau of Biological Survey
Fisher, A. K., 33, 57, 113–14
Flagstaff AZ, 9, 15, 74, 75, 107, 118
food chain, 94, 156
Forest and Stream, 16
Forest Service, and administration of
    Kaibab, 21, 29, 31, 42–44, 49, 62, 67,
    70, 75, 78, 79, 84, 86, 87, 96–97, 100,
    109, 110, 121, 128, 129, 143, 149, 151,
    164, 170–71, 175, 177, 183–84, 187–89,
    196
Frederick, Karl T., 136–37
Fredonia AZ, 8

Gabrielson, Ira, 197–98
game, 18, 41; annual reports of, on Kaibab,
    87, 121–25, 159–60, 171, 173, 183–85,
    189–90, 198; decreasing numbers of,
    in West, 18

Game Management (Leopold), 28, 176
game management, 28, 42, 149; definition
    of, 63; pioneering efforts of, on the
    Kaibab, 43, 82, 91, 103, 112, 115, 127,
    136, 145, 147, 150, 181, 182, 203–5. See
    also management of wildlife
game protection, 26, 194–95
game surplus, 80, 84, 107
Gatlin, John, 194, 197
General Land Office, and jurisdiction of
    Kaibab lands, 14
Gery, R. E., 102
Glen Canyon Dam, 9
Goldman, Edward A., 38, 40, 44–46, 50,
    52–56, 80, 83–85, 88, 104–7, 111–15,
    137–38, 148–49, 165, 172, 179, 205
Grand Canyon, 8; as tourist destination, 6,
    17, 145
Grand Canyon Cattle Company, 74
Grand Canyon Forest Reserve, 14
Grand Canyon National Game Preserve, 3,
    17–18, 29; as described by Hornaday,
    27; jurisdiction of, 3, 157
Grand Canyon National Monument, 33–34
Grand Canyon National Park, 19, 21, 181
Grand Canyon Village, 119
grazing, 3, 14, 20, 90–91; habits of cattle,
    41. See also livestock; ranching
Greeley, William B., 43–44, 48, 50, 79, 97
Greenland Point, 11
Grey, Zane, 3, 19, 29, 68–77, 237–38 n.37
Grinnell, George Bird, 16
Grinnell, Joseph, 36, 52, 53, 85, 125, 137,
    144–45

Hall, E. Raymond, 85–87, 113–14, 138,
    144–45, 148–49, 163
Hamblin, Jacob, 13
Hansen, Q. David, 122
Harrison, Benjamin, 14
Harrison, C. L., 89
Havasupai, 12
Hayden, Carl, 19, 195–98
Heller, Edmund, 52
Henderson, W. C., 36, 113, 194
Holman, George E., 33, 36–37
Hoover Dam, 9
Hornaday, William T., 26

Hough, Donald, 79, 88
Hough, Emerson, 21, 34, 42, 59
House Rock Valley, 9, 18, 19, 44, 73, 118,
    136
Howell, A. Brazier, 111, 137–38
Howell, Joseph, 17
Hualapai, 12
humblebees, 94
Hunt, George W. P., 66, 68–71, 96–97, 101,
    131, 141, 143, 148, 150, 152
hunting. *See* sport hunting
Hunting Trips of a Ranchman (Roosevelt), 16
Hyde, Arthur M., 150

Ickes, Harold, 194–97
Illinois State Natural History Survey, 159
Indian Hollow, 132
irruption(s), 1, 201, 204, 210
Izaak Walton League, 135–37, 140

Jackson, Maria, 161, 163
Jacob Lake, 9, 14
Johnson, Fred, 198–201
Johnson, Harlen G., 187–88, 191, 193
Johnson, Stephen S., 66, 77–79
Jones, Charles J. ("Buffalo" Jones), 18, 19,
    73, 118
Judd, W. D., 131
Julander, Odell, 162, 172, 173–75
Jumpup Point, 11, 44, 122

Kaibab, meaning of, 8
Kaibab deer, legacy of, 19, 155–57, 169–70,
    181–82. *See also* deer
Kaibab Indian Reservation, 13
Kaibab Investigating Committee: of 1924,
    61–64, 157; of 1931, 135–50, *141, 142,*
    157
Kaibab lesson, 2, 158, 184, 205, 206–15.
    See also textbook lesson
Kaibab myth, 207, 212, 217–18 n.5
Kaibab Plateau, 9. *See also* Buckskin
    Mountain
Kaibab Suspension Bridge, 10
Kanab UT, 13, 15, 17
Kanab Café, 79
Kanab Canyon, 10, 45
Kartchner, K. C., 131, 133, 137, 141, 143,
    194–98

Keeton, William T., 207
King, Keith, 208, 214
Kittredge, Frank, 196
Kneipp, Leon F., 32

Largent, Mark A., 218 n.8, 232–33 n.22,
    246 n.1
Laws, Edward, 98
Lees Ferry, 9
Leopold, Aldo, 1, 27, 28, 41, 91–93, 104,
    127, 149, 158, 170, 176, 181, 198, 201–5,
    207, 210–11
Ligon, J. Stokely, 28
livestock: companies, 20; conditions of, 18,
    35; increasing numbers of, in
    nineteenth century, 22, 143, 157, 209–
    10; and industry opposition to game
    protection, 27, 67, 68, 78, 129–31, 133,
    138; and industry support for predatory
    animal control, 27, 66, 114, 116, 193;
    reductions in, 42, 143. *See also* grazing;
    ranching
Locke, S. B., 30, 40–44, 91, 104, 127–28,
    132–33

MacFarlane, John M., 137, 143–44, 145,
    152
Madsen, David, 162–63, 166–67, 177
management of wildlife, scientific, 2, 4,
    28, 62–63, 85, 116, 144, 148, 164, 172,
    180–81
Mann, Walter G., 87–88, 103, 118–25, 129,
    131, 142, 148, 151, 152, 159, 163–65,
    166, 172, 173–74, 179–80, 183–87, 190,
    198, 200–201, 205, 213
Marble Canyon, 9
Marvin, C. F., 69
Mather, Stephen, 21, 34, 42, 48, 64–67,
    70, 76–80, 86, 89, 96, 101, 109
McCormick, Charles, 66–67, 68
McCormick, George, 68–73
McCullough, Tom E., 118–19
McDougall, W. B., 189–91, 198
McGinnies, W. G., 108, 123
McKee, Edwin, 193–94, 196
Merriam, C. Hart, 22, 35
migration patterns. *See* deer, migration of
Milwaukee Public Museum, 2, 3
mining, 14

Mix, Michael, 208, 214

Mount Pleasant (Utah), 126

Mount Trumbull, 14

mountain lions, 11, 92, 114–15, 158, 182, 190, 205; control of, as predators, 45, 59, 85; estimate killed, 37, 56; estimates of numbers, 31, 89–90; food habits of, 24, 32, 57; hunt of, for sport, 19

mountain sheep, 16

mule deer. *See* deer

Museum of Vertebrate Zoology (Berkeley), 36, 85, 163

Musgrave, M. E., 75–76, 123

National Association of Audubon Societies, 61, 135–37, 183

National Park Service, 17, 19; and administering Kaibab, 21, 29, 34, 49, 62, 64–68, 78, 88, 101, 106, 118, 128, 158, 166–67, 169–70, 177–78, 185–87, 195–96; attempts by, to expand boundary of Grand Canyon National Park, 47, 66–67, 118–19, 140, 170; and promotion of deer display, 29, 66, 80, 100, 106, 109, 110, 121, 128, 143, 160, 167–68, 170–71, 175, 181–82, 187, 195; and opposition to predator control, 86–87, 143, 146, 161, 194; and opposition to sport hunting, 106, 118; and promotion of tourism, 29, 117, 119, 121, 128, 193, 195

National Parks Association, 61

Natural History, 204

natural history, nineteenth-century approaches to, 23, 40, 93, 126, 153–54, 209, 224 n.3

Navajo Bridge, 9

Navajo Indians, 12, 20, 102

Nelson, Edward W., 39–40, 52–53, 79, 84, 113; and deer utilization, 46–48

New Mexico Wool Growers, 28

New York Times Magazine, 76–77, 79

Nichol, A. A., 106, 141, 179, 184

On the Origin of Species (Darwin), 94

Otero, Eduardo M., 28

Outdoor America, 65, 66, 77, 79, 88

Owens, James T. ("Uncle Jim"), 19, 31, 33, 36, 37, 56, 73, 184

Paiute Indians, 12, 20

Park, Robert H., 121–22, 131–32

Park Service. *See* National Park Service

Pearson, T. Gilbert, 61, 137, 141, 144, 162, 183

Pelican Island (Florida), 16

Phillips, John C., 101, 106–8, 131

Pierson, Karl, 121

Pine Cone (Leopold), 27

Pleasant Valley, 10

poaching, 20

poison, for predatory animal control, 24, 37, 53, 83, 85, 110–15, 137–38

Powell, John Wesley, 7, 13, 220 n.1, 221 n.7

practical conservation, 55

Pratt, George, 137, 139, 152, 161–62

predators, 4, 11, 24, 37, 59, 127; absence of, as explanation for game increase, 91, 94, 133, 157, 201, 204, 210, 210–11; first-time use of term, 25; role of, 52, 58, 94, 105, 123, 158, 165, 193; value of, 52, 57, 59, 60, 123, 165. *See also* varmint

predator-prey relationships, 6, 20, 51, 65–66, 158, 166, 190, 195, 209

predatory animal control, 20, 24, 29, 33, 36, 43, 50, 51–60, 62, 65, 75, 79, 83, 91, 110–11, 113, 146, 161, 191

predatory animals. *See* predators

predatory mammals. *See* predators

Prescott AZ, 78

preservation-minded nature lovers, 6

preserves, wildlife. *See* refuges

President's Forest, 34

Presnall, Clifford, 186–87

quadrat(s), 102, 122, 125, 173, 182. *See also* sample plots

Rachford, Christopher, 43, 64, 70, 78, 86–87, 135–36, 139–40, 162, 176–77

railroads, 15, 160

ranching, 6, 14, 18, 56, 112. *See also* grazing; livestock

Rasmussen, D. I., 125–27, 131, 153–59, 172, 198, 201–2, 205, 213

Redington, Paul, 106–7, 110, 137, 140, 144–45, 152

Refuge(s), 15; purpose of, 59, 65

Report on a Game Survey of the North Central States (Leopold), 176

resorts, 15

Roak, J. C., 30, 38, 42

Robinson, F. W., 160

Roosevelt, Theodore, 10, 15, 16, 18, 19, 29, 69, 164, 182

Rust, Bill, 160

Rutledge, R. H., 69–71, 100, 107, *108*, 135, 140, 142, 151–53

Ryan site, 14, *30*, 190

Saddle Mountain, 11

Salt Lake City, 15

Salt Lake City Tribune, 145

sample plot(s), 80, 146, 174–75, 179, 184, 187. *See also* quadrat

A Sand County Almanac (Leopold), 203, 210

Saturday Evening Post, 21, 34

Scoyen, E. T., 78–80

seasonal changes, 42, 122, 127, 138, 175. *See also* deer behavior; vegetation

Seymour, Edmund, 118–21, 136, 148

Shantz, Homer L., 106, 108, 123, 143

sheep. *See* grazing; livestock; ranching

Shelford, Victor, 125–26, 153, 154, 156, 159, 202

Sherman, E. A., 64

Silent Spring (Carson), 211

Simpson, George Gaylord, 207

Smithsonian Institution, 13

Smoot, Reed, 17

Sowats Point, 11, 44, 122

sport hunter(s), support for game protection by, 27, 221–22 n.12

sport hunting, 6, 15, 16, 70, 121, 178; as a means of limiting game populations, 84, 146; and opposition of preservationists, 30; prohibition of, 20; and support of government officials, 43–44, 110

State Livestock Board (Utah), 36

Stephan, Sol, 89

St. George UT, 17

stomach-content analysis, 54, 57, 79–80, 113

Storer, Tracy, 111

Storm, Earl, 98, 103

Stuart, R. Y., 110, 119, 130, 137–38, 150–51, 162, 167, 170

Swamp Point, 132, 142

Taylor, Walter, 155

technology, 5, 219 n.13

textbook lesson, 1, 206–10. *See also* Kaibab lesson

"Thinking Like a Mountain" (Leopold), 203, 210

Thompson, Ben, 162, 173, 177, 179–83, 205

Thornber, J. J., 108

Tillotson, M. R., 98, 100, 106–7, 118–21, 129–31, 133, 138–39, 143–44, 148, 150, 161, 167–68, 177–79, 186, 188

Tomlinson, T. W., 61

tourism, 6, 21, 62, 71, 100, 124. *See also* National Park Service; VT Park

Tucson Daily Citizen, 129–30

U.S. Bureau of Biological Survey. *See* Bureau of Biological Survey

U.S. Department of Agriculture. *See* Department of Agriculture

U.S. Fish and Wildlife Service. *See* Fish and Wildlife Service

U.S. Geological Survey, 13

varmints, 27, 28, 51, 147. *See also* predators

Vasbinder, D. L., 149–50

vegetation, 4, *49*, 116; browse line of, 99, 179, *203*, *204*, *208*, 233 n.29; damage to, 35, 85–86; forage studies of, 45, 103, 157, 174–75. *See also* winter conditions

vegetative conditions, 29, 40, 45–46, 65, 82–85, 104, 121–25, 127, 132, 140, 142, 146, 154–55, 164, 168, 171, 173–75, 180, 183, 193, 200–201, 209, 212

Vorhies, Charles T., 108, 114

VT Park, 117, 118–21, 125, 126, 138, 139, 142, 144, 146, 160, 161, 162, 167, 175, 178, 179, 187, 188, 221 n.4. *See also* DeMotte Park

Wagner, Louis A., 78

Walcott, Frederic, 169, 171

Walhalla Plateau (Greenland Plateau), 11

Wallace, Henry A., 178

Wallace, Henry C., 48–50, 63, 69

West, 3, 15, 18, 114, 182

Wild Life Division (National Park Service), 162–63, 166, 177–80, 187, 189
wildlife management: as an "applied" science, 5, 93, 218 n.8, 219 n.12; research of, 58
wildlife refuges. *See* refuges
Willard, G. M., 70
Williams, R. W., 47–48, 64, 97–98
Wilson, James, 18
Winkler, Ernest, 35, 41
winter conditions, 22, 45, 78
wolves, 11, 18; control of, as predatory animals, 24, 25, 59

Wool Growers. *See* New Mexico Wool Growers
Work, Hubert, 48–50
Worster, Donald, 211
Wright, George, 162, 166–71, 177, 180–81, 205

Yard, Robert Sterling, 48
Yellowstone National Park, 18, 20, 41, 168, 180, 182

Zion National Park, 21

11/12/02